THE RIGHT TO *USEFUL* WORK

The Right to *Useful* Work

Planning by the People

edited by Ken Coates

with contributions by Michael Barratt Brown, Stephen Bodington, Mike Cooley, Pete Thomas, The Community Development Projects, The Socialist Environment and Resources Association, The Lucas Aerospace Combine Shop Stewards' Committee and the Vickers' Combine Shop Stewards' Committee.

Published for the Institute for Workers' Control by
Spokesman

First published in 1978
by Spokesman Books
Bertrand Russell House
Gamble Street, Nottingham NG7 4ET
for the Institute for Workers' Control

Cloth ISBN 0 85124 219 7
Paper ISBN 0 85124 220 0

Printed by the Russell Press Ltd., Nottingham

Acknowledgements

Pete Thomas' article on *The Green Bans* first appeared in *Taming the Concrete Jungle,* published in Sidney in July 1973 for the New South Wales Branch of the Builders Labourers' Federation. We are grateful to the author and to Jack Mundey for permission to reproduce this passage.

'Decline in Industry, Decline in Towns' was first published in January 1977 in the Community Development Projects (CDP) paper *The Cost of Industrial Change.* It was prepared by the CDP Inter-Project Editorial Team. 'Alternative Energy Plans' formed part of the evidence submitted by the Socialist Environment and Resources Association (SERA) to the 1977 Public Enquiry into the application by British Nuclear Fuels Limited to establish a plant for reprocessing irradiated oxide nuclear fuels at Windscale, Cumbria. It was drafted by Judy Bartlett, Dave Elliott, Mike George and Andrew Watson. We are grateful to CDP and SERA for permission to reproduce these pieces.

We should also like to thank the Shop Stewards' Combine Committees of Lucas and Vickers for permission to reproduce information on their alternative plans featured in Chapters 10 and 11 of the book.

Contents

Conclusion

Introductory

Chapter I

Planning by the People

Ken Coates

This book seeks to braid together a number of threads. First, we take the thread of unemployment. Contrary to the expectations of most politicians during the post-war decades, mass unemployment has not only returned, but has, for the Establishment which governs Britain, now taken on all the aspects of permanence.[1] Second, there is the thread of democracy: never more threatened than at a time of mounting social stress, democratic ideals are nonetheless reasserting themselves in increasingly clamant demands that rulers be held more accountable for their actions, and in a growing insistence that the autocratic centres of power in industry must be brought to answer for their actions to the people they employ. Above all, planning is seen, more and more plainly, as an area which must be emancipated from the domination of professional planners. Thirdly, we follow the thread of unmet social need: as men and women collectively gain ever greater insight into the remedies (which had eluded their parents) for a whole variety of human disabilities and afflictions, so it becomes plainer each day that vast achievements are now possible in the fields of welfare, education and health if only the wholesale current waste of living resources can be stopped.[2] Fourthly, we have the related thread of environmental concern: so much of the alleged "prosperity" which boomed out across the expanding post-war decades was based upon human and natural spoliation, that a major communal effort of husbandry, care and cleanliness has become imperative, and very much overdue.[3]

Considered separately, each of these four threads is a thin filament of moral concern, abstracted in all honesty from an intolerable political and economic muddle, but too frail in its abstraction, by itself, to bear the great strain of heaving a lumbering and slow public opinion over the obstacles of a kept press and inert public institutions. The problems which need to be faced have often already been identified, sometimes with a degree of sharp clarity. But they can only be resolved if these threads can be jointly seized, by large numbers of people, so that all their distinct concerns may begin to melt together, each reinforcing the other. Morality may only then begin to become a compulsion instead of a reproach.

To abandon the metaphor, any political programme for the restoration of full employment will remain a demagogic chimera, until it embraces the need to transform an economic power structure within whose limits productive advance can only exacerbate the loss of jobs. Power structures tend, within our polity, to assume an aspect of "outsideness", to be accepted as given, immutable, inevitable as ill weather. When it becomes necessary to indict them, the indictment cannot effectively be a flimsy one, because it can only take its course when vast numbers of people have been persuaded that it must. Even two million unemployed are not enough, on their own, to provide such a force. Of course, unemployed workers are isolated, so that their role in this process tends to be that of witnesses of breakdown rather than its prosecutors. The about-to-be, or might-be, unemployed are a different army altogether, until the moment they are disbanded from their works.

But the fight to establish and impose a right to work depends for its success on the support of those who have not yet been, and are not about to be, deprived of it. Few will nowadays stand forward to insist upon the need to dig holes and fill them in again, particularly when it is socially possible to hand out a measure of relief which does not require any such futile justification. Yet today, the right to work, if it is to become real, must still assert itself against, and over, the rule of market forces.

Industrial concentration not only distils great economic powers in the shape of transnational corporations, but it foments remarkable growths in productivity, which imply that, in a rational world, economically compulsory labour could become a very small part of every person's life occupation. Yet the same market which stimulates unprecedented efficiency in the manufacture of some commodities, totally ignores large and growing areas of human need in which associative forms of consumption become imperative. Several hundred pressure groups will testify to this: from the all-too-feeble lobby for adequate provision of speech therapy, to the ramified network of organizations to help and teach mentally and physically handicapped people, to the numberless local groups which seek to assist the old, or the deprived, or the poor. All of these bodies are a permanent reproach to the hidden hand which regulates the market: this hand is not only invisible, it is unfeeling, they all insist. To seek redress for the wrongs they suffer, or have seen to be suffered, such groups are compelled to join together to levitate themselves, too often by their own bootstraps, over the blind cruelties of their economic inheritance. That the ill-housed or homeless could benefit if tens of thousands of workless builders might only pick up their tools again, is plainly evident. Teachers join dole-queues while children still crowd into classes which are far too big for the methods of modern pedagogy. Legions of school-leavers are innoculated with the brutalising serum of pointlessly

imposed idleness, while want and waste still face each
other out in all our cities. In each of these great follies,
a greater still subsists: the late capitalist market is a
near-total failure when we confront the overall problem of matching needs to resources.

Libraries have been written about this affliction, and
yet each generation needs to face it as its own problem, almost as if for the first time. Much insight may
be found in the treatment of it by numerous classic
socialist writers. But the socialist movement, like all
other large human institutions, tends to prescribe and
codify its behaviours and its ideas in accordance with
doctrines it has received from early ages, so that in its
present theory there is commonly an element of con-
servatism, not to say ritual, which may actually prevent
it from facing current realities.[4] Even the most intransigent and belligerent radical groupings are not immune
from this syndrome, as may sometimes be seen in their
treatment of these four key issues.

Yet, happily, the growth of awareness about such
matters is not, in a working class movement which has
been the beneficiary as well as the victim of considerable educational and technical advances, solely (or
even mainly) a resultant of conventional political agit-
ation. Today, with whatever perils, working people are
increasingly willing to think and act for themselves,
and to experiment in the working out of their own
ideas. Among such a population, socialist concepts
may catalyse thought and activity, but they will seldom
require their spokesmen to "lead" in the conventional
sense. Indeed, any valid contemporary socialist
project is bound to challenge received notions about
"leadership", in order precisely to stimulate and
extend that high spirit of self-reliance and popular
self-confidence which alone can begin to create the
human conditions which are necessary to promote
real changes in the order of things.

This is not to say that there is no need for initiative in the present-day labour movement. The contrary is true. Much of this book is given over to recording attempts by shop stewards to elaborate plans enabling them to avoid unemployment by diversifying their production to meet established social needs and environmental concerns. The path-breaking exercise in this field was the thousand-page study by Lucas Aerospace workers, a summary of which is reprinted below. This was, of course, a triumphant assertion of the demand for industrial democracy in practice, and so it has, with considerable effort and skill, already comprehended all four themes of this book. Yet it was not a simple act of spontaneity. To begin with, the Lucas shop stewards have their own developed ideas, and have worked through a rich ferment of socialist discussion. Further, the demand for their project arose when they lobbied Tony Benn, then Industry Minister, for help in facing anticipated dismissals. He asked them to work out their alternative proposals. Soon after he was purged from his Ministry, which was regained for inertia and the loving support of the status quo by Eric Varley, so that there could be no response from Government when the Lucas men had completed their work. We shall return to this matter later, but what it is necessary to say here is that this illustrates a complex dialectic between rank-and-file and central-ised political initiative, in none of which does conven-tional elite theory offer the least explanatory help. Workers' control is like that. It is far from an unstruc-tured process, but its great advances are not simply in the original distillation of its programmes, but in the res-ponses these set off in the imaginations of other men and women. The Lucas stewards and their imitators have excited sympathetic discussion among disarmers and friends of the earth, conservationists, and socialist radicals, on a world-wide scale. Yet they also are part of a wider dialogue within the British Labour Movement, which embraces all that movement, from top to bottom, however fast run those who wish to get away from it.

These issues raise themselves in a variety of ways, only some of which can be covered in these pages. Outside the industrial responses at Lucas and Vickers, there are the related arguments of people involved in community action and environmental protection. This book exemplifies a vast body of such material in two chosen cases, which raise, very specifically, the whole question of who plans, for whom, in a world where powers of decision are daily more closely concentrated. State choices about energy sources are not, in principle, far removed from those about military policy, so there is a clear and close relation between what happened at the Windscale enquiry and what is happening at Vickers. As jobs crumble in old industries, they also crumble in particular townships, so that the concerns of the Community Development workers about inner-city decline are simply a complementary facet of that urge to protect employment which has swept through British industry since the Upper Clyde Shipbuilders' work-in of 1971.

But just as the urban ecologists may reinforce the efforts of trade unionists, so, too, there can be a welcome reciprocity, which is beautifully highlighted in the example of the 'green bans' in Australia, where the Builders' Labourers Union undertook a truly staggering programme of initiatives.

Australia shares many British problems: 400,000 people are without proper houses, most hospitals require modernisation, repair or extension, an enormous school building and reconstruction programme is needed, and although two-fifths of all workers are women, there are hardly any pre-school facilities for their children.

At the same time, speculative development has gone

on with great vigour, environmental vandalism is widespread, and the office-building boom has destroyed numerous civic amenities in most major cities.

Fortunately, Australia also has a very strong trade union movement, which recently gave rise to an organised movement for workers' control. Among the unions which have been actively concerned with the problems of industrial democracy, one of the most persistent is the Builders' Labourers Federation of New South Wales whose recent secretary, Jack Mundey, is also a figure of national standing, as a result of the campaigns which he has waged with the active involvement of his members.

The Builders' Labourers have not merely taken the idea of workers' control to heart: they have obviously begun to practise it: and not only in defence of their own immediate interests, but in favour of much wider social objectives as well.

There can hardly be any clearer examples of the scope of such actions than the New South Wales Builders' institution of "green bans" on undesirable speculative developments. As Jack Mundey said on Australian TV:

"As far as we're concerned, we believe that a union in this day and age must be concerned about things other than just bread and butter issues. When we live in a country that is so sparsely populated, yet the most urbanized country on earth: when we find that our cities are growing in such an unbalanced way, at such a pace, it's only natural that people will rise up in anger at the destruction of our cities . . . "

'Rise up in anger' is exactly what the builders' labourers have done. They banned the development of the vast Sydney Opera House car park in the interest of the preservation of trees. The public supported them, and the $2m scheme was killed.

They blocked a major, billion-dollar road project in a working-class housing area of Sydney, with the active

support of the residents. Another $70m project was
next hung up by the union's fight to preserve the
Newcastle Hotel, a rendezvous for writers, dockers
and artists.

Similar actions aroused widespread support at
Woolloomooloo, an area of cheap housing which
would have been levelled to make room for a $400m
redevelopment, but for the appeals of residents and
the energetic responses of the union.

Green bans of this kind, involving contracts to the
value of billions of dollars, have been able to focus
public attention on official civic barbarism. As Jack
Mundey explains:

> ". . . all that we've done is to support residents or progres-
> sive architects, engineers and other people, town planners,
> in trying to slow down the destruction, to slow down the
> erection of a concrete jungle, and make cities a place where
> people should live . . . "

Few people in England trust planners any more
than do Australian builders, although urban planning
in England is probably fractionally less capricious
than it seems to be in Sydney. Nonetheless, in spite
of the liberalising prescriptions of the Skeffington
Report, industry still tends to get very much its own
way, at the expense of local authorities and the
people who suffer them. The case study, featured
below, of the National Coal Board's influence upon
Nottinghamshire County Council's structure plan points
a moral which is obvious, and which itself has painful
implications for the future of employment, and even
worse ones for the future of Community, if the
mining neighbourhoods and unions cannot develop
their own appropriate counter-plans.

'Planning' is a word which has carried over from
the interwar years a whole series of 'progressive' conno-
tations, based on the assumption that it must, in
some way, be inherently just and rational. Undoubtedly,

during the 1930s, the experience, imperfectly understood, of five year plans in the Soviet Union, led very
many Western reformers and socialists to see their
entire function in terms of working towards "planned
production for community consumption" as the Webbs
characterised it. Such formulae are not devoid of value
as half-truths, but they lamentably fail to pose the crucial question, who-whom?, so tellingly put by Lenin.
Who plans, for *whom*? In centralised state controlled
economies, undemocratic institutions will warp the
most reasonable plans into fearful shambles, as a prodigious Soviet literature makes plain. The considerable
weakness of fabianised versions of communist doctrine,
which accepted, through the Webbs' selective spectacles,
a "vocation of leadership" which could be fulfilled by
Gosplan and the Politbureau, produced some revealing
indiscretions, as for instance this one by John Strachey:

> "If it were true . . . that the fascists are the agents of a
> separate class, able to set up a workable economic system,
> which would end the present chronic state of crisis . . . then
> there would be a great deal to be said for the fascists."[5]

In the same very popular work, *The Nature of Capitalist Crisis,* Strachey told his readers that "the master
question" was "whether the occurrence of crisis is accidental to or inherent in the capitalist system". If the
answer were to be that they were accidental, he went
on, "then we shall certainly work for their gradual
elimination by appropriate reforms. For who would be
so mad as to recommend the scrapping of the system
itself if the catastrophes which it is bringing upon us
were remediable?"[6] This train of thought certainly explains how, once Freud had helped him to read the
gospel according to Keynes, Strachey found it possible
to take up a very much more "moderate" position in
the late forties than that he had felt justified ten years
earlier. But it also explains a vast difference between
socialisms old and new. For those of us who survived

the traumas of the cold war, the socialist future had to
come to grips with a world which required challenge
whether or not capitalism could expand and control its
propensities to slump. That world was unjustifiable because it marked out completely unsupportable frontiers
between men, based on a mutilating division of labour
which systematically stunted the capacities of vast
numbers of employees, whilst elevating the powers of
handfuls of entrepreneurs over people and even
Governments themselves.

In this sense, the more "efficient" the growing global
companies were, the worse their effects became.
Whether or not their powers might be curtailed by
reform, they could certainly not be limited without
vast and intelligent working class organisation, and at
the same time they could not be passively tolerated
without surrendering more and more of the lingering
advantages of parliamentary democracy and autonomous
nationality.

In Britain, by 1973, 100 companies, almost all of
them multinational, produced half manufacturing
output and employed half the relevant labour force.
Half direct exports were controlled by 75 giants, while
half existing assets or capital was in the hands of 50
such Leviathans. Properly these were identified by
Stuart Holland[7] as a "meso-economic" sector, immune
in many ways from conventional economic controls
by national governments, and growing increasingly
powerful and irresponsible all the time. Behind them
they left the remainder of an ailing economy, struggling
against all odds to survive hostile competition, and
doomed to be squeezed into more and more restrictive
employment policies.[8]

Of course, the "system" also failed to perform
"efficiently", in that crises emerged ever more openly.
For that reason it is pointless to talk about what
might have happened "if" something else had hap-

pened: but it is necessary to insist that postwar capitalism at its most "normal" operation was a brutal and greedy master, creating vast areas of social squalor and misery. Even supposing a new formula could be found tomorrow to resuscitate the beast, it would hardly be a friendly monster to have among us. The fact remains, no-one in authority knows how to get it going again at full employment levels, and its life-expectation cannot be assumed to be indefinite.

Yet in urging the restoration of the right to work, as we must, we can in no way look to "planning" of the kind defended by John Strachey or the Webbs. No civil servants have the unaided power, still less the unprovoked will, to over-ride those who need a renewed slump in order to purge their ailing industries. Without such power, planners must necessarily want for effective knowledge. The planning of the 'eighties will have to be *popular* planning, a democratic convergence upon agreed goals according to argued priorities, rather than a series of edicts by commissars or state agencies. It will need to win support for its aims in the process of determining them, by wide and uninhibited democratic discussion. It will create, in the process, not only a body of technical resources, but also and essentially, a live political movement.

This is the pioneering importance of the ideas of the social audit and the alternative corporate plan, discussed below. Only secondarily are they to be seen as blueprints: in the first place they are charters, campaign platforms, an offer of an alternative future. That future is not to be entered by permission of an executive committee, or an official commission. We shall go there ourselves, because we choose to do so. Jerusalem was not rebuilt by any Sanhedrin, but by all the people; with a trowel in one hand, a sword in the other: and it may well be that the greening again of England will begin in a similar way.

FOOTNOTES

1. For a detailed analysis, see *Full Employment – Priority,* published in 1978 by Spokesman, as a companion to this book.
2. See *Resources and the Environment,* ed. Barratt Brown, Emerson and Stoneman, Spokesman, 1976.
3. See *Socialism and the Environment,* Spokesman 1972.
4. Even when, as in 1973, the Labour Party unanimously carried at its Conference a far-reaching motion on environmental questions, no positive action was to ensue.
5. *The Nature of Capitalist Crisis.* Gollancz, 1935, p.342.
6. *Ibid.,* p.19.
7. See Stuart Holland: *The Socialist Challenge,* Quartet, 1975 and *Strategy for Socialism,* Spokesman 1975.
8. See Michael Barratt Brown: *From Labourism to Socialism,* second edition, Spokesman 1978.

Part One

THE SOCIAL AUDIT

One of the earliest efforts of the Institute for Workers' Control to open up the argument about social planning priorities was in the initiation of the idea of a social audit, deliberately assessing the community impact of changes and their overall social costs, as a corrective to narrow commercial profit and loss accounting. A pioneering study of these questions was made by Karl Kapp, in his The Social Costs of Business Enterprise, *published by Spokesman at the same time as this volume. The notion of the social audit took this kind of thinking to the Labour Movement, to stimulate trade unions into tabling their own priorities in all planning discussions.*

The first detailed attempt at a social audit in the IWC's terms was the Scottish TUC's public enquiry into the circumstances of the closure threats at Upper Clyde Shipbuilders, which provoked the celebrated "work-in" of 1971.

More than two hundred work-ins and sit-ins have taken place since that event: less spectacularly, perhaps, but with considerable impact nonetheless, the idea of the social audit has also burgeoned into numerous other fields.

Chapter II

Profits and Losses and the Social Audit

Michael Barratt Brown

Profits and Losses and the Anatomy of Bankruptcy*

Workers who work-in or sit-in do so primarily to
protect their jobs. This, they are told by economists,
is either pointless or actually self-destructive because the closures or bankruptcies they are resisting
are inevitable. The firm or plant must be inefficient
or redundant or it would not be going out of business. To keep it in business is to stop capital and
labour from being transferred to more efficient
management producing goods and services that are
wanted. Workers must be expected to suffer a move
when management is inefficient or product demand
changes. The rationality of this argument depends
on the rationality of the market where goods and
services are bought and sold and through which
profits or losses are made for the capital employed.
An efficient firm producing the goods and services
people want and at the right price is one that makes
profits on capital. Losses are the proof of inefficiency or failure to produce what people want.
Bankruptcy provides the sanitary system for the
market. This is its inherent logic.

It is not, however, a logic that workers should

---

*In this chapter I have drawn heavily upon Robin Murray's book *U.C.S.:
The Anatomy of Bankruptcy* (Spokesman, 1971). We are deeply in his
debt.

be persuaded to accept. Bankruptcy does not
necessarily imply long term unprofitability.
Profits and losses may reflect other factors besides
efficient or inefficient management. What sells
in the market may not be just what people want.
Workers made idle by a closure or bankruptcy may
not easily be transferred to other work. Capital
withdrawn may not be reinvested. It is necessary
to ask who gains from the closure of a plant or the
bankrupting of a firm. The question of social
accounting and of social costs and benefits involved in decisions about the best allocation of
resources to meet what people want will be considered
later. Here we shall concentrate on the meaning of
bankruptcy and the source of profits and losses in the
private accounting of companies.

The Causes of Bankruptcy

Bankruptcy means literally that the bank is broken;
it cannot pay up; and so this can be applied to any
person who cannot pay his bills when the creditors
call for cash. Trading companies have been granted,
since the middle of the nineteenth century, the
legal status of being persons. They have what is
called corporate personality, and if they are "limited
companies" the claims of creditors upon them are
limited to the assets of the company. Neither owners
nor managers can be sued for a penny more than the
face value of the shares they own. This arrangement provides the most valuable protection for
private capital. Its introduction made possible the
transition from the partnership or individual entre-
preneur of early nineteenth century capitalism to
the great joint stock company established at the
end of the century as the typical agent of economic activity. The risk of a loss of capital could be

spread by capitalists over many different companies. A single giant enterprise could call upon the capital of many hundreds, or even thousands of share holders.

This special position of the company in law is of interest to trade unionists for another reason than its relevance to bankruptcy. In claiming protection for trade union property from liability at law for damages arising out of industrial action, trade unionists are often charged with attempting to establish themselves above the law, at least to be claiming a special position at law. They are in effect claiming no more for labour than private capital established for itself under the Companies Acts. Indeed the comparison between these two "special positions" was made by Frederick Harrison, the Trade Unionist advocate on the Royal Commission on Trade Unions a hundred years ago. It was on these grounds that trade union legislation was built in the Act of 1870; but it has required a succession of later Acts of 1906, 1965 and 1974 to reaffirm this "special" trade union position against the adverse judgement of judges and the Acts of Conservative governments.

When a company goes bankrupt this means that the directors of the company have found that there is not the cash in the company's name to pay the bills and there is no possibility of borrowing to tide over the shortfall. This is where the future profitability of the company is the crucial test. A company has to start operations with capital, to buy land and buildings and plant and to pay staff and workers and buy in stocks of raw materials and parts and other goods and draw upon supplies of fuel and power, before any money begins to come in from the sale of the products it is in business to produce. There may be a long gestation period, as it is called, between taking orders or signing contracts and having anything ready to deliver against payment. This was one of the problems that forced Rolls Royce into bankruptcy over the RB211 contract, but there were many other aggravating problems.

Robin Murray in his study of the Upper Clyde. Shipbuilders case, *The Anatomy of Bankruptcy,* listed several possibilities that can cause problems of cash flow between initial outflows of cash and subsequent payments.

1. Once payments begin to be received there may still be cash problems if new orders have to be started on before payment is received to cover outgoings on previous orders;

2. Costs may rise (or, less likely today, sales prices may fall) so that planned margins between costs and prices are squeezed. This is most serious in a period of inflation where the contract is made for a fixed price. This again was one of the problems of Rolls Royce with the RB211 and was the cause of the downfall of Court Line's holiday business;

3. Output may have to be stepped up in an expanding market (entry into the Common Market for example) for the competitive position of the company to be maintained;

4. New models may have to be more costly because of increased sophistication requiring both more expenditure (even though this is ultimately allowed for in the price) and a longer gestation period. Robin Murray quotes the case of British Leyland's expenditure of £45m over three and a half years on development of the *Marina,* which nearly bankrupted this giant company early in 1970;

5. New capital equipment may be needed to maintain the company's competitive position just when and just because profits are falling. This was crucial

in the case of Upper Clyde Shipbuilders;

6. Credit may be squeezed by government action or by general uncertainty about future lending prospects.

In all these cases which involved new capital outlay the funds set aside for depreciation of plant and equipment may be inadequate to meet the actual replacement costs. It will be helpful at this point to indicate what funds are available to make up what is called the Cash Flow of a company over any accounting period:

These are primarily contributions from trade

(i) Net profit, i.e. receipts *less* expenditure, taxes due and depreciation;
(ii) Depreciation provisions;

At any moment a company will have certain sums in cash available to it and certain outstanding creditors and debtors, and also certain sums locked up in stocks and work in progress. Its *current assets* are generally regarded as including

Cash and bank balance and deposits
Stocks
Debtors

while its *current liabilities* will include

Creditors
Current taxation
Bank loans and overdrafts
Proposed dividend

Two measures of liquidity can be made

a. the so-called 'current ratio' of *current assets* over *current liabilities*

b. the so-called 'quick', 'liquid' or 'acid test' ratio of *current assets* minus *stock* over *current liabilities*.

It is assumed that debts are collected and creditors
are paid within the accounting year but individual
debt collection may be of the order of three months
or so and credit may be shorter or longer. Changes in
these periods will be crucial for a company's liquidity.

In addition to such cash flows, working capital may
be increased by:

a. Sale of assets or long term investments
b. Proceeds from the issue of additional share capital
c. Proceeds from the issue of debentures or long
   term loans
d. Increased overdrafts or other short term borrowing
e. Increase in current assets over current liabilities,
   i.e. mainly increase in trade creditors over debtors
   (may be increase of creditors or reduction of debtors
   or both).

Of course not all these items will be positive; some
may be negative and the working capital to that extent
reduced. If on balance the figures are negative then
the company is bankrupt. Presumably all possible
short term borrowings have been made and credits
extended while all possible debtors have been asked
to pay up; and the cash is inadequate to meet the
creditors' demands. This is a terrible moment for a
company because the merest breath of suspicion that
bankruptcy is imminent will bring every creditor
demanding immediate payment and any banks
involved to the point of foreclosing. Thus it was
only enough for the Conservative Government to suggest
that it might no longer guarantee Upper Clyde Shipbuilders the further 'long stop' credits they needed of
£6m, to cover a current cash flow deficit of £165,000
and capital investment needed of £5m, for £53m of
credit to be blocked and the deficit raised to £6.4m.

The evidence of the Ridley Report drawn up by the
Conservative front bench spokesman on Trade and

Industry in 1969 indicates clearly that Upper Clyde Shipbuilders was deliberately bankrupted by the new Conservative Government in October 1970. The Government's reasons will be considered in a moment. Its action was supported by a panel of four so-called "wise men". Their judgement was based entirely on the past failure of UCS between 1968 and 1971. The company's position was as follows:

Assets in Issued capital — 5m
1968 Unsecured Loan — 0.9m
Overdrafts, bank loans and other
short term loans — 4.2m

Total — £10.1m plus guaranteed
government credits.

Liabilities Profit and Loss account — 10.6m
1968- Later raised to 28.1m
1971 Provision for contract losses — 8.4m
Later raised to 21.8m
of which inherited contract losses — 3.5m
Later raised to 12m
new contract losses — 4.8m
Later raised to 9.8m

But this was only to look at what had been inherited from the past. The annual losses had been reduced steadily as follows:

1968 = 9.5m (17.0m at annual equivalent)
1969 = 12.1m
1970 = 4.1m
1971 = 2.4m (3.2m at annual equivalent)

There was strong evidence from the results of the new management and the new policy of rationalised production that future profits were assured. Why then drive UCS into bankruptcy?

The Results of Bankruptcy

Bankruptcy was described earlier as the sanitary system of capitalism in that it flushes out the inefficient management and the obsolete means of production. The multiple bankruptcies of a slump are even a more essential part of capitalist economy. Cycles of boom and slump have been associated with the whole history of capitalism. By more and more state intervention it has proved possible for governments to manage aggregate movements of demand and supply so as to offset the worse crises and the deeper depressions of pre-Keynesian days. But as capital becomes more and more concentrated in giant transnational companies competitively seeking to profit from establishing individual monopolistic positions, so the state has to step in further and further to tax these giants and their employees so as to maintain something near to full employment in the less profitable fields that the giants have abandoned. But boom and slump were not only the modalities through which capital became centralised in giant monopolistic competitors the world over. Nor were they merely unfortunate blemishes awaiting a Keynes to reveal the less ugly face of capitalism. It appears that they were, as Marx had always said they were, an essential part of the working of the system.

In the early years of a boom profits are raised well ahead of other incomes. So long as these are reinvested the boom will go on, but the longer the boom lasts the greater grow the doubts in the hearts of the owners of capital about the profitability of still further investment. The share of other incomes rises and with it the purchasing power to justify new investment but this very fact of increasing wages and salaries cuts into the rate of profit. Old plant and equipment are still working well enough alongside the new. Only special conditions of the invention of still newer machines and discovery of still newer materials will stimulate still more investment; and only the largest companies can afford the increasing scale of new investment. The slump with its multiple bankruptcies was apparently and paradoxically necessary to restore the rate of profit and start a new cycle of investment.

How did the slump and especially the spate of bankruptcies restore the incentive for capital investment?

a. old plant and equipment is written off and disposed of, leaving the more productive new machines at work and the prospect of new investment becoming worthwhile.

b. unemployment rises and the bargaining power of labour is reduced. Workers laid off are only slowly reemployed as the cycle of economic activity restarts.

c. the paper values of capital are marked down so that the rate of profit appears to rise. For those who sold out in time and preferred liquidity it really does rise again.

Without a slump or at least a spate of bankruptcies and mergers these essential elements in the system are missing. The 1960s saw a great wave of mergers in Britain as firms hit by declining rates of profit were taken over and absorbed by their more powerful rivals, but still the profit rate declined. In 1970 a Conservative Government was returned to office with the stated intention of reasserting the natural forces of the market in the economy. This it hoped to achieve by four main measures:

a. reducing state spending so as to raise the number of unemployed;

b. imposing upon the trade unions legal restraints and pay controls that would reduce their bargaining power;

c. hiving off the more profitable parts of the public sector to jack up profits in the private sector;

d. closing down the more unprofitable parts of the public sector and selling off the assets at knock-down prices.

Since the heavy rates of unemployment typical of pre-war slumps were regarded as politically unacceptable, although unemployment was pushed up to the million mark in 1971, most of the reassertion of the natural forces of the market had to be achieved through the other three means. This was combined with an opening up of trade and capital movements with the Common Market. This supplied a new element of competition that sent many firms into bankruptcy and a new field for investment that led to a great outflow of capital. This last would hopefully one day bring back higher rates of profit than those available at home. We can see, then, how bankruptcy was an element in Conservative Government policy and the bankrupting of UCS a deliberate act. The most profitable part of UCS, its share in the Yarrow Yard was returned to the Yarrow company with Government finance and at a loss of £1.7m to UCS; the rest was to be liquidated. Likewise the most profitable part of the River Don works in Sheffield was exchanged for its stainless steel business with Firth Brown's and the heavy forgings were prepared for closure.

But what was the special advantage to private capital of the bankrupting or otherwise shutting down of publicly owned plant? Many of the creditors could be supposed to be companies in the private sector. What could they hope to gain? The answer lies, first, in the nature of the very precise pecking order established in a liquidation process; second, in the particular creditors involved at UCS and, thirdly, in the great advantage to the buyers of the knocked-down assets at bargain prices.

First, then a liquidator must settle with the preferential creditors. Overdrafts from banks must be paid off. Loans that were secured by mortgages or debentures must be reimbursed. Creditors whose credit was unsecured will be paid from what the sale of any remaining assets realises and the shareholders may expect nothing. But the main shareholder, as Robin Murray showed in the case of UCS, was the government; and the tax payer in effect lost £24m through the bankruptcy in shares, loans and grants. The Yarrow Company gained and since those of the other three yards that were merged in UCS, John Brown, Stephen and Connell faced bankruptcy themselves when they entered UCS they lost nothing. The shareholders in Fairfields, the last of the merged yards, were not losers if Fairfields profit forecasts, made prior to the merger, are to be accepted. Again the main Fairfields' shareholder was the government. Of the ordinary creditors for goods and services at UCS, Murray shows that a half was accounted for by public corporations and outstandingly the British Steel Corporation.

And who gained then from the bankrupting of UCS apart from the Yarrow Company? One must note first from Robin Murray's analysis of the assets of UCS that £30m of assets as of 1968 were realised at about £4m in 1971. He gives three sets of figures:

Assets in £m	1968	*1971 Book Value*	*1971 Estimated Realisable Value*
Land and Buildings	5.8	2.5	2.1
Plant and equipment	3.5	4.1	1.0
Goodwill	1.2		
Stock and Work in Progress	7.9	0.35	0.25
Debtors and Bills	5.3	0.34	0.34
Grants and Deposits	6.0		
Total	29.6	7.4	3.7

In practice the work in progress, thanks to the work-in, realised much more than the estimate; and the loss to the shipowners was that much the less. It can be seen, then, that it was the writing down of plant and equipment that was the most drastic. Liquidators must sell up for whatever price they can get. If times are bad, as they were for shipbuilders in Britain in 1971, offers will be sparse and the few offering will get a bargain. But of course many of the assets would be of little use, and costly to remove, off the site. Keeping the assets intact for a revived public company, which was the effect of the UCS work-in, saved plant and equipment for use in the public sector that would otherwise have been a bonus for private shipbuilders and other companies in the private sector which could have picked up the plant for a song. The work-in very largely foiled a direct transfer of capital from public to private hands.

The Role of Government

At this point we need to review the extent of the impact of modern government not only upon the economic environment but upon the direct financial position of companies. In Britain direct employment by the state and employment in state corporations do not together exceed one fifth of all employment; but the state is responsible for channelling, through grants to persons and to companies as well as through direct expenditure, more than half of the total national expenditure. Moreover, the public sector of central and local government and of the public corporations accounts for a half of all capital investment; and on top of this, as Tony Benn kept reminding everyone while he was still Secretary of State for Industry, grants and loans to private industry are equal to half the total even of private investment. Finally, government controls over credit, over prices and incomes, over the movements of goods and capital into and out of the country, over the location of industry and over safety and health and building standards must be added to the powers of government of taxation and expenditure.

Let us now consider how these great powers impinge upon the finances of a company. We may think in terms of changes in government policy because it is such changes that will affect the company's planning of its flows of funds:

a. interest rates may be changed by government action. These have been steadily raised in the last few years as national governments have sought to capture mobile funds in a period when the postwar international money system has broken down and international exchange rates move from day to day. Each nation state plays catch-as-catch can. Much of the world's inflation of prices follows from this breakdown; the effect on the costs of a company's operations is obvious.

b. credit terms and the availability of credit through banks and other financial institutions can be altered by governments with obvious effects for companies; and especially those which are relying heavily on credit as a normal practice or in particular circumstances;

c. rates and forms of taxation can be altered by governments and the timing also of tax collection. The requirement of advance payments of corporation tax introduced in recent budgets had the most stringent effect on companies' cash flow;

d. prices may be fixed or profit margins controlled. Public corporations have been subject to government price fixing for 30 years. Controls over the profit margins of private companies are a more recent introduction under price control legislation. The particu-

larly stringent margins on food retailing in 1974 resulted in a huge number of bankruptcies during
the year.

e. grants and loans and credits may be provided by
   governments for many different purposes. Some of
   these may be regarded simply as allowances or
   remission of taxes for certain general economic purposes, such as the encouragement of employment in
   regions with high unemployment rates. Increasingly
   government funds are being made available to specific
   companies for the purpose of rationalising production
   or resisting foreign competition. This has sometimes
   led to outright nationalisation; and current Labour
   Party policies envisage a considerable expansion of
   public share holding in specified companies in the
   private sector including oil companies operating in
   the North Sea.

Such public power over private finance has two
major implications for the connection between bankruptcy from short term cash difficulties and profitability in the longer run. The first is that the judgement of the capital market about long term profitability is made dependent upon predictions of government
policy changes. The most obvious example of this arises
in the public sector where nationalised industries are not
permitted to raise prices, with the result that heavy losses are inevitable. This tells us nothing about the efficiency of their operation, which we shall consider in a
moment; but it also implies that decisions about the
continuing or closing of a plant or bankruptcy of a
company cannot be made to depend on current losses.
They must be made by government in the light of
long term prospects. This was the message that the
work-in at UCS and the work-on at the River Don works
of the British Steel Corporation so clearly established.
   The second effect of growing public power on private

finance is that state intervention has to become increasingly discriminatory. It is a part of the mental equipment of all British Civil Servants, based upon their studies at University of John Stuart Mill and Walter Bagehot, that governments must treat all private citizens and therefore all companies equally, or at least equitably, so that groups and classes are treated together and individuals are not discriminated against. Thus it was always argued that monetary regulation was the best instrument of government because all persons alike were equally affected by higher interest rates or reduced credit. In fact, of course, this discriminated against those with the smallest capital reserves who had to borrow and rely on credit. No *specific* discrimination, however, was involved. In the same way, and even more fundamentally, the allocation of resources was left to the market where prices were determined by supply and demand — whether this was a market for goods or capital or land or labour. In fact, of course, this discriminated once more against those with most limited funds. If they could not pay, it was assumed that they did not need, or did not contribute so much to society as those who could. For every giant firm whose bankruptcy becomes headline news thousands of small firms go out of business without comment or notice.

Now, if government is to intervene more in ways that require state decisions about the allocation of resources and long term prospects, then it will have to discriminate more and more. Already, grants are given for the use of funds in specified new capital investment, premia are paid in certain regions, loans are made for certain mergers, credit is guaranteed for firms that export. Many new forms of discrimination are adopted in other capitalist countries and will no doubt come to be applied in Britain; for example, special funds available for increasing a company's net exports, easier finance for firms that collaborate with government in long term planning agreements, special assistance to the development of cooperative enterprise, not to mention financial support for companies in which the state takes a major shareholding.

Profitability

We have seen that the explanation given in a market economy for the closing of a plant or the refusal to lend money to save a company from bankruptcy is always based on a judgement of profitability. By this is meant the return of the capital as quickly as possible plus a rate of interest. The uncertainties of the future make capitalists hesitant to tie up their capital over periods much longer than five years though very big firms will go to ten years. It may be an extremely important argument for trade unionists to use that a too low time horizon is being employed in judging profitability. Hydro-electric power was very little developed in France until the electricity authority was permitted to repay capital on hydro schemes over a longer time than that applying to oil and coal burning plants.

What matters is future and not past profitability, because in capitalist economics bygones are bygones and capital investment decisions always start from 'now'. But we have seen that today judgements about long term profitability depend not only on the future efficiency of the company in market terms but also on an estimate of future government policies concerning prices, profit margins, credits, taxes and grants. Profitability will also depend upon the market situation of the company's products. If it has a monopolistic position for one or more of its products, prices can be raised well above costs on these items. If it is in a very competitive market, profit margins will be squeezed. It is for this reason that giant companies, and particularly giant financial holding companies, close down the plants and product divisions that are least profitable, not necessarily unprofitable, and switch investment into products in which they have a monopolistic position. The closures of Merseyside and other plants after the merger of GEC, AEI and EEC which aroused thoughts of the first work-ins were for this purpose. Most of the subsequent work-ins and sit-ins were occasioned by such calculated closures of plants that were not unprofitable but were producing for a highly competitive market. Increasingly, as we have seen, the government has been forced to step in to help finance such production in the sectors of industry where competition keeps down profit margins. Production is not necessarily inefficient. Efficiency is nonetheless judged by profitability.

How then should efficiency be judged? We may say that efficiency itself results from the most effective use of the factors of production — land (including materials), capital and labour. Where more than half the costs of a company's operations are labour costs, such activity is called labour-intensive. Where more than half are capital costs, it is capital intensive. Efficient use of labour will be more important in the first and of capital in the second. The test in both cases is the saving of time, labour time and machine time.

The output of the two together — of machines and workers — are generally measured as productivity, in terms of output per man hour, in money terms or real terms, i.e. of tens and units. Increased productivity is a function of several variables;

a. the capacity of the machines employed in production;

b. the organisation of production and especially the supply of parts and materials and repairs so that machines and workers can be kept working to capacity;

c. the motivation or incentive to workers actually to
   keep machines working to capacity.

All three are of equal importance, but frequently the
situation is that the machines are given and cannot
quickly be changed. If they are obsolete or unreliable,
little can be done by organisation and motivation to
increase their capacity, although the miracles of maintained output during the three day working week early
in 1974 show what can be done with shortages of power
which may be subsumed in the category of machine
capacity. Organisation of production and particularly
the standardisation of products and flow of parts were
the crucial elements in the changes made by new
management at UCS. Before these changes were introduced, the evidence was that workers were only involved
in productive work for about a fifth of their time, three
fifths was spent waiting for supplies and one fifth doing
work that was abortive. No amount of worker motivation can overcome that sort of organisational weakness;
indeed, such organisational failings will make incentive
schemes impossible to apply. But UCS revealed weaknesses in the organisation of shipbuilding which went
beyond the process of production. When a ship was
completed a large part of the work force was laid off
until new orders were at hand in one or other of the
yards. Naturally, workers tended to spin out the com-
pletion of jobs and to restrict particular jobs to
specified groups of men. All of this led to uncompetitive
prices and long delivery times with the result that
British shipbuilding stagnated at around a million tons
a year in the 25 years after World War II while world
output of ships grew six fold — and not only in Japan
but in high wage countries like Sweden and West
Germany and France.

Similar problems have been typical of other industries
in Britain, and especially in steel making and large

sections of engineering, worst of all in machine tool manufacture. In all these cases the final resort of government has been to nationalisation to carry through the modernisation and rationalisation that private capital had failed to achieve. We saw earlier that the refusal of governments to permit nationalised industries to raise prices has inevitably led to their showing losses. The private sector industries which obtain their supplies from the public sector thus get a cheap product; and nationalisation is said to be inefficient. If the test of greater efficiency is, however, increased productivity, the nationalised industries in fact achieved much bigger increases in productivity over the decade of the 1960s than did private manufacturing industry.

The implications for the development of workers' control over the work process must, however, be confronted fairly and squarely. First of all, these processes of rationalising production inevitably involve a reduction in the labour input per unit of output. If output is thereby expanded, the work force may not be reduced but the likelihood is that there will be some reduction, so wasteful of labour have been many of the processes. Where alternative work is immediately available, the saving of labour is a clear advantage; but suppose it is not. Some of the implications of this situation will be examined in the next chapter. Even the rescue of all three yards involved in UCS, after Yarrow was hived off, found employment for only 350,000 men out of an original 700,000.

There is a second implication for workers' control, which is even more serious though less discussed. Robin Murray has emphasised that flow processes to produce a standardised product with interchangeable parts not only involve the deskilling of labour but what he calls in the words of Alfred Sohn-Rethel the "measured atomisation of labour". This is the way that all other industries have gone since F.W. Taylor, the father of the principles of scientific management, set out in the Midvale Steel Company of Philadelphia in 1880 to speed up the work so that time was saved and capital turned over more quickly. The principles applied are principles of 'scientific management' and not of 'scientific workmanship'. In Taylor's own words the system which Taylor transferred with even greater success to the giant Bethlehem Steel Company was "aimed at establishing a clear cut and novel division of mental and manual labour throughout the workshops". The mental labour was reserved to management.

Nearly a hundred years after Taylor his principles, which have been applied successively to the production of sewing machines, typewriters, bicycles, motor cars, radios and television sets, have at last reached ship-building, and other sectors of heavy engineering. But they have done so just when the human element in production, the workers themselves, have attained a level of education and understanding which makes the atomised tasks of the modern process and conveyor belt factory intolerably boring. Schemes of 'job enrichment' and the study of human relations at work serve only to treat the symptoms and not the cause of the worker's increasing alienation from his work. He not only has no control once he clocks in to his work place over the uses to which his labour is put, he is increasingly removed from any control over the way he sets about his tasks. The division between mental and manual labour has been made complete and the subsequent tensions and frustrations break out in all directions.

The challenge of workers' control is a fundamental challenge to the productive process in which the saving of time and the dictates of capital accumulation take precedence over all other considerations – the

health and safety and sanity, the very humanity of
the worker himself. To go back to the point where
Taylor broke down the labour process into isolated
tasks subject to managerial control will not be easy.
With the machines of Taylor's age it would not be
possible, but the introduction of automation and the
use of the computer and data controlled machinery
makes possible the replacement of the most boring
and repetitive human tasks by machinery. What is
still required is the reorganisation of the work process
so that mental and manual labour can once more be
reunited. There are no prospects for increased human
and mechanical efficiency along any other route. But
the implication of such a change is that workers themselves will have to become increasingly involved in the
big decisions about the use and allocation of resources
both inside the company and in the community as a
whole. And to that we turn.

Social Responsibility and Social Audit

As we saw above, the single criterion for judging the
continued viability of a company was its profitability in the relatively long term. But we saw at the
same time that this could depend on government
action and on monopolistic positions in markets for
products as much as upon any kind of productive
efficiency. Productivity, moreover, was seen to have
been generally increased at the expense of the safety
and health and job satisfaction of the worker even
if it did not involve his being rendered unemployed.
Such are the dictates of the market and of the competitive accumulation of capital; for even where the
giant companies enjoy monopoly positions for some
of their products they are in competition for capital
and must accumulate or go to the wall.

The "Social Responsibility" of Business

Since some time around 1970, there has been much
talk and some writing particularly in the United States
about social responsibility in business. A United States
Committee for Economic Development report issued
in June 1971 was entitled *Social Responsibilities of
Business Corporations.* Revelations of the 'ugly face of
capitalism' in Britain too led to the setting up by the
CBI of a Committee on Company Affairs in March 1972
to report on corporate responsibility. About the same
time the Industrial Educational and Research Foundation changed its name to the Foundation for Business
Responsibilities and John Humble of Urwick Orr, the
business consultants, wrote a pamphlet published by
the Foundation on a "Social Responsibility Audit".
None of this should be confused with Social Audit Ltd.
which was founded by Michael Young in 1971 and
began the publication of *Social Audit* in 1973. Nor with
the proposals for a Social Audit made way back in 1968
by the Institute for Workers' Control in a pamphlet
entitled *Opening the Books.*[1] (We shall come to that in
a moment.)

What is most interesting in the growing talk about
"social responsibility in business' is that there is
evidently a real ambivalence amongst business men
about the whole affair. As propaganda, it is fine and
does something to put a smile on that ugly face but
many businessmen appear to be genuinely frightened
even of a face lift. The CBI report referred to above
makes a strong defence of the profit motive and em-
phasises "a company's duty to trade profitably", adding
"but with a sense of responsibility towards the whole
community". When it comes to recommendations, most
of these concern the responsibility of shareholders and
of the non-executive directors appointed to company
boards and "fostering genuinely constructive relationships with their employees". Mr Humble begins his

pamphlet by insisting that "since business is the wealth producing institution of our society, it *must be profitable* (his emphasis). The greatest social irresponsibility would be so to manage business that wealth was not produced for the community's fabric of schools, houses, roads and so on."

The first point to be made here is that all the acts of social responsibility recommended by Mr Humble would cost money and most would reduce profits:

— the employment of staff to monitor social responsibility;
— involvement of staff in joint planning with government;
— honest labelling and packaging;
— control of pollution, and care for the environment;
— equal pay and employment opportunities for women and minorities;
— improvement of heating, lighting, ventilation, noise levels, office design, load lifting and other conditions of work;
— higher safety and health standards and more flexible working hours;
— better redundancy compensation;
— better canteen and other welfare provision;
— elimination of degrading and inhuman tasks at work;
— recognition of trade unions and provision of facilities for union representatives;
— release of employees including trade union representatives for education and training programmes.

Now, of course, some of these improvements would be likely to raise long term profitability but some would imply a straight addition to short term and even long term costs, which could only cut into profitability. The second point is just this, that profitability is evidently not an absolute concept. If all firms are required to meet the same legal standards — in respect to labelling, packaging, pollution control, equal pay, non-discrimination, health, safety, working conditions, redundancy payments, training facilities, trade union recognition etc. — then all should be on an equal basis. Yet, rather strangely, the CBI Report comments that the law can set only "minimum standards of conduct". "A company should behave as the good citizen in business" and pay attention to informed public opinion. It seems clear that in fact the law will be required to set rather more than minimum standards if even the businessman's concept of social responsibility is to be met.

There is, however, a third point to be made about the insistence on profitable business as "the wealth producing institution of our society", from which our schools, houses, roads etc. are produced. Now it is, of course, well known that these services are publicly financed although buildings, equipment and supplies are generally produced by companies in the private sector. What is implied in the statement is that, if our basic needs of food and clothing and of the goods that go into supplying these public services were not produced in the private sector with higher productivity, i.e. with less and less labour, we could not have the rising standard of living of both private goods and public services that we look forward to. This is a somewhat smaller claim than that of being "the wealth producing institution of our society". Those who teach in schools, build roads and houses and nurse in hospitals also produce wealth. They are not 'productive workers', not in the Marxist sense of not necessarily producing for profit and not therefore accumulating capital, but because they cannot increase productivity. It is the productive sector in this sense that is subject to corporate taxes from which a part of the public services must be supplied. The "non-productive" are of course subject to personal taxation, often heavy, to meet the greater part of just these services. Given that return to private capital was the dynamo of the capitalist engine, it is clear that private company profitability would be *the* wealth creating institution; but in fact we have seen that the state is responsible, already even in our mixed economy, for generating at least a half of the capital and thus of the wealth creation. It is not, then, surprising that from UCS to Meriden those who have fought for the right to work have looked to the state to support their claims.

Social Audit or Private Profit

The concept of a social audit was proposed in the pamphlet *Opening the Books* in 1968 and developed in relation to the threatened closure of UCS in 1971 in a further pamphlet entitled *UCS: the Social Audit*.[2] The object from the start was to challenge the principles of private accounting in a market economy, which "may leave resources of man power and equipment unemployed and thus fail to assure the optimum resource allocation". It is, of course, just against this possibility that work-ins and sit-ins have been mounted, and it is because other criteria than that of private profitability have been invoked that they have been successful in obtaining government support. What then are the social considerations that are left outside the private profitability accounting of companies, which must lead trade unionists to question the claim of the profitable business to be "*the* wealth providing institution of our society"? For it is obvious that a plant that is closed down, like a business that goes bankrupt ceases to be a "wealth providing institution".

We shall consider first the case for a social audit as

a corrective to private accounting and then the criteria
for judging between alternative schemes when the test
of profitability is not to be relied upon.

We must start by repeating what has been said already,
that profitability is not necessarily an indication that
urgent demands are being met. Monopoly positions
result in high profits and these may or may not have
been the reward for innovation ahead of rivals which
can be generalised for the good of all. It is almost inevitable that a company with a new technique or new
product should attempt to keep its secrets and even
restrict sales to raise the price since it may make a larger
profit that way. Cornering the market and buying up
rivals only to shut down their business are a commonplace of capitalist enterprise; and the emergence in the
last decade of giant conglomerates and financial holding
companies has made the practice of asset-stripping in-
famous. It was such practices that the workers at
Plesseys in Alexandria and at Tube Investments in Wal-
sall resisted by their actions.

It would probably be claimed by defendants of the
profit motive that all this is exceptional, that normally
profit is made in highly competitive conditions by daily
attendance to the needs of the people as expressed by
what they will and will not buy at the going prices in
the market. But this is to pass over in silence two major
obstacles to the credibility of such a delightful picture
— first the unequal pull of different sized purses on
the market and, second, the use of advertising to persuade us that what has been produced is indeed what
we want. We may take them one by one. Of course, the
market men will say, the purses may vary in length but
everybody in the market can buy what he or she wants
within its limits. We will not consider here why some
purses are longer than others, although this too could
be found to be closely connected with the demands,
and the results, of capital accumulation. The fact is

that what influences the market is not the number of
people buying but the amount of money spent. If
one third of the people spend as much as the remaining
two-thirds, then they have an equal pull on the market.
Meeting the needs of the better off one third is likely
to be more profitable than meeting the needs of the
poorer two thirds; for many types of goods it will be
possible to push prices up a bit and the goods will still
sell. You only have to look at the prices in the West
End of town compared with those in the East End.
Sainsburys and Marks and Spencer respectively operate
wholly and mainly in the Southern half of England.
The Cooperative Societies sell mainly in the north.
We have seen already how government funds have been
required to maintain full employment where spending
power is weak — in the areas of high unemployment
and in products where competition has cut sharpest
into profit margins. This situation is of the greatest
importance for workers threatened with the closure
of their plant. It may well have been producing just
what poor people need but with too many competitors
for profitability.

The second main objection to the market as allocator
of resources to supply what people want can be seen in
the role that advertising and the "hardsell" now play in
determining what it is indeed that people want. The
fact is that with many products the planning and design
and tooling up for production take so long that what
has been produced must be sold. We met this fact before
as the long gestation period that causes such problems
of cash flow. In introducing a new model car, market
research and study of previous sales trends have to be
carried out many years before a single car appears in
the show rooms. But this disadvantage is aggravated
by the further fact that competitive secrecy (not to
mention the building in of obsolescence) prevents the
canvassing of public opinion in advance of the decisions

on design and other specifications. Where the gestation
period is long, some of these difficulties in determining
what the public wants may be inevitable; but where it
is much shorter, it is still the practice to produce first
and rely on advertising to sell; and in this process we
never know what alternatives we might have had, and
on what grounds they were rejected. Those things
that are not measurable in the market, the air, the
sun and the rain, and human happiness, moreover,
the market neglects.

The effects of advertising, however, are most evident
in the general atmosphere of sales pressure which en-
courages the proliferation of goods for private purchase
at the expense both of heavy social costs and of im-
poverished public services. Thus we all want more money
to buy things for our private needs and resent paying
taxes for ensuring that social needs are met. It might
appear that since companies in the private sector not
only produce for direct sale but also for sale to the
public authorities, to build schools, houses, roads,
hospitals and to maintain them when they are built,
that private capital would be just as happy to see money
for spending in public as in private hands. Indeed many
of them are; their operations are largely dependent on
public contracts — for defence, public works and so
forth. Why then the outcry from private capital when
the share of state expenditure is raised? There are
several reasons, all of which are deployed not only
against an extension of state ownership but also
against more state grants, even though they go to
companies in the private sector. They are all epitom-
ised in the claim, so widely accepted, that we must
have more "growth", that is of productivity in the
private sector, before we can have more public services
— to reduce it to absurdity that we must have more
cars before we can build more roads.

Here are the reasons why private capital resents, while

yet benefiting, from an expanded public sector.

1. Companies pay a part of the taxes; and these cut into their margins of profit, and if they are higher than those paid in other countries can be said to reduce the competitive position of British companies;

2. For many companies it is true that more public expenditure reduces the spending power available for the private purchases of their products;

3. The private consumer can be captured more securely as a market than can public authorities, whose policies may change and who may be able to exercise more vigilance over standards of quality and margins of profit than the individual consumer can (whether they do exercise such vigilance is another question);

4. An expanding public sector would tend to increase competition for scarce resources of materials and skills and might be a source of inflation;

5. Too large a public sector, finally, would begin to challenge the whole status of private business as "the wealth producing institution of our society".

All these arguments, assiduously peddled through the media of press and television, mean that workers threatened with plant closures and redundancies will have to fight hard to win support for public spending on their behalf. In doing so, they should not assume that public funds can rescue every threatened plant, though they must insist that where plants are closed new work is found.

The Social Audit and the Economics of Resources

By what criteria should governments be expected to judge between rival claimants for public funds if the test

of profitability is not to be relied upon? We may start
with some tests of the social costs and benefits flowing
from the provision or withholding of funds and then
examine some much wider aspects of resource allocation
where the judgement of the market is replaced by a
social decision. The social costs and benefits will be
looked at in relation to the level of unemployment, the
utilisation of existing social investment, the foreign
balance of payments, the general welfare of communities, the use and conservation of natural resources and
the effects on the environment.

1. *The level of unemployment*

We have already challenged the assumption that workers
made redundant from an unprofitable or marginally
profitable activity will necessarily or quickly be reab-
sorbed into more productive employment. Where local
rates of unemployment are particularly high, as they
were on Clydeside and in Scotland generally (respectively 8% and 5%), compared with a national average of 3%
in mid 1971, this in itself provides a strong indication
for public finance. A high proportion of unemployed
to vacancies for employment in the particular occupa-
tions involved would reinforce the argument as it did
in the case of the Upper Clyde Shipyards. To have unloaded onto a labour market with already 120,000
unemployed, 5,000 shipyard workers plus another
23,000, who would have been indirectly affected by
the closure of the yards, was a prescription for local
disaster. Moreover, given the current trends of employment opportunities in that part of Scotland, and even
allowing for wives continuing to find work, the cost
falling on social security plus redundancy payments was
estimated at £15m a year. The sum asked for from the
government by UCS was £6 million. A similar argument
was pressed by the National Union of Mineworkers for
keeping pits open that were not making a profit. The

costs in redundancy payments and the absolute loss
of most of the men from further employment should
have been set against any actual losses from maintaining production.

2. *Existing Social Investment*

Supposing that it were decided that local employment
in an area of massive redundancies, as was proposed on
Clydeside, really had been impossible to reestablish,
then presumably some number, between say 5,000
and 15,000 men, would have had to move elsewhere.
A calculation was made in evidence to the Committee
of Inquiry on the UCS closure of the costs of re-
establishing that number of families in houses with
roads, schools and hospital provision in another part
of the country. The figures worked out at £40m
and £120m respectively — again enormously in excess
of the £6m that UCS had asked for. It might have been
argued against these calculations that such social
provision was in any case due for replacement; but
in fact Clydebank had been largely rebuilt after Nazi
raids during the war. This would have become a wasted
investment.

3. *The Foreign Balance of Payments*

Most of the problems of the British economy in the
last two decades have arisen from a failure to balance
the foreign payments account. Special consideration
for public funds can therefore be recommended for
import saving investment and for companies which
succeed in increasing their net exports (i.e. exported
goods and materials minus imported goods and
materials). It was a major argument in the case of
UCS that, although about a half of all shipping built
in the UK was exported, nearly a third of all shipping
ordered by UK shipping lines came from abroad. What
is more, only about a half of the goods leaving and

entering this country were being carried by UK shipping lines. The argument became immensely stronger in relation to the coal industry when the cost of net imports of oil rose in 1973-4 to a third of the value of all imports, and provided the most powerful support for the warnings, which the miners had been issuing for years, against too great reliance on imported fuels as the coal industry was steadily run down. It was generally argued against the miners that cheap fuel was the basis of the competitive position of Britain's general exports — an argument that proved in the event to be particularly wide of the mark.

4. *Community Welfare*

It appears to be a well established fact about British communities that most people in this country would prefer to stay near to where they were born and in the communities with which they grew up. The high mobility of families in the United States if often cited as part explanation of high rates of divorce, delinquency and alcoholism. Without pressing the point too far, there is no doubt about the demoralisation of communities which have been steadily decimated by the collapse of employment opportunities. There is a special argument in the case of coal mining that the break up of mining communities may lead to a situation where it will no longer be possible to find men prepared to go down the mines, if those that are closed should have to be reopened at sometime in the future.

5. *Conservation of Natural and Especially of Non-renewable Resources*

The world is only fairly recently being made aware of the fact that many of the natural resources upon which we rely for our industrial development — minerals and fuels — are non-renewable and are rapidly running out. To close down the working of any mine or quarry with workable reserves left in it, in such a way that it is difficult to reopen — and this is the result of most pit closures — is to perpetrate a crime or at least to act in a most shortsighted manner. To use up new sources of fuel and power at a maximum rate, because they are cheaper to obtain — as we are doing with oil and natural gas — so that in 30 years they may all be gone, whether or not it is a fact — which it is — that there are 300 years of coal reserves under the ground, is to compound the felony. While conservation of resources may indicate the need to continue with the operation of plant and processes that appear more costly in their use of labour, it is even more likely to demand a far less wasteful use of natural and non-renewable fuels and materials than has been typical of industrial capitalism. Man, the great despoiler, can be replaced by men and women who care.

6. *Environmental Effects*

The threat of pollution and the destruction of the environment are, like the failure to conserve non-renewable natural resources, crimes for which the naturally exploitative instincts of capitalist enterprise have been responsible, but until recently they have been mainly concealed from us. Now that the rich as well as the poor are beginning to suffer from the deteriorating environment, much more attention is being given to the matter. From our point of view, it is already being established that smaller, more decentralised plants are not only less wasteful of resources and more humane in their working conditions but that they are also less damaging to the environment than the giant plants that the savings from economies of scale, have been indicating as the most appropriate to our needs: 'Small is beautiful', is the argument of E.F. Schumacher and it applies perhaps most of all to the total working environment in which human beings must spend most of their waking lives. It is not only the external costs of large scale operation that must be considered before scrapping small scale plant, it is the internal costs of such an environment for the worker. Where work is made an objective – even *the* objective – of economic activity, both how the work is done as well as what is done, may become central criteria of resource allocation.

The costs and benefits reviewed above, though they are not necessarily all measurable, leave a wide un-answered question about the use of resources and the balancing of internal costs and benefits against external costs and benefits. Quite often this means (only!) the balancing of *our* benefits against *our children's* costs; but in another sense there are real dilemmas of resource use and of the balance of the dangers to health and amenity against the pleasures of extra goods and services. What is clear is that the market will not give us answers to the questions. We cannot, for example, buy health and amenity (except for the few who can buy ducal estates) the way we can buy goods and services. We have to find a means for putting these big questions of the allocation and use of resources to the vote. The market was one way of voting and, while it served enor-mously to increase our productive powers for a hundred years, it serves us ill today. The world wide division of labour through the market has created both our powers and our perils, it is because the single minded pursuit of money has encouraged both the most prodigious human effort and the most reckless neglect of all other con-siderations besides money. All the wisdom of the ancients tells us that nature is not to be mastered but to be wooed. When work ceases to be satisfying and meaningful in itself, then not only men and women but the whole natural order are exploited and despoiled as a means to a single end. The demand of workers, who work-in and sit-in for the right to work, is in effect a challenge to the market system of allocating resources. Intervention by government with state finance can only mark the beginning of a long process in which the allocation of resources through money and the private ownership of wealth is replaced by social determination of social provision, and work itself becomes an object of economic activity.

The market has had the effect of dividing society into producers and consumers who are apparently in conflict, although they are of course the same people. In the next chapter we shall look at the implications of workers' control for reuniting consumer control and producer control. What needs to be said here is that the logic of the work-in movement is that the workers have to look to the local community in their actions to overcome the division between worker and consumer. The strength of the UCS workers rested on their deep roots in the Scottish community and its support for them. Had they not been able to re-establish the four yards in production because there was a real demand for their products, they would have been bound to look more broadly at the social needs of the Scottish community, which they were being denied the right to contribute to meeting; and at how these might be met from the labour and other resources that were unemployed.

The special case of Scotland with its high level of unemployment and strong nationalist sentiment in favour of self government, should not be allowed to conceal the fact that a similar claim could be made for each of the ten regions of Great Britain; and that further decentralisation to District Councils (roughly now half a million population) and local communities (a thousand households, perhaps) would be needed if social formulation of social need were really to begin to take the place of the market allocation of resources.

It is clear enough to workers in nationalised industries
who have found their jobs rationalised and their plants
or pits closed down without alternative employment
that the mere change from private to public ownership,
however important as a basic condition, is not a sufficient condition for the full employment of human
and other resources in our economy. For that, a major
extension of social planning is needed, based upon
local and district as well as regional and national
determination of needs and resources.

The efficacy of the market in allocating resources
of capital and land and labour and of distributing the
output of economic activity was based originally (by
Adam Smith) upon the assumption that no sovereign
(or group of bureaucrats) could ever know enough to
bring together the myriad points of production and
the millions of consumers. The concentration of production into far fewer and far larger units and the
information systems available to us by use of the
computer and modern telecommunications make
possible a wholly new form of economic organisation.
Money, at present, conveys most of the information
upon which our market system works – prices, wages,
profits – but money provides but a crude and easily
distorted system of communication. Some of the
political and economic implications of working out
an alternative system of establishing priorities will be
discussed in the next chapter. Suffice it to say here
that the demands of workers expressed in their work-ins
and sit-ins, have no logical stopping place before they
have found such an alternative.

REFERENCES

1. IWC Pamphlet No.4.
2. IWC Pamphlet No. 26. An abbreviated version of this pamphlet, now
   out-of-print, forms Chapter 3 of this book.

Chapter III
Upper Clyde Shipbuilders*

Michael Barratt Brown

The considerations that would have to be taken into account in a social audit may now be summarised and applied to the case of the Upper Clyde Shipyards.

1. The starting point cannot be the sums of money that have been made or lost in the past, although lessons would need to be learned from past failures of management and trade union practices and their interaction; nor can it be merely the direct accounting of competitive return to capital on any scheme that is considered.

2. The starting point must be the resources available
   a. land and water
   b. plant and machinery and buildings
   c. labour of many different skills, including managerial
   d. housing and other local amenities.

3. External economics of integration and diseconomies from any spillover effects must be taken into account.

4. The next consideration must be the needs of people for different types of goods and the price they will pay for them — in this case for ships and shipping services.

---

*This chapter is an abbreviated version of *UCS: The Social Audit*, published as IWC Pamphlet No.26 in 1971.

5. A parallel consideration must be the balance of home consumption and export earnings.

6. Full employment of resources and particularly of labour in the whole national as well as regional economy must be a prime objective, both as being desirable in itself and as the only basis for maintaining economic activity and encouraging the investment in improved living standards.

7. An absolute increase in the share of real income in the hands of poorer families must be taken in conjunction with the objective of full employment.

8. Account must be taken of the general welfare and that of those most directly involved by taking them into consultation upon all the major decisions.

Thus, a most detailed review must be made under each of these headings of the claims of UCS to the investment of public funds. No more can be done here than to indicate the lines which such a review might take. The actual review by the Social Audit, hearing expert witnesses and consulting public opinion at every stage can alone determine the upshot of such an enquiry. What follows must therefore be regarded only as a preliminary survey of the ground, and may well be faulted in many respects.

1. *Past failures.* There had been widespread criticism of the failure of management in the rather tightly-knit family concerns involved in building ships on the Clyde. This was already being discussed in the . late 1950s when the industry was booming. It was the main burthen of Sir Iain Stewart's criticisms when he took over the running of Fairfields in 1967 and when he declined to continue under the merged UCS. There is, however, evident confidence

among the workers in the new management of
UCS led by Mr Ken Douglas.

There has been equally widespread criticism of
labour practices on Clydeside and of industrial
relations in general.[1] A part of this has been a
management problem resulting from three special
economic factors in shipbuilding: first, the difficulties of forecasting demand in a sharply fluctuating
market, and the tendency of managements therefore to take men on in large numbers when orders
were good and especially when delivery dates were
tight and to lay them off when orders were thin;
second, the difficulties arising from the product
mix of different types of ships at different stages of
construction in a yard at any time requiring different
types of labour; third, the great amount of subcontracting with the resultant tendency for workers to spend
much of their time waiting for the particular work
on which they are involved to be ready for them.
The fact is that although wage costs per hour were
not particularly high in British yards, productivity
per hour was relatively low. Table 1 gives the figures.
figures.

Table 1: Wage Costs and Productivity in Different National Shipbuilding Industries 1960-65

Country	Wage Costs per hour (£) 1965	Productivity (man hour per ton)	
		1965	Av.1960-65
U.K.	0.40	140	187
U.S.A.	1.19	220	164
Germany	0.44	135	155
Sweden	0.67	62	82
Japan	0.26	39	70

Source: K.J.W. Alexander and C.L. Jenkins, *Fairfields.* Allen Lane
1970 pp.38-9.

Although the gap between Japan and the rest is
very wide on both counts the gap between UK and

Germany, Britain's other major rival, is quite narrow.

It is, moreover, reported that productivity has been doubled at UCS in the last year; and there is little doubt that reduction in duplication of overheads, improved planning and programming, more specialisation in output and improved manpower utilisation had begun to show important results. What is of quite crucial importance is that evidently both workers and management had begun to believe in the possibilities of successful shipbuilding, if only the inheritance of past financial difficulties could be wiped out.

2. *Available resources.* Only expert opinion can establish the resources available on Upper Clyde as a viable basis for future investment. Four points may, however, be made without danger of contradiction:

a. The members of the Advisory Group — the so-called 'Four Wise Men' (Mr Alexander MacDonald, Chairman of Distillers; Sir Alexander Glen, Chairman of H. Clarkson, Shipbrokers; Mr David Marchand, Director of Hill Samuel, Merchant Bankers; and Lord Robens, Chairman of Vickers) — which took four weeks to produce a four page report with no evidence whatsoever included to support their decision, must be pressed to supply this evidence.

b. The costs of unemployment pay and of resettling 5,000 or more workers elsewhere, must be taken into account in any decision.

c. The morale of the workers and management at UCS, which has led to the occupation of the John Brown's yard, must be regarded as an extremely positive factor.

d. If Fairfields is a viable production unit in the view of the 'Wise Men' then it is likely to be much more viable with the addition of other production facilities since there are major economies of scale in overheads, subcontracting etc., in shipbuilding.[2]

3. *External Economies and Diseconomies.* A proposal by John Hughes[3] for a joint operation by the British Steel Corporation and UCS on the Upper Clyde, or for a diversified state corporation on the lines of the Italian IRI which would develop not only Clydeside, but a range of shipbuilding, shipping services, engineering and associated undertakings. The coastal shipping of Great Britain has for long required nationalisation to bring into efficient publicly controlled operation the thousands of small and unscrupulous operators in this business. Instead of hiving off British Rail's ferry boats, hovercraft and freightliners and dismantling the publicly owned Atlantic Steam Navigation Company, which pioneered roll-on-roll-off services, these might appropriately be integrated with other coastal shipping and orders for ships programmed in association with the steel suppliers and shipbuilders. Quite contrary to the impression being given by the Conservative Government the public corporations have a much better economic record than private industry in the last decade.[4] As for diseconomies, there can be no doubt that the River Clyde will have to be looked at as a whole in the next decade and a major enquiry should be put in hand to this effect immediately.

4. *The Market for Ships.* Once again this is a matter for expert witnesses, but there are a number of points that can be made with some assurance:

a. UCS has an order book of £90m[5] all due for delivery in 1971-2 or 1972-3 and it is understood that the order book would have been very much larger had the company not felt unable to take on orders beyond 1972-3 in view of the Government's threat of witholding cash flow.

b. The Clyde cargo ships which are the specially designed standardised 18,000 ton ships pioneered by UCS are proving extremely popular. Seven are already made and it was orders for these which were cut back earlier this year. Similar standardisation principles have been applied to the 26,000 ton bulk carriers of which 14 are on order.

Table 2: U.K. Merchant Fleet and Shipbuilding Industry

Year	(m.tons)	% of world	000 tons	% for export	% tankers	As % of world output	Shipbldg. Empt. Construction	
							All (000)	Only (000)
1913	18	42	1,932	22	—	58	—	—
1929	16	29	1,523	17	—	55	—	—
1939	17.7	26	630	12	—	25	—	—
1949	18.3	22	1,268	41	28	41	250	67
1955	19.6	20	1,474	37	47	28	—	64
1956-60	19.5	16	1,380	20	42	17	227	61
1961-4	20.4	14.5	1,060	21	38	12	240	41
1965	21.4	13	1,204	12	39	10	224	—
1966	21.5	12.5	1,130	25	35	8	219	—
1967	21.4	12	1,192	51	12	7.5	218	—
1968	21.7	11	1,046	52	23	6	207	—
1969	22.3	10.5	814	39	6	5	201	—

Note: All employed includes naval vessel building and marine engineering repair work.
Merchant Fleet is of all sizes, output is of 100 gross tons available only.

Sources: U.N. *Statistical Yearbooks*, U.K. *Annual Abstracts of Statistics*, W.S. & E.S. Woytinsky *World Commerce and Governments*.

c. UCS is only responsible for about 10-12% of the tonnage being built in British shipyards and British yards are only now building about 5% of world output. In view of the sharp recent reduction in this share shown in Table 2 it should not be impossible at least to hold on to this share if not to build it up. What is involved is really quite marginal — about half of one per cent of world output, 100;000 tons out of the world merchant fleet that now tops 200 millions, a third of this being tankers in which UCS is not involved.

d. Demand for ships is a function of the growth of world trade. This has been advancing for the last decade at the rate of 10% per annum (nearer 12% in manufactured goods). Even if we exclude the most rapidly growing inter-trade of the Common Market most of which is carried overland, the growth rate is 8% per annum. Then the fact that the world merchant fleet has been growing at 5% a year in terms of tonnage, 4% excluding tankers tonnage which has been increasing at 8% a year, gives reason for hope that this market is still expanding. In view of the fact that the underdeveloped world has had little part in this rapid growth of trade it is to expansion there that Britain should look, as will be argued in a moment.

e. The tonnage of new ships being ordered mainly consists of giant tankers, giant ore carriers and giant container ships. It is possible, on the one hand, that the boom in these is over; it is certain that they will greatly reduce the number of ships required both because of their size and speed and because of their rapid rates of turn-around in port. This last point particularly applies to container ships. The Rochdale Report

recently commented on the basis of the
Australian trade:

"The tonnage of the UK deep cargo line fleet may well
be nearly halved over the coming decade as container
services develop. The number of vessels would show
an even greater reduction."

This was in line with a Board of Trade estimate
for the world demand for dry cargo tonnage.
Even more rapid changes have been predicted
in private studies like the Lambert Bros. (Shipping) Ltd., Study of 1970 which suggested
the displacement of between 500 and 850
vessels by 1975.

James MacDonald the *Financial Times* Ship-
ing Correspondent was already reporting in
1970 that shipowners were finding once more
that they had ships which were not at the end
of their useful lives with no employment for
them.[6]

These developments have huge implications
for dockworkers and for sailors. Dock labour
is expected to be halved between 1970 and
1975.[7] British seamen employed between 1964
and 1968 dropped by an eighth but the volume
of goods carried in British ships rose by a quarter. The new 400,000 tonners have actually
smaller crews than the old 40,000 tonners.[8] On
the other hand there may be a growing demand
for smaller ships to feed into the big carriers.

5. *The Balance of Payments.* A combined strategy
for shipbuilding, shipping and port employment
becomes an evident necessity, if unemployment on
a mass scale in the major ports of Britain is to be
prevented. Shipbuilding and shipping services, as
can be seen in Table 3, are important items in Britain's
balance of payments. Nobody would nowadays

defend the erstwhile activities of the "Shipping Conference" lines in excluding developing nations from
the carrying trade of the world.[9] What may be suggested here is that the needs of the underdeveloped
countries for increased trade and their own shipping
services may provide opportunities for a reconstruc-
ted approach by British Governments to the whole
question.

Table 3: U.K. Imports and Exports of Ships and Shipping
Services

Year	Ships (£m)			Shipping Services (£m)		
	Imports	Exports	Balance	Imports	Exports	Balance
1964	19	30	+11	724	687	− 7
1965	26	34	+ 8	728	725	− 3
1966	9	48	+39	716	718	+ 2
1967	22	69	+47	780	798	+18
1968	34	82	+48	895	956	+61
1969	39	62	+23	914	959	+44
1970	31.5	61	+30	1,087	1,073	−14

Source: Overseas Trade Accounts of the U.K.

It has already been suggested that these countries
have not enjoyed the same growth of trade as the
more developed lands. Indeed, while the trade of the
more developed lands has grown in the last decade by
10% a year; that of the underdeveloped has been
growing by only 5% a year. Britain with a long history of trade with the less developed nations has
been particularly affected by this event. This is one
of the main arguments adduced for entry into the
Common Market where trade has been growing
rapidly. An alternative conclusion might be that
Britain should plan to increase her trade exchanges
with the underdeveloped countries by agreeing upon
increased purchases of the goods they have to offer
for increased sales of the products excluding ships
which we have to offer. The result of entry into the
Common Market is that we buy even less from

the underdeveloped countries — not only of agricultural products but of textiles and other semi-processed goods and manufacturers, and have to concentrate our sales in the Common Market where the fiercest competition for markets not only for ships but many other staple UK exports already, exists.

In the case of containerisation there may be a specially important point here since underdeveloped lands are not going to be able for some time to develop the dockside facilities or the organisation and computer programming techniques required to operate container systems except perhaps at a few points on each continent. Feeder shipping from these points by sea and river will remain of key importance; and it is this type of ship which UCS is most suited to produce. Plans to increase the sale of ships for the products of underdeveloped countries would of course require Government aid and support in the first instance and a major measure of Government planning. Such plans would come up against powerful opposition from the banks and the giant companies including the shipping lines which would fear quite rightly that funds which they would wish to control for their own profitable enterprises would become directed to other purposes.

The crucial questions for a Social Audit of the future of British Shipbuilding are first whether a product can be made in a standardised form to reduce the costs to meet the needs of the underdeveloped countries and second whether Government arrangements can be made to market these in exchange for guaranteed imports of goods which British people want from the underdeveloped countries. It is as simple (and as difficult) as that once we speak in terms of the use of resources to meet needs instead of in terms of the competitive market.

6. *Full Employment and the Right to Work.* It
should hardly need repeating here that the crucial
question to be asked again is how we may make
use of the skills and capacities of human beings in
Britain to make more goods which others in this
country and abroad would be most anxious to
obtain for goods which they could offer in exchange and we should like to have more of. What
in fact happened as we saw earlier in examining
the competitive market system, is that funds are becoming concentrated on giant companies who
have established some monopolistic position in
the market at the expense of the ordinary needs
of men and women. Since these companies operate
at high levels of technology with few workers
and much capital equipment, capital resources
are denied for providing employment in meeting
such ordinary needs. What appears as a technological advance, like supersonic transport and space
research, becomes a monstrous dragon devouring
the resources of whole peoples. Only the expenditure of governments out of the taxation of companies and the richer individual taxpayers serves
to offset this process and to maintain full employment. Any move towards relegating the allocation
of resources once more to the arbitrament of profit
and loss can only mean the reappearance of mass
unemployment. We may quote the words of a liberal
Professor of Political Economy at Cambridge
University:

"There would be a similar number of exceedingly
wealthy property owners; the proportion of the population required to man the extremely profitable auto-
mated industries would be small; wage rates would then
be depressed; there would have to be a large expansion
of the production of the labour intensive goods and
services which were in high demand by the few multi-
multi-multi-millionaires; we would be back in a super-

world of an immiserised proletariat and of butlers, foot-
men, kitchen maids and other hangers on. Let us call
this the Brand New Capitalist's Paradise."[10]

It must be perfectly obvious by now that all
investments cannot be siphoned off into the most
profitable lines of business without leaving a desert
surrounding them. What is more and what James
Meade does not proceed to examine is that such a
process would be self-defeating. As we have already
indicated, somebody has still to earn enough to
buy all the products of the most advanced auto-
mated factories. The fact is that the role of Governments and of the public sector has to be extended,
not contracted. We have to tax the multi-multi-
millionaires and other rich individuals so that the
rest of us do not have to find ourselves working as
their shoe shine boys and to have the chance to
produce the whole range of goods and services that
automation cannot produce. This is not of course
to say that we should behave like Luddites and
resist the introduction of new labour saving
machinery where sweat and danger of human
labour can be reduced. Our aim, however, must be
different — the full use of human capacities. It may
well be that a smaller labour force working longer
hours may be more efficient than a large labour
force working shorter hours. Unit costs may be
lowered that way — through reduction of overheads, lower National Insurance payments, redundancy and industrial training contributions and the
costs of payment calculations, canteens, car park
and worker space. Once more these are the private
costs of the company. The social costs of the
leisure forgone of those at work and the unemployment of those made redundant must however be
set in the scales against them.

Where it appears that the reduction of manpower in a particular enterprise is inevitable — and this must be faced — the demand of the right to work must still be maintained. Some years ago I put forward a proposal based upon a suggestion of Sir Roy Harrods taken up by John Knapp of Manchester that unemployment should be abolished for ever.[11] All that was needed was that every man and woman requiring work should present himself or herself to a Labour Exchange and choose from one of three alternatives.

a. transfer to another part of the country in his own skill with costs of removal covered and housing guaranteed in the new area;
b. retraining for a new skill with wages paid at 75% of rates in his previous job during training;
c. employment at Trade Union negotiated rates on jobs required by the local authority with Government grants to cover them, to improve local amenities, remove dereliction, clear pollution, create parks and social centres.

The cost I argued would be likely to be little more than the cost of unemployment benefit and social security and redundancy pay; important work would be done to improve the environment in run-down industrial areas; and a new atmosphere would be created of job security in which it would be more rather than less easy to encourage flexibility and mobility of employment. If there are to be concessions in the numbers that should man up the new shipyards on Clydeside, they should only be made after guarantees of the implementation of such a proposal have been obtained.

7. *Increases in the Income of the Poor.* Scottish households in 1967 achieved an average household income equal to that of the average for the UK

only because they had 8% more persons per household on average and 7% more persons in the household at work. Only Northern Ireland of all the regions showed large figures in these respects. The earnings of full-time working men and women were the lowest in the Kingdom, once again barring Northern Ireland.[12] A year later men's and women's earnings had relatively improved but they remained some 8% below the national average. With the above average rise in Scottish unemployment during 1969, the improvement largely disappeared. On the principle that an increase in the share of real income in the hands of the poor must increase public welfare (unless it involves a decrease in the total income) the claims of Scotland, and particularly of the Glasgow area, must have a high priority. Glasgow has above average earnings for Scotland as a whole, but much below average for all the major cities

Table 4: Relative Male and Female Earnings in Big Cities of the U.K. 1967-68

Region and City	Average Weekly Earnings	
	Males	Females
U.K.	100	100
London, GL Conurbation	115	125
Manchester	110	99
Southampton	102.3	101.1
Cardiff	100.9	100
Bristol	100.9	93.8
Edinburgh	98.9	104.1
Sheffield	95.9	87.5
Newcastle	95.1	92.5
Liverpool	94.9	92.1
Nottingham	93.5	92.8
Glasgow	92.1	98.9
Leeds	90.2	93.1

Source: Regional Statistics Department of Economic Affairs 1969 from Ministry of Social Security returns.

of the UK with which it should properly be compared. Only Leeds of the big cities showed lower male earnings in 1967/8.

One must add once again that with higher rates of unemployment after 1968 the position of Glasgow may well have declined.

8. *General Welfare and Popular Control.* The population of Scotland in the Eighteenth Century comprised some 15% of total population in the UK. In the first half of the nineteenth century it remained at about 13.5%. A hundred years later in 1966 it had fallen almost to 9%. Yet the area of Scotland makes up a third of the UK total. Population density is thus about 165 per square mile compared with 830 per square mile in England and Wales. Employment which has increased in England by 7% in a decade has not increased at all in Scotland. Some 30,000 (net) have migrated southward, every year, half of them from Glasgow. Is this really what we want in a world that is increasingly overcrowded? Is it what the Scottish people want? The fact is that they have never been asked.

This paper cannot be brought to an end without emphasising that whatever the final decision about UCS, the rights of the people concerned to have a say in the decisions, to be free to use the skills that they have to build the goods, that other people want, to live among the friends and relatives they know are inalienable rights, that cannot be overruled by any decisions of Governments in London or Commissions in Brussels, unless it can be proved that the general welfare of the whole people of Britain requires that they be overruled. That is the case that those who would close the UCS yards must establish. It is not necessary for the workers at UCS to prove their rights. They know what they want

and they have the support of the whole Scottish
people in defending them. It is necessary for those
who would overrule those rights to establish their
reasons for doing so, in the full light of English
and of Scottish public opinion. The burden of proof
lies with the Conservative Government in London
and it is the task of the Committee of Inquiry set
up in Clydebank this month of August 1971 to
detail the case which that Government must answer.
In so doing let it be understood that they are chal-
lenging its right to govern.

The Committee of Inquiry should thus be required to call as witnesses not only industrial and
economic experts, but the social workers, clergy-
men, representatives of all the many facets of
Scottish life. What results should first be truly a
social audit, not merely an economic cost-benefit
analysis.

Conclusion

It must be clear from the foregoing that a social
audit, to establish the case for public investment
in UCS, will have to go beyond the direct accounts
of the company, and even beyond the direct costs
and benefits of its continued operation as a public
concern. It will have, in effect, to open up an
inquiry into the full use of the human and natural
resources of Scotland.

What is required is a Scottish economic plan for
full employment. The resources of universities,
technical colleges and all industrial and trade union
research departments should be called upon immediately to provide staff:

First, for making an inventory

a. of the urgent social needs of the people,
b. of economic resources including manpower,

education and training facilities and plant and equipment existing in Scotland,
c. of resources needed for outside Scotland and Scotland's capacity to pay for them;

and *secondly,* for drawing up an emergency economic plan leading on to a longer term plan for economic development.

Funds would have to be made available immediately for teams to get down to this work and for local authorities, trade unions and other voluntary bodies to take part in what would become a national audit. Nothing less can save Scotland from becoming a derelict area on the periphery of an increasingly concentrated Western European Common Market.

REFERENCES

1. See for example A.K. Cairncross and J. Parkinson "The Ship-building Industry" in D. Burn (ed) *The Structure of British Industry* 1958, pp.122-3.
2. See K.J.W. Alexander et al, op. cit. p.46 ff.
3. *UCS:* Institute for Workers' Control Pamphlet No.25.
4. See M. Barratt Brown and R. Pryke *Stop Messing Them About* — Public Enterprise Group.
5. Details are given in *UCS,* the Institute for Workers' Control Pamphlet No.25.
6. *Financial Times* supplement on Containers, June 1 1970.
7. Report in *The Post* January 30 1969, quoted by Tony Topham in *Trade Union Register 1* Merlin/Spokesman 1969, p.124.
8. *The Observer,* February 8, 1970.
9. For details see M. Barratt Brown *After Imperialism,* p.272.
10. J.E. Meade *Efficiency, Equality and the Ownership of Property,* 1964, p.33.
11. See *Tribune,* 14 November, 1967.
12. *Family Expenditure Survey Report* for 1967, Regional Table.

Part Two

COMMUNITY ACTION, COMMUNITY PLANS

Community Action, like industrial action, will be contained and neutralised if it does not give rise to its own alternative plans.

Pete Thomas, in his graphic description of the Australian "green ban" movement, explains one of the most dramatic modern rebellions against urban destruction. Subsequently, the Builders' Labourers' Union in Sydney came under sustained criticism and attack.

The Community Development Projects in Britain gathered considerable experience in a number of cities while they were allowed to operate. Our excerpt is taken from a comprehensive report on decline in five of the inner-city areas which were involved. The account of the failure of Skeffington-style consultation in Nottinghamshire, in spite of the earnest intentions of a most dedicated group of professional planners, is still not complete, since the argument about the future of mining in the area is only just beginning.

In the same way, the evidence given by the Socialist Environment and Resources Association to the Windscale Enquiry is hardly likely to be the last word on the questions it treats.

In all four of these case studies, the problems are still increasing, and the pressures will not abate.

Chapter IV

The Green Bans in Australia

Pete Thomas

Australian newspapers have described New South Wales builders' labourers as Sydney's "social conscience". The British weekly *Guardian* has said that Jack Mundey, New South Wales secretary of the union, could claim to be "Australia's most effective conservationist", and it went on: "Middle-class groups are a little embarrassed at having to turn to a rough-hewn proletarian Communist to protect their homes (and values) from flats and motor-ways, and their theatres and pubs from office developers. But approach him they do . . . "

An architect, in a letter of appreciation to the union's office, described the union as "the last line of defence against the pack-raping of things of quality".

This has been part of the recognition of NSW builders' labourers' actions — mostly by bans on demolitions, and also bans on certain constructions — to preserve history, people's homes and what remnants survive of a gracious and natural environment. What the builders labourers' union has done on this has won for it a respect of a character never before accorded to a union.

Issues of the environment, conservation and preservation have been rising in importance in the community's mind in Australia, as elsewhere. Public concern has grown as Big Business marauders' course of demolition and destruction has quickened, and as authorities have stood indulgently aside.

Some countries have taken positive action. In France,

laws to preserve structures recalling the history of
France may apply to whole areas, such as the Marais
quarter of Paris. Owners can be compelled to do work
necessary for preservation, or the Minister for Cultural
Affairs may take over a building if the owner is misusing
or neglecting it. In return, owners receive various benefits.

In England, when a building is scheduled for preservation, then funds are made available for its restoration
and upkeep.

But in New South Wales and most other parts of
Australia, history and the environment are elbowed
aside by the dollar.

Sydney architect Norman Edwards wrote in the
National *Times* in July 1972 that, in Australia, "progress
is defined as newness for its own sake, and the consequence of this environmentally is that of bushland bull-
dozed out of existence, of polluted rivers, and of fine
old buildings and streets ripped up for the urgency of
turning over a fast million bucks."

Mr Peter Keys (a Federal councillor of the Royal
Australian Institute of Architects) wrote in late 1972
that every building of historic importance in Australia
is in danger of being demolished. This could happen
because State Governments had no legal rights to stop
owners from pulling down their buildings. He said
also:

> "Of course, the cost of preserving these buildings must be
> weighed against the need for continued economic growth . . .
> But it seems the powers-that-be in this country think
> economic progress and growth are related to demolition
> and erecting multi-storey buildings."

The Sydney Strategic Plan, calling for measures to
preserve places and structures of historic or architectural significance, noted wryly:

> "The history of Sydney is unique to Sydney, and its old
> buildings, precincts, structures and details are the physical

expression of this history . . . An invaluable part of the city
is being destroyed through redevelopment and there is a
real danger that Sydney will become a 'faceless' city because
the buildings that are replacing the old ones are more and
more international in style and homogenous in appearance . . .
Economic pressure for redevelopment is strong and economic
incentives for preservation are weak . . . "

The union's initial intervention in NSW was over the
Kellys Bush issue.

Kellys Bush is a much-loved surviving piece of natural
bushland on the Parramatta River in elegant Hunters
Hill. The A.V. Jennings group with State Government
connivance, planned to move in there with home-unit
construction.

Local people and others protested in every way they
could devise – meetings, deputations, petition, newspaper items, the lot. But to no avail. In desperation,
they sought union aid, and they got it.

Building unions, including the Builders Labourers',
were among those who responded. The Jennings group
was warned that, if it persisted with desecration at
Kellys Bush, it could face a ban on all its Sydney
projects, which would be left stark and uncompleted
as memorials to Kellys Bush. The threat was effective:
Kellys Bush survives, in testimony to that, Parkland
remains where otherwise stone and concrete would
have taken over.

The next case was Eastlakes. Parkes Developments
zeroed in on some remaining green land there; they
intended to build more home units on it. Eastlakes
people were indignant; the existence of this parkland,
they said, had been one of the inducements used to
attract some of them to move into Eastlakes units.

Faced with the threat to the parkland, they turned
to the Builders Labourers', which put a ban on the
project. Again, it succeeded. The parkland is still parkland.

A unionist coined a happy phrase for such bans to save natural bush and park. "They're not black bans," he said, "they're green bans."

Next came one of the most dramatic and significant of the union's bans: the ban which checkmated a project to dismember Sydney's Rocks area for the sake of a $500 million redevelopment, much of it for foreign interests, into commercial skyscrapers.

The Rocks area lies at the heart of Sydney's history from the time of the First Fleet. This stubby finger of land, on the western side of Circular Quay, stretches to the tip of Dawes Point (which is now beneath the southern end of the Harbour Bridge).

It was Australia's first colonised settlement, and was seen by Governor Phillip as the cradle of the new colony. A ship's surgeon at that time wrote (as recalled by Charles Sriber in a 1972 Sydney *Morning Herald* article) about "the stupendous rocks . . . hang'g over in a most awful manner from above and forming the most commodious quays by the water." Settlers built wherever they could find a flat piece of ground: wattle and daub huts, and buildings of sandstone quarried almost on the spot.

It grew in a haphazard cheerfulness that was the delight of most but the despair of the predecessors of today's civic officialdom. Wrote one of these in the latter 1880s:

> "How can you expect righteousness when one householder . . . is using as his backyard the roof of his neighbour's house placed low in the street behind; or does it make for riches when the roadway suddenly narrows to a cart's width and this man is growing roses in what should be the centre of the street?"

Seamen from clippers and whalers came to the Rocks for their sprees after savage months at sea. They were welcomed at such pubs at The Sailor's Return and The Ship & Mermaid, where Joseph Conrad, Robert

Louis Stevenson and Jack London stayed when in Sydney.

(Some of the taverns around the Rocks and Circular Quay in the early days weren't the best places for a seaman to do his boozing. When he came to, he might be out to sea on some strange ship bound for a faraway port – victim of a gang recruiting for a short-handed crew.)

Times and ways have changed, but the Rocks remains rich in community spirit. Its pubs still carry names associated with long-gone personages and events: the Hero of Waterloo (built originally as a dwelling in 1804 and then, as a pub, named amid the exuberance about the final defeat of Napoleon on that Belgian battlefield in 1815), Lord Nelson (he came to his end at Trafalgar in 1805), Fortune of War, and Palisade. The convict-built Holy Trinity Garrison Church still stands, as Australia's oldest church, where officers and lesser mortals of the NSW Corps attended in between their other and less godly doings in a colony where rum was once the currency and the NSW Corps controlled the rum. The village green of Argyle Place and its drinking fountain are still there.

Cedric Flower has written: "To walk through the West Rocks is to experience a breath of calm, it restores our sense of balance, gives back our human scale, allows past hands to touch ours."

The rows of terraced houses, monuments to the past, remain to help preserve the close-knit neighbourliness of those who live in the Rocks, some of them from families which – like that of Rocks Resident Group secretary Mrs Nita McCrae – have been there for generations and can conceive of no other place as being home.

Newcomers, too, quickly feel the spirit of the Rocks community. A migrant woman told one of the public meetings in the Rocks: "When I came to Australia, I felt a stranger. But then I came to live in the Rocks and

I found new friends all around me."

Then trampling into all of this came the monster of development. The State Government, owning the Rocks, set up its Sydney Cove Redevelopment Authority, headed (in deference to the bygone NSW Corps?) by a former army colonel.

The attractions of the Rocks as a site for profitable development were hawked around the world. The prospects made some foreign interests drool. Plans were initiated for a programme with a first stage of some $50 or so million and to cost altogether around $500 million, including 40 and 50 storey towers, an international hotel and other ugliness rearing high.

Some of the historic spots and terraced homes were to be preserved — but not for people who now live in the Rocks; homes were to be restored as suites for professional men, and any history retained was to be virtually some sort of quaint and gimmicky annexe for the hotels and gaunt commercial highrise.

Tenants in the East Rocks were told that they'd have to go. Many left. But then remaining Rocks people rebelled. They asked for, and got, a ban by the Builders Labourers' on any demolition or other work connected with the scheme.

The Sydney Cove Redevelopment Authority tried to push ahead and to bust through the ban. On January 24, 1972 — two days before the anniversary of the First Fleet dropping anchor so near to the Rocks in 1788 — early in the morning residents heard bulldozers rumbling into destructive action.

In outraged indignation, some 30 locals, mostly women, rushed out and sat in the path of the bulldozers and trucks there. As an added buttress, they moved a station wagon also into the way. And they called up the unions.

In response, the Federated Engine Drivers and Firemen's Association (FED&FA), whose members

operate bulldozers, joined the Builders Labourers' in
the ban, and prevented a resumption of the bulldozing.
Australia's biggest union, the Amalgamated Metal
Workers' Union, also joined the ban. Other unions,
including the Building Workers' Industrial Union, have
declared their support for the residents.

The Government and its Sydney Cove Redevelopment Authority have tried in a variety of ways — some
of them subtle, some crude — to penetrate or get
around the ban. There have been sugared approaches
to tenants. There have been threats. There have
been court proceedings. But the ban stays.

Residents themselves have been resolute and spirited,
and have taken their campaign out widely into the
Sydney community. In one of its leaflets, the Rocks
Residents Group said:

> "The buildings of the Rocks are part of our history. They can
> never be replaced. They belong to all Australians . . .
>   "Planning is for people and progress, not for profiteers,
> politicians and pollution."

It acknowledged that, "once again, in the face of the
usual apathy, inaction and favouritism of the Askin
Government," it had been left to unionists "to show
leadership in protecting our citizens and their historic
buildings."

Another of the Rocks Residents Group's leaflets,
calling for protests, asked people at large: "Do you want
a city with a dead heart, a concrete jungle, increased
noise and air pollution? . . . If you are concerned
about the past, present and future of Sydney, you
must act now . . ."

The Australia Party candidate for Sydney in the
December 1972 Federal election, Allan Sorrensen, said
in a leaflet that the Rocks community are the guardians
of the national heritage of all Australians. He said that
the Askin Government, the Sydney Cove Redevelopment

Authority and the faceless developers were indifferent
to social upheaval to families and destruction of the
community spirit of the Rocks, overloading of transport,
and other essential services, and "cramming people into
high-rise slums, like chooks in a battery farm."

From a public meeting in the Rocks in October 1972,
a Rocks People's Plan Committee, including architects
and others well qualified for the task, set out to examine
what was known of the authority's redevelopment plan
and to put forward a people's plan. By hard work, it
was able to publish its plan on the day of the annual
Rocks celebration in April 1973, when the people cheer-
fully take over and the Hero of Waterloo, and the other
pubs are almost burst apart in the crush of hundreds,
in happy carnival mood.

After seriously examining the options, the People's
Plan came out in favour of maintaining the Rocks as
an integrated residential and historic area, separated
from the functions of the Central Business District of
Sydney. Any new development, it said, "should be
either infill or replacement of derelict buildings and
should conform to the style and mass of the area."

The objectives of the Sydney Cove Redevelopment
Authority, the People's Plan said, should be redrawn
so as to revitalise the area through a return of residents,
an injection of cultural and entertainment centres, and
an extensive programme of historic preservation. The
operations of the Authority, it said, should be opened
up, and full and ongoing consultation instituted between the Authority and residents, tenants and
interested citizens.

It said that the future planning of the Rocks should
be a cooperative endeavour of the planners and public,
in place of secretive conflict and bad feeling. Decisions made about the future of the Rocks should involve as fully as possible, "and even to the point of
veto", those who now live and work there or who will

come to live there over the next years.

Earlier, in 1972, a report by the NSW Division Committee of the Royal Australian Planning Institute said:

"The Rocks area is not a privately-owned piece of real estate to be exploited in the most profitable way. The land in question has been acquired or is controlled by the Government on behalf of the people of New South Wales. It is part of the national heritage, paid for many times over by the generation since the continent was first settled . . . "

A subsequent press statement by the NSW branch of the Builders Labourers' said that it agreed with the conclusion by the Institute that the State Government was sidestepping the moral issue; that is, to use the land in the way that would bring the greatest benefit to the most people. This, it said, "implies the same courage and foresight as must have been exercised by early decision-makers in this State, when areas such as Hyde Park, the Domain and Centennial Park were set aside for public use and enjoyment in perpetuity."

The Askins and the developers huff and puff, and the Sydney *Morning Herald* and other dailies write venomous editorials against the union ban. But the Rocks still lives. Workers and their families are still there. They don't intend to go, and the Builders Labourers' and other unions are right beside them.

During 1972 and onwards, the Builders Labourers', and often the FED&FA, were called on for a succession of other bans. They responded. In every case, the ban imposed was at the request of residents or other concerned people. The unions were meticulous not to intrude, unasked. (Not that this stopped the Sydney *Morning Herald* and others from accusing them of intruding.)

One such ban was to save the lovely Sydney Botanic Gardens — with their profusion of trees, shrubs and plants — from the effects of an underground car park project, dreamed up in the last stages of that massive

saga of Opera House construction. The idea was that
the AMP Society (whose insurance money takes it into
a vast complexity of industrial and commercial undertakings) would build a $4 million car park excavated
beneath the Botanic Gardens.

This project would for a start, have doomed three
venerable giant Moreton Bay fig trees. More than this,
fumes from the cars going into and out of the underground parking area could extensively damage the
Gardens. But, in the Government's thinking, gardens
for the people were rated subordinate to cars for those
who can afford the Opera House prices.

The Builders Labourers' help was invoked. It laid
down conditions for doing any work connected with
the project: the Moreton Bay fig trees must be saved
and effective measures must be taken to ensure that
the health of other Gardens' flora be not jeopardised.
Unable or unwilling to comply, the Government gave
in. In August 1972, the plan for the underground
car park was shelved. The Government had to devise
an alternative proposition.

The Botanic Gardens thrives, saved from the car-
park threat.

About the same time, the Builders Labourers' found
itself in another eyeball to eyeball conflict with the
Askin State Government; this time over Moore Park
and Centennial Park.

The Askin Government got enthusiastic over a
notion to try to have the 1988 Olympic Games in
Sydney. In some sort of a brainstorm, the Government conceived the idea of using the Moore Park-
Centennial Park area, to the south of Sydney city,
for a grandiose sports complex for the Games.

There were immediate and strong objections.
Some were on the grounds of the unsuitability of the
location, because of transport and other problems.
Others, even more emphatic, were because the project

would commandeer acres of natural parkland.
The Save the Parks organisation wrote:

> "These parks already suffer from the effects of too many
> visiting cars and too much noise pollution and would suffer
> further irretrievable loss from the destruction of breathing
> space and greenery, including many ancient Moreton Bay
> figs lining Anzac Parade. It means chaos and the permanent
> downgrading of all nearby residential suburbs.
>
> "The western suburbs have a crying need for this very same
> sporting complex. In that area, there are several relatively
> uncongested sites available, adjacent to railways (the present
> site is not) which would actually benefit from this plan. These
> other sites are not beautiful parks and playing fields. They are
> not, as are Moore Park and Centennial Park, used by thousands
> of terrace-house inner-city suburbanites with inadequate
> gardens or growing room for children.
>
> "We must stop this plan. For everyone's sake. It's the right
> idea in the wrong place!"

It asked: "A lot of park, or a parking lot?"

Feeling the hot angry breath on the back of its
neck, the Askin Government got out from under. In
June 1972, it announced the appointment of Mr
Walter Bunning, Sydney architect and town planner,
to investigate the submissions on the project: an
investigation that obviously should have been carried
through before, and not after, the Government made
a decision.

The upshot was a vindication of the public protest
campaign. The Bunning report recommended that any
such Games complex should be built not in the Moore
Park-Centennial Park area but in the Homebush area,
which is what the campaigners had advocated.

Another campaign, in which Actors' Equity, the
Builders Labourers' Federation and the Federated
Engine Drivers & Firemen's Association (FED&FA)
were involved, ran up against the Lend Lease empire,
headed by Mr G.J. Dusseldorp. Lend Lease, together
with the MLC insurance company, had an inner-city

development project which involved a lot of demolition.
One building marked for destruction was the Theatre
Royal, with its historic and sentimental links going
back far into last century.

The campaign to save the Theatre Royal brought
together in common activity people from right across
the social and political stage; a judge, Liberal Party
and Australia Party and Labour Party people, and
communists and others from trade unions. They pulled
together in concerted effort. An attempt by Mr Peter
Coleman, a Liberal MLA far over to the Right, at one
public meeting to redbait against Jack Mundey rebound-
ded against himself.

In the end, it was not possible to save the Theatre
Royal from demolition. But the pressure had been so
strong that Lend Lease's Mr Dusseldorp bent to it and
promised to erect a new theatre (to be named the
Theatre Royal, to maintain the lineage of Theatre
Royals in that area). It would seat at least 1000, it
would be devoted to live professional theatre, with
preference to performances using local talent, only
an "economic" rent would be charged (that is, a minimum rent related to costs), and so on.

Actors' Equity, as one of the initiating forces in the
campaign, applauded the outcome. In a pointed comment on Sydney's lack of theatres, an Actors' Equity
spokesman said that, with the rebuilding of the burnt-
out Her Majesty's and now the promised rebirth of a
Theatre Royal, Sydney's three million people might
by the end of 1973 have two working city theatres —
"one more than Hobart".

Another campaign was for preservation of Sydney's
historic Pitt Street Congregational Church, self-styled
as "the church with a heart in the heart of the city".
The National Trust rated this church as "a highly significant building" and strongly recommended its preservation. But the church leaders had plans for demolition

and a redevelopment, to include a high-rise office block, restaurant, and other amenities, as well as a chapel and church offices.

In a letter to the Sydney *Morning Herald*, Mr Mundey said that the union's members would not demolish the building. He went on:

> "If architects, engineers and building workers combine to preserve a little of our history, people in the future will be grateful for our belated action. In the building industry, we will strive to continue to make our presence felt, not only in our members' interests but in the interest of the general public as well."

The church's minister, the Rev J. Bryant, said that the office block and other aspects of the redevelopment were needed to provide the "financial sinews" which were "necessary for the church to minister to the people". Demolition, redevelopment, money, for sacred purpose.

As well as its social and environmental significance, the affair had its piquant aspects. On the one hand, church leaders were wanting to knock down the church; on the other hand, a union with a communist secretary was intervening to preserve the church. A Molnar cartoon in the Sydney *Morning Herald* had Jack Mundey saying to the Rev J. Bryant: "Nothing personal, you understand; actually I'm an atheist."

The campaign got results. A satisfactory alternative plan was devised, to save the church.

Another union ban has saved from demolition what used to be Jim Buckley's Newcastle Hotel, in downtown George Street on the fringe of the Rocks area and for long a lively haunt of artists and young people. Following the ban, it stayed in business for months after it was originally supposed to close its doors and, though it is now no longer operating as a hotel, the building remains.

In Canberra, the Builders Labourers' Federation barred an attempt by the McMahon Goverment's

Interior Minister (Mr Hunt) at demolition of Reid House
hostel to make way for a car park. Canberra's Labour
MP Kip Enderby and others urged that it be retained for
temporary student accommodation, and the Builders
Labourers' Federation backed them with a ban on demo-
lition. The union said that the only way that Minister
Hunt could get it demolished would be to do it himself.
Mr Hunt chose not to do so.

Other bans imposed by the Building Labourers' in response to approaches to it have kept demolishers away
from a variety of Sydney buildings.

At one point in 1972 the list of union bans covered
the Rocks project, Opera House car park, Moore Park-
Centennial Park sports complex, construction of high-
rise buildings on single blocks at Botany, and demolitions
of the Pitt Street Congregational Church, Regent
Theatre, three gracious buildings in the Martin Plaza
area (ANZ Bank, National Mutual, and Colonial Mutual),
Lyndhurst (a historic Glebe house threatened by an
expressway) and many others.

The union's branch executive secured from the environment committee of the NSW Chapter of the Institute of Architects a National Trust list of about 1700
historic buildings and declared that the union would not
demolish any of these.

In 1973, residents of Woolloomooloo appealed to
the Builders Labourers' to stand with them against a
massive redevelopment scheme there.

Woolloomooloo, adjoining King's Cross and sloping
down to Woolloomooloo Bay, has been called "the
most Sydney-like place in Sydney". Poets Victor Daley
and Christopher Brennan lived there. Artists have pain-
ted adornments on brick walls; the 9 in a house number
has been made into a many-toothed face.

A Woolloomooloo Residents' Action Group (WRAG)
was formed. Its secretary was a lively young Roman
Catholic priest, Father Edmund Campion. They fought

to keep the 'Loo residential, to save it for the people and not let it be devoured by a vast tower development, an associated office project and other plans. The Federated Engine Drivers & Firemen's Association and the Builders Labourers' Federation responded, with bans, to WRAG appeals.

The outcome was an announcement in July 1973 by a company spokesman that the $400 million Woolloo-mooloo scheme had been abandoned. A company direc-tor referred to there having been "new thoughts about the scheme after considering residents' opposition and the ban on demolition at Woolloomooloo by the Builders Labourers' Federation."

In another episode, in Woollahra, residents plus the Builders Labourers' Federation halted demolition of Helen Keller House by the Royal Blind Society.

Helen Keller House and houses around it had a National Trust C classification ("considerable interest", and should be retained) and a higher rating for them was possible. But the Royal Blind Society, in asso-ciation with a developer, intended to demolish Helen Keller House and to replace it with new buildings to increase the Society's income. Demolition had already started when, alerted by an urgent phone call, union organiser Joe Owens got there and had it stopped — and also got tarpaulins for protection of places where the demolishers had begun.

Community-union solidarity won. The Society backed off from its intention to knock down Helen Keller House.

Other examples of Sydney bans include those on demolitions for the Western Distributor roadway and for the eastern expressway. The union rates people's homes as being more important than more roadways for cars and commercial vehicles.

The Builders Labourers' involved themselves also in the campaign to save King's Cross's picturesque Victoria

Street, with its venerable plane trees and long asso-
ciations with the identity of the Cross. In response to
an urgent appeal from those resisting a multi-million
redevelopment scheme there, the union put on a ban.
The developer was forced to get an alternative plan,
much reduced in dimensions. The union ban remained,
pending a decision being made by the people concerned
as to whether the alternative was or wasn't acceptable.

An article by Marion Macdonald in the Bulletin in
May 1973 said that Sydney development projects
worth $2500 million had been halted by "green bans"
and "cultural bans". Two months later an article written
by Oliver Harvey and published in the Brisbane
Courier-Mail said that the union in NSW "has invoked
an incredible 36 bans against using labour on projects
worth a massive $3000 million because the projects
would mean the tearing down of historic buildings or
could violate parklands within metropolitan Sydney."

There have, too, been builders labourers' bans for
other reasons. One such ban was on new work at Mac-
quarie University. This ban, in June 1973, was over the
exclusion of a homosexual student from the Robert
Menzies College at the university. A week or so later,
a similar ban was put on new work at Sydney University; this ban was in support of the strike by students
and staff members in the Philosophy Department over
the Professorial Board's refusal to agree to a course by
post-graduate students Elizabeth Jacka and Jean
Curthoys on "Philosophical Issues in Feminist Thought".
(The course later got the go-ahead.)

In Victoria, too, some notable successes have been
achieved on environmental issues and the defence of
the people's amenities.

There was, for example, the Carlton affair. In Carlton,
an inner suburb that starts where the city itself leaves
off, some land ("big enough for a football field", says
football fan Norm Gallagher, the Builders Labourers'

Federation Federal and Victorian secretary) belonging to the railways was being handed over to private interests. The company concerned wanted a warehouse there for tissues.

At one stage, the projected deal was that a developer would get the land on a 51-year lease (and with an option for another 30 years) for $3000 a year. The developer was to build the warehouse and then get $30,000 a year from the company for the land and warehouse: a handsome margin of profit for little outlay.

But the people thought differently, and got the Builders Labourers' to back them. Pickets guarded the site. Men who went there to work despite the pickets even went to the extent of masking their faces. There was a clash between Norm Gallagher and a company man. Police arrested Norm Gallagher, who had two of his ribs broken as they did so.

Sentenced to 14 days jail for "assault", he refused on principle to pay the costs ordered against him. He spent 13 days in jail.

But the land was saved. Instead of it being used for an insightly warehouse, the railways handed it over to the people of Carlton for use as a park. It is being administered by a people's committee. One member of the committee is Norm Gallagher.

Then there was the case of the City Baths, in Swanston and Franklin Streets, close to the Trades Hall and the union's office. It's on land that would attract hungry eyes. There were rumours that both Ansett and some Japanese interests wanted the land for a motel or some such commercial purpose.

The City Council said it was going to close down the baths, as being "uneconomic" — though a check showed that 190,000 people a year used them.

The land on which the baths stand is held by the Council under a lease from the Victorian State Government. Under the terms of this, if the site ceased to be used for the baths, the land would revert to the Government — a Government which, like the Askin Government in NSW, is acutely sensitive to the requirements of the developers and other big business.

On behalf of the protesting people, the Builders Labourers' moved in with a ban. The union also let the Council know that, until it got adequate assurances, then there would be a ban also on the Council's cherished City Square project. The demand put to the Council was that either the baths stay as they are, or else that an Olympic-size public baths, under council ownership and control, be included in any development on the site. So the baths are still there, in use.

The union also banned demolition of the Beaurepaire pool, which the Council had closed (again on the ground that it was "uneconomic"). After the ban, the Council offered to build a new indoor all-year-pool in place of the one closed.

Earlier, in 1972, the Builders Labourers' Federation in Victoria joined in the successful efforts to save Fitzroy's Blanche Terrace, birthplace of authoress Henry Handel Richardson, who won worldwide repute for her book *The Fortunes of Richard Mahoney.*

A property development firm wanted to demolish No.169-171 of the terrace in order to build medical consulting rooms. But protests and threats of a ban succeeded in having the plans revised, in order to save and restore the main double storey section of the houses, including the facade.

The Victorian chairman of the National Trust, Mr Rodney Davidson, wrote to the Victorian secretary of the Builders Labourers', Mr Norm Gallagher, saying that "this result was undoubtedly achieved by the action taken by your union and other organisations". Cr. Brian Lennon, of Fitzroy Council, wrote to the union saying that its help had been "crucial", and he added: "If other unions and unionists shared your sense of overall responsibility, our country would have far fewer problems internally and externally."

An environmental ban by the union in Victoria on a proposed Newport power station brought expressions of appreciation from the Port Phillip Conservation Council and the Williamstown Conservation & Planning Society. A letter from the Council said that the fact that some of the union's members were losing work because of the ban gave it greater cause for gratitude.

In another episode, in mid-1973, the union banned work on a projected factory in Albert Street, East Brunswick. The plans for the factory, for which a home had been demolished, envisaged the factory being built right alongside the weatherboard home of a frail 69-year-old woman pensioner, who has an invalid-pensioner son living with her. The factory would, among other things, block the sunlight and natural warmth from her living room.

The woman pensioner has lived in this home for almost 50 years.

On being approached, the local Council said that the plans for the factory must be altered, to move the factory some feet away from the boundary between it and the pensioner's home. But then, without the woman being told, the company appealed to the State Building Regulations Committee and a referee gave approval for the factory to be built right to the boundaries.

The East Brunswick Progress Association called to the Builders Labourers'. The union responded: work on the factory was put under a ban.

In June 1973, to the delight of many, the Victorian branch of the Builders Labourers' put a ban on demolition of Melbourne city hotels, so as "to preserve some watering holes for workers". The old pubs where a man could go in working clothes and get a drink at normal prices were disappearing, the union said, and they were being replaced by taverns with inflated prices and dress rules. Hence the ban on demolition.

The NSW builders labourers' bans were in keeping with what was virtually a testament of the union's social principle, set out in a letter from Jack Mundey to the Sydney *Morning Herald* in January 1972.

A snide paragraph in the Sydney *Morning Herald*'s titbits section, Column Eight, had implied that the union was two-tongued in expressing concern about unemployment in the industry and, at the same time, putting bans on projects which could have provided some jobs. In reply, Jack Mundey wrote:

" . . . Yes, we want to build. However, we prefer to build urgently-required hospitals, schools, other public utilities, high-quality flats, units and houses, provided they are designed with adequate concern for the environment, than to build ugly unimaginative, architecturally-bankrupt blocks of concrete and glass offices.

"Likewise, we wish to build for those aged people who gave their working lives to improve our country only to end up in some pent-up squalid room in the City.

"In the whole building industry — both the public and private sectors — there is a crying need for an overall programme, not only to arrest the unemployment but aimed at overcoming our building industry's inadequacies.

"The Federal Government, the Master Builders' Association and the building unions should meet, not to engage merely in an empty exchange of words but to draw up and implement a meaningful programme for 1972 and 1973.

"Though we want all our members employed, we will not just become robots directed by developer-builders who value the dollar at the expense of the environment.

"More and more, we are going to determine which buildings we will build. Following our bans on the Eastlakes parkland, where a developer intended to erect more units, our ban on the intended destruction of the last remaining bushland on the Parramatta River at Kellys Bush, and our ban on the Rocks project because the scheme destroys the character of this historic area and ignores the position of the people affected, our union was inundated with congratulatory messages.

"People from all walks of life expressed their support for a union not being myopic but truly acting in the real public interest and in the interest of future generations.

"This union will stand with the National Trust, forward-thinking architects and engineers to protect buildings of historical or architectural significance. In fact, in future we will refuse to demolish any building so designated by the Trust.

"Those of us who build must be more concerned with what we build. The environmental interests of three million people are at stake and cannot be left to developers and building employers whose main concern is making profit.

"Progressive unions, like ours, therefore have a very useful social role to play in the citizens' interest, and we intend to play it."

Some other unions — though not enough of them — have acted on similar principles. In NSW, the Federated Engine Drivers & Firemen's Association (with Norm Hockney as its State president and Jack Cambourn as State secretary) has consistently joined in "green bans" and other bans, notably at the Rocks. The Amalgamated Metal Workers' Union (with Frank Bollins as State president and Merv Malcolm as State secretary) is another which has associated itself with such bans.

The NSW branch of the Building Workers' Industrial Union has supported such campaigns as those over Kellys Bush and the Rocks. It also put a ban on a projected marina for the Royal Sydney Yacht Squadron which would have usurped for private use part of the Kirribilli-Neutral Bay inlet and which aroused strong protests from the public and also from ferry-masters.

The demand for a say in what is to be built has been asserted in other States as well as NSW and Victoria.

Queensland unions, through the Queensland Trades & Labour Council, have notched up some important successes on issues of ecology and the environment. Black bans halted the Bjelke-Petersen Government's

plan to allow oil drilling in the Barrier Reef area
(Premier Bjelke-Petersen himself has been shown to
be a big shareholder in an oil company, Exoil) and also
barred mining of the unique Cooloola coloured sands
area on the Sunshine Coast north of Brisbane.

In South Australia, too, in another area of union
challenge, the builders labourers played a significant
part towards securing the eventual legislation which
eliminated employers' rights to institute Supreme
Court proceedings over industrial disputes.

The builders labourers' actions on this issue included
a refusal to attend a Supreme Court case seeking
damages against the union for a black ban. In a subsequent case, a similar refusal was followed by the jailing
of the union's State secretary, Les Robinson, and organiser Ron Owens for ten days for "contempt". It was
after this that the Dunstan Government legislated to end
employers' access to the Supreme Court on such matters.

In Western Australia, builders labourers' were able to
stave off for three months demolition of Perth's gracious
old Esplanade Hotel. When it did eventually go, the
union was able to have some parts of it saved from destruction, for incorporation in the new building there.

The January 1972 Mundey letter to the Sydney
Morning Herald set a cat among the chooks. There
were squawks and much fluffing of feathers, as developers and their political friends saw the implications to
their cherished fortune-building projects.

When the events of the following months showed how
much in earnest the union was in its concern for people
and the environment, the voices of the developers and
their publicists became hoarse in their desperation. But
there were influential voices raised on the side of the
union and its principle.

After the Sydney *Morning Herald* had returned (for
want of any valid argument) to its pious protestations
of concern over loss of workers' jobs through bans,

answers came from, among others, Professor Neil Runcie and celebrated writer Patrick White.

The union's policy is for establishment of a Building Investigations Committee, made up of representatives of architects, the unions and employers. Others could be co-opted to it. This committee would determine which buildings should be erected and what priorities should apply in the public and private sectors of the industry. Its aim would be to serve maximum community needs.

The committee, in the union's concept, should assess the needs and value of any proposed buildings. It should see that no buildings are undertaken unless they meet the needs of the environment in the areas involved.

Factors to be considered when assessing any proposed development should include:

— Are the most urgent needs of the area catered for in this development?
— Will the project displace families in the area of development? If so, have the plans been on public display for at least six months before acquisition of any properties? Has the matter been discussed in open forum with the residents? Has adequate reimbursement been offered and accepted?
— What changes will the development make to the natural environment? Will any such changes be in the best interests of the future in that area?
— Will this development cause any manner of pollution? If so, what measures will be taken to prevent or control it?
— What effect will this development have on transport in the area?
— Where the development is housing or home units, are adequate parks and playing spaces being provided?

The union plan proposed that, where any one member of the committee disagrees with a project, this project shall not proceed until such disagreement is withdrawn or alterations are made to the project to the satisfaction of the disagreeing party.

In the meantime, many buildings which earlier were marked for demolition, at the Rocks and elsewhere, still stand. This is to the credit of the initiatives and determined efforts of very many in the community — the Resident Action Groups and so many other principled organisations and socially-conscious individuals in all walks of life. Supplementing the efforts of all these, the union bans have brought muscle and leverage to bear against those who would destroy.

After the Kelly's Bush victory, the Sydney *Sun* acknowledged that the people who had battled for a year to save it had, before they turned to the unions, "believed the battle had been lost".

Sydney architect Norman Edwards, in a newspaper article which referred to Builders Labourer's interventions, said: "For the first time in Australia, it is being shown that the power of big business to demolish and build where it pleases, despite informed opposition, may be thwarted."

He saw resort to strikes as extreme. Then he added: "But, in the absence of other effective powers, good luck to the Jack Mundeys."

Chapter V
Decline in Industry, Decline in Towns

Community Development Project

The symptoms of industrial decline — derelict land, empty factories, run-down housing, unemployed workers — are painfully apparent in Batley, Benwell, Canning Town, North Shields and Saltley today. Yet their present state is the result of a process that has been going on for many years — in some areas for three-quarters of a century.

The industrial decline of each area started for different reasons and at different times, and has proceeded at varying speed. The first signs of stagnation and decline were evident in the north-east by the turn of the century, while in Saltley the new phase of investment in the motor industry staved off decline until the 1950s.

All five old industrial areas now lie enclosed by more recent industrial and housing development. Beyond Canning Town lie Dagenham and Barking, and the post-war new towns of Basildon and Harlow. On Tyneside, Benwell and North Shields are overshadowed by interwar estates like Team Valley, and, beyond them, the new towns of Cramlington and Washington. But the process that spells decline for the local areas is not a simple one of capital withdrawal. Sometimes it is the very process of investing in new and more productive techniques that is responsible for the loss of many jobs; even increased profitability for industry can mean economic decline for a local community. Furthermore,

where major traditional employers have reduced their
local operations or even closed down altogether, this
is not the end of the story. The decline of the traditional
industries has been the signal for new capital to move
into these areas, and these new economic activities have
rarely provided equivalent new jobs to replace those
lost from the older industries. Increasingly, the old
working class communities are coming to depend upon
a low wage economic structure.

Decline is not a simple process, but one which has
many complicating factors and many different stages.
The decline of the traditional industries is only the start.

The old industries collapse

The traditional industries of North Shields had suffered
a major collapse by the 1930s. The dramatic decline of
local shipbuilding was highlighted by yards closing in
the Howdon and Willington Quay areas, next to North
Shields. Benwell's local industry underwent more
gradual decline, interrupted by the booms of the two
wars and the severe slump between them. A more rapid
collapse with several closures began in the 1960s.

The textile industry in Batley, after reaching its peak
in the First World War, declined steadily from then
onwards. The process of contraction was only temporarily arrested by the Second World War and the years
immediately following it. The fifties and sixties have
seen the closure of mill after mill and a belated attempt
to rationalise the remainder of the industry, with the
loss of many jobs.

In Canning Town many firms were subject to takeovers and mergers from the early 1900s onwards in the
face of falling profitability. Some of these mergers laid
the foundations of what are now multinational companies. As in Saltley, serious economic decline in Canning Town has only become apparent in the last ten

years. The early industrial pattern in Canning Town
and Saltley, and in west Newcastle to a lesser extent,
survived longer than that in North Shields. In these
three areas most of the traditional industries maintained some local presence until the mid-1960s. As
a result, in Canning Town and Saltley especially,
a relatively stable local employment structure persisted up to then.

The disparate rate of change in the industrial bases
of the different areas is reflected by the fact that in
1966, the traditional sector in North Shields provided
less than a fifth of all jobs (shipbuilding, docks); less
than two-fifths in Batley and Benwell (textiles and
engineering respectively); but three-quarters of all jobs
in Canning Town and Saltley. In general though, jobs
in the traditional industries have been disappearing
steadily in all five areas over the last forty years, and
this trend has accelerated in the last ten years especially
where the traditional sector had been large. A relatively
small number of companies are responsible for cutting
these jobs. They are often established firms, frequently
the subsidiaries of major corporations pursuing rationalisation policies. In some areas less than half a dozen
firms have been responsible for three-quarters of local
job losses.

North Shields

At the end of the nineteenth century, shipyards on the
Tyne were hit by the growing problem of foreign competition. The owners tried to reorganise in order to keep
their share of the shipbuilding and shiprepair industry.
There were mergers and rationalisation throughout the
shipbuilding towns of the Tyne — Wallsend and
Jarrow as well as North Shields. The 1899 merger of
the Smith and Edwards firms created the largest dry
dock in the world at the time, Smith's Dock at North

Shields, now part of Swan Hunter Ship Repairers. Up river in Wallsend, Swan Hunter merged with Wigham Richardson, and the new firm launched the *Mauretania* in 1906, built with state financial assistance and designed as a prestige ship to answer the growing competitive threat from the German shipbuilding industry. The booms and deepening slumps of the early 1900s were relieved by the great demand for shipping during the First World War and immediately afterwards when the losses in merchant shipping had to be met. But after this, in the 1920s, shipbuilding began to collapse, and the process continued and grew worse in the thirties.

In 1926 the last coal mine in North Shields closed, and long term unemployment came to stay, with two out of three workers on the dole. Shipbuilding (as distinct from ship-repair) disappeared from the town altogether during the depression. Yards at Willington Quay and Howdon were closed by the National Shipbuilders Security Ltd – a kind of trust made up of shipbuilders and bankers which masterminded the reduction in British shipbuilding capacity. The Second World War provided renewed naval work, and some Tyne yards opened up again, but not the ones near Shields. The boom following the war meant that modernisation programmes were delayed and slump set in again in the late fifties. Further centralisation and rationalisation took place in the sixties. Now another stage in this process – nationalisation of the industry – has arrived.

The docks of North Shields declined too, especially after the Second World War. As the centre of the south east Northumberland coalfield gradually shifted northwards, North Shields, until then a major outlet for coal export by sea, began to suffer while ports like Blyth took over their trade. Jobs in the transport industry were also badly hit. Over a quarter of them went as the coal trade disappeared, the rail back-up once needed became redundant and freight handling came to use more capital equipment and fewer workers. By the 1960s, the coal staithes in the North Shields docks were derelict and disused, and the Northumberland dock was closed, reclaimed and covered in. Only a relatively modern staithe at Whitehill Point remained, and this was eventually closed in 1974, signalling the end of North Shields as a coal port.

Tied up with this was the creation of the Port of Tyne Authority in 1968 to take over from the old Tyne Improvement Commissioners. One of its functions was to look at ways of increasing port usage (and revenue) as the coal trade declined. In North Shields, the new Authority had been left with a general passenger and cargo trade with Scandinavia, the import of petroleum oils, and a large amount of derelict land. It introduced roll-on, roll-off containerised handling and more dockworkers' jobs were lost. The separately based fishing industry in North Shields has also recently faced a crisis of investment. With plans for a new fish dock turned down by the government, the industry plods on, although resources for the new forms of fish handling are inadequate.

By 1966, then, the traditional industries of North Shields were a pale shadow of their former selves. Once they had dominated employment in the town. Now shiprepair employed only 8% of the workforce, and transport, which included the docks but also road haulage and public transport workers at a local depot, only 9%. From 1966-75, Swan Hunter's shiprepair yard had fairly full order books, and kept a relatively stable workforce; but still rationalisation reduced jobs by about a fifth.

The workers of North Shields not only experienced concentrated long-term unemployment during the depression, they were also amongst the first in our five areas to see the ownership and use of the industrial land around them change dramatically, first in the 1930s and then again, as elsewhere, in the late sixties. Today, industrial estates and trading estates dating from both these periods with a variety of activities like light engineering, warehousing and so on, are their major source of work.

Benwell

The First World War brought boom to the riverside firms of west Newcastle. Employment rose to match — reaching an all-time peak at Armstrong's. But soon after the war ended, the enormous expansion of production and employment collapsed again. The 1920s saw a return to general stagnation and decline. There were several dramatic closures, such as that of Spencer's Steel works at Newburn which threw thousands out of work.

The inter-war period also saw some restructuring of local industry. The West Newcastle firm of Robert Stephenson's merged with Hawthorn's during the general rationalisation of the locomotive industry in the late thirties. Armstrong's had already merged with their great rival Whitworth's by the end of the nineteenth century, because of competition from Vickers. After the First World War, the company attempted to adjust to peace-time conditions and an altered market; it tried to diversify into consumer goods, but with little success, and no dividend was paid on its ordinary capital from 1923 to 1926. By 1927, Armstrong-Whitworth were massively in debt, and were forced to merge with Vickers who had by then diversified into more buoyant sectors like Saltley's railway carriage industry and embryonic motor industry.

The Second World War brought another boom and another dramatic expansion of employment for

Benwell. But once the fighting stopped, this too
came to an end. The downward drift of profits and
jobs continued.

Through this period of stagnation and decline,
the industrial pattern built up during the nineteenth
century remained broadly the same. The local industrial
land was occuped by the same industries as before
although there were far fewer jobs. But after the early
1960s there were considerable changes in the old
pattern: older factories in the inner-city belt were
closed, among them Robert Stephenson's (1960),
Hawthorn's locomotive works, Elswick gas works
(1968), and Elswick leather works (1971). By 1974
only four engineering firms apart from Vickers were
still to be found in the inner west end. The ownership
of that west end industry has changed a lot too. The
major national and multinational companies control
an increasing amount of it.

These closures have brought a permanent loss, a
fundamental change in the use of the riverside after
100 years as a centre of engineering. The future rests
upon insecure, static or declining employers like
Vickers, who are unlikely to generate more jobs and
see any future expansion largely in terms of re-invest-
ment in more efficient machinery not more workers.
Although the numbers working there have steadily
declined, Vickers still dominate employment in manufacturing, employing 50% of the workforce and a
large area of the riverside. The firm has responded to
changed markets by trying to diversifying its operations
and investing in new plant but the Newcastle factories
have seen little of this new investment. While completely new works have been built at Crayford and
Swindon, only marginal adjustments have been made
within the existing plant on Newcastle's riverside.
In Newcastle, particularly at Scotswood, Vickers has
been saddled with out-of-date factory buildings

and machinery. The pressure to increase productivity
has grown. The company's response seems to have
been to make more intensive use of labour, coupled
with modest reinvestment in new machinery. Both at
Elswick and Scotswood the firm is now manufacturing on only a part of its original land — large areas of
the sites have been cleared, and a section at Scotswood
is being redeveloped for warehousing.

Other local firms left in the area have similarly
relied in their efforts to increase productivity on more
intensive use of their workers, such as the introduction
of shift-systems. Most are based on relatively crude
technology; none of today's most advanced sectors
of capitalist production are to be found in Benwell's
local industry.

The riverside strip which was the focus of nineteenth
century growth now houses the oldest technology in
the city. The most modern is in the new towns away
from the city centre. In between lie the peripheral inter-
war estates like the Team Valley Estate to the south
across the Tyne or westwards at Newburn, itself an
old riverside mining area now incorporated in the growing city of Newcastle.

Throughout the inter-war and post-war periods,
industry in the inner areas of Newcastle has declined,
while on its fringes and in the new estates beyond
there has been expansion and investment. There are
few cases of firms actually closing their works in the
older areas and transferring activities to alternative
sites. It is new investment that has gone to the new
sites.

Batley

Like many other parts of the country, the First World
War brought business and peace brought decline to
Batley. After 1918 the shoddy industry lost its military

outlets and the more open competition of peacetime showed up the general inefficiency of the industry. The employers cut back production and laid off many workers. Yet Batley remained an industrial 'monoculture' long after the First World War had seen the start of the final decline of its staple industry. Textiles still employed three-quarters of Batley's workers in 1929 (most of the remainder were then in coal-mining) and nearly two-thirds of the total after 1945.

The shoddy industry's steady retreat after 1918 was temporarily arrested during the Second World War and the boom years which followed. Its effects were also mitigated by the movement of some local firms into the more 'upmarket' and profitable sectors of woollens and worsteds and by the arrival of the carpet industry which took advantage of surplus textile labour and build- ings. Shoddy's steady retreat became a complete rout from the late 1950s onwards, as it came under increasing competition from more efficient European competitors, as well as from artificial fibres. More recently, other sectors of woollens and worsteds have experienced a similar fate.

In 1959, textiles still employed half the local work- force, a decade later the proportions had fallen to one- third. Between 1961 and 1971, the industry had shed 31% of its jobs in Batley. Closure followed closure; more than one-third of the seventy-eight textile firms present in 1966 have since ceased production. Over the same period, the 'Top Ten' local textile firms have between them shed over half their workforce — 2,500 jobs lost — while three of them have closed altogether. A similar picture of closure and contraction has characterised the smaller local firms. New firms opening up replaced only a fraction of the jobs lost in those closures.

Jobs have not only been lost from the more back- ward sectors of the textile industry like mungo and shoddy; the carpet industry in Batley, the only major

textile growth sector represented here, has also been
responsible for several hundred redundancies. With the
closures and redundancies have gone a spate of take
overs and mergers, like those which had occurred much
earlier in the basic industries of the other four areas. In
1966, nine of the top ten local textile firms were still
independently owned; by 1975 only three remained so.
Major national companies like Homfray's, Scottish
English & European Textiles, Thomas Tilling, and Sirdar
have now established interests in Batley's textile industry — usually by taking over firms in the more
profitable sectors like carpets, bedding and some areas
of yarn production. These, and the independent companies which survive usually in the more marginal areas
of production, took advantage of the relatively low
wage-rates paid to Batley workers, a bonus which the
textile employers in the town have always enjoyed. The
industry took on a new lease of life when large numbers
of Asian workers arrived in the early 1960s. By replace-
ing women workers with Asian men, the employers have
been able to extend shift-working and still keep wages
down. Three-quarters of Batley's Asian community now
work in the woollen textile industry, although few have
been allowed into the better-paid carpets sector.

Batley's textile industry now represents a diverse
range of operations from the relatively sophisticated,
capital-intensive, externally controlled carpet industry
at one extreme to the last remaining elements of primitive, small-scale shoddy production at the other. Alongside the surviving small firms of the traditional kind
which increasingly operate in areas of marginal profitability, there are now branches of the larger multinational
and national companies, which operate largely in technically 'more advanced' areas of production. The technological differences within Batley's textile industry are
immense. Throughout the local industry, differences of
process are reinforced by differences of company owner-

ship, size, investment, profitability and company prospects. These differences are not reflected to the extent which might be expected, however, in job security and prospects, working conditions or wage rates. While Batley's textile industry combines different levels of technology and stages of economic development, it does so within a common, and generally low-paid and shrinking, employment structure.

Canning Town

For the owners of industry in Canning Town, the First World War also brought a return of high profits and a respite from the growing competition of French sugar refineries and German chemical works. But the danger signs were already pronounced and the need for them to re-structure and re-invest was urgent.

Their earlier investments in plant and machinery were beginning to age. Too many docks had been built in the early speculative years and now cut-throat competition between them was taking its toll and giving the dock-owners cause for alarm. The private dock companies along the Thames, suffering from over-capacity, were effectively nationalised in 1901 into a public trust company — the Port of London Authority. Decisions on reinvestment at this time favoured Canning Town's Royal Docks over those docks upstream or Tilbury downstream. Two new docks were announced. The George V was opened in 1913, but as trade fell away the second was never built.

In the peace-time slump, considerable re-structuring took place in the refining industries through a series of mergers and takeovers. The two sugar firms of Lyle and Tate had up till then survived intense competition from foreign refiners by unspoken gentlemen's agreements, but in 1921, they eventually merged. The collapse of the raw materials market led to competition in soap

and animal feeds production with Lever Bros. taking
control of almost all the major processing mills in
Canning Town between 1920-37. Bruner Mond was incorporated in the new ICI, while ITT took over the STC
site, and P&O and Vestey's secured control over large
parts of shipping, ship repair and stevedoring. By the
end of the thirties the area's relatively dispersed economy had become highly concentrated into the hands of
a few companies. These big companies continued to
invest and expand, but little of the new investment
at this period went into the traditional activities —
and little therefore into Canning Town.

War again brought temporary relief. The Second
World War meant a quick solution to high unemployment amongst dockers and workers in the refining
industries. And afterwards the reorganisation forced
on local firms in the period of crisis between the two
wars laid the basis for the prosperous fifties and early
sixties, when there was full employment for the first
time. At last workers in the docks were decasualised
after almost a century and won a real rise in their
living standards, but it was a short-lived victory. By
the mid-sixties there was a new and permanent fall
in the number of jobs for local workers as a result
of productivity increases throughout a range of
local industries. Tate & Lyle alone cut 1,700 jobs
between 1966 and 1972 by redundancy and wastage,
and introduced a system of continuous shift working, with a complicated and ever changing pattern of
rest days, reducing their need for workers and closing
one refinery. But as the sixties wore on, the pattern
became one of very widespread closures for the first
time in Canning Town's history.

Because two-thirds of its traditional industries had
survived successfully for so long, decline came very
rapidly in the end. Since 1966, when 67% of jobs
were still in traditional industries, recent rates of

decline have been high. 24,000 jobs have disappeared in this time. Between 1966 and 1972, employment fell in the docks (42% fewer jobs), in ship repair (70% fewer), food jobs (down 30%), chemicals (68% fewer), gas (completely closed), and most other sectors. Three quarters of the jobs were cut by just six companies – P&O, Tate & Lyle, Unilever, Harland and Wolff, Furness-Withy and Vestey's.

Rapid changes in shipping techniques with containerisation and bulk tankers many times the size of existing ships meant the ports had to be in deep water sites. So the focus moved from Canning Town to Tilbury or away to Southampton, Felixstowe and other new ports where new systems were installed, needing fewer workers.

The development of North Sea Gas supplies saw the mighty Beckton Gas Works close and 5,000 jobs disappear. Changes in the supply of grain and radical changes in distribution methods brought the closure of the long-established, port-based mills providing animal feeds. Instead, smaller mills were established in a number of county towns throughout the South East, supplied by local wheat producers and serviced by bulk carriers.

Throughout the fifties the insulated cables firms in the area, like BICC and STC, were developing new tele-communications technology. But when it came to building factories for the new production the companies sited them elsewhere, in the ring of new towns around London. In the same way, with the development of plastic and fibre optic cables, 2,000 jobs at STC will disappear by 1977 from Canning Town, the original seed bed of the industry.

The 1944 Greater London Plan had described industry in Canning Town as 'immovable' and overall few firms physically moved their existing operations out to new towns. (The main exception was Jeyes which left for Thetford in the late sixties, taking away 280 jobs.) Rather, most of the closures were allied to new investment programmes in which the area no longer figured. By 1975, thirty major sites once used by refining industries had been abandoned. In the space of ten years, the huge expanse of the Victoria Dock lay virtually empty and the 500 acres of Beckton Gas Works had been cleared.

Canning Town's traditional economy has now collapsed, leaving only a handful of firms like Tate & Tyle offering less than secure prospects.

Saltley

The motor industry, whose arrival seemed to be the saving of Saltley, turned out to provide only a temporary reprieve. In the event, it too is now declining and only slightly after the decline of the earlier generation of industry. Saltley's early industries were railway carriages, gas and the railways. Amalgamation in the railway carriage industry brought Wright's works and four others together in 1905 and by re-organising, the companies succeeded in holding onto their overseas markets. By 1919 the north-east firm of Vickers had bought into the company, and then in 1928, at the height of the slump, it reorganised to produce Metro-Cammell out of the rolling stock interests of Vickers and Cammell Laird shipbuilders. The workers of Saltley were lucky in the rationalisation which followed. The works in Nottingham and Leeds were the ones which were closed.

Although the company can point to its mark on London's tube trains, most of Metro-Cammell's profits came from selling goods abroad which it succeeded in doing until the market finally faltered, bringing severe and rapid rationalisation in the late fifties. It tried unsuccessfully to raise productivity but there was little scope for significant productivity increases in this craft industry. As a result, there have been many redundancies, especially in the years 1959-64. The Saltley site of Metro-Cammell, which in 1958 employed 1,800 workers, was sold off in 1962. The company has diversified production at the later, adjacent Washwood Heath site which now produces railway carriages and buses.

The four gas works which had been taken over by Birmingham Corporation in the 1850s, and then by the Gas Board, survived successfully until the late 1960s, when the search for cheap fuel rapidly eliminated them. In the railways too there was a similar rapid decline as major technical change in signals and maintenance brought rationalisation. Other light industries like Hughes Biscuits, a subsidiary of Rowntrees, closed down, and Southalls only survived without more losses by closing other factories elsewhere.

While all this was happening things were still going relatively well for the motor industry. But decline, rationalisation and reorganisation was to begin there too, soon after. Between 1966 and 1974, employment in the local plants of Leyland Motors (itself a product of several mergers since it first moved into the area as Forward Radiators in the 1920s) fell from over 14,000 by nearly 5,000. Reorganisation had already brought about the closure of the old Morris Commercial site in Adderley Park which had figured so significantly in the area's early growth. Production was concentrated in the later and larger works at Common Lane, removing 4,000 jobs in the overall reorganisation.

Between 1966 and 1974, 8,400 jobs were lost in Saltley. Three quarters of those were cut by two firms — British Leyland and Metro-Cammell. Vehicle manufacture fell by 31%, gas making was eliminated and jobs halved. The workers of Saltley did not lose

their jobs because firms actually relocated. There is
only one example of this. The jobs were eliminated
as the companies reinvested and directed their capital
towards concentrating production somewhere else.

So far the changes in the older parts of Saltley's
industry like gas are less important in terms of employment than in terms of land use. Over the last decade
one third of the land once occupied by thriving
traditional industries had fallen empty. And the process is still only in its early stages. Although many
jobs have been lost, Saltley has probably not yet
suffered the full effects of the decline of the motor
industry. The area still contains a major British Leyland
works at Washwood Heath.

COMPANIES RESPONSIBLE FOR INDUSTRIAL JOB LOSS SINCE 1966

Company	Activity	Job Losses
Batley (1966-71)		
1. G.H. Hirst	Textiles	− 273
2. Geo. Sykes	Textiles	− 217
3. William Holton	Textiles	− 205
4. Waldran & Herregan	Textiles	− 125
5. J.T. & J. Taylor	Textiles	− 461
Benwell* (W. Newcastle 1964-7)		
1. N.E. Co-op	Distribution	−2740
2. Vickers	Engineering	−2471
3. Wm. Leech	Construction	−1562
4. Scottish & Newcastle Brewer Co	Brewers (food and drink)	− 755
5. Northern Gas	Gas	− 245
6. Troldahl	Vehicle distribution/ cold storage	− 157
7. Adams & Gibbon	Garage	− 149
8. Adamsez	Manuf.	− 103

Company	Activity	Job Losses
Canning Town (1966-72)		
1. P&O	Shipping/ship repair	−4000
2. Tate & Lyle	Sugar	−2400
3. Unilever	Animal feeds/soap	−1500
4. Harland & Wolff	Ship repair	−1460
5. Furness Withy	Stevedores/shipping	−1410
6. Vestey	Stevedores/shipping	−1200
7. Rowntree Mackintosh	Confectionary	− 370
8. Ellerman Lines	Shipping	− 340
9. British Commonwealth	Shipping	− 340
10. C.W.S.	Flour/animal feeds	− 340
Saltley (1966-74)		
1. B.L.M.C.	Cars	−4800
2. Metro-Cammell (Laird Group)	Railway carriages	− 640
3. W.M. Gas	Gas Making	−1400
4. Rowntree Mackintosh	Biscuits	− 450
5. C.H. Pugh	Lawn mowers	− 220
6. Southalls	Sanitary towels	− 200
7. British Rail	Loco sheds	− 200
8. Thos. Smith	Metal manuf.	− 350
9. Birmingham Co-op	Bakery	− 190

Source: Department of Employment returns/Local sources
*Benwell: these are the only figures currently available for job losses
which cover Benwell. They relate to a wider area of West Newcastle,
including part of the city centre.

LOCAL DECLINE OF BASIC INDUSTRIES

% of jobs (1966)   *Recent Job Loss*

Saltley 80%

1964-74	Vehicle Manuf	−31%(5,450 jobs)
	Gas making	−54%(1,400 jobs)
	Food, drink, tobacco	−37%(640 jobs)

Canning Town 75%

1966-72	Transport (including Docks)	−42%(4,320 jobs)
	Food, drink, tobacco	−30%(2,260 jobs)
	Ship repair	−70%(3,860 jobs)
	Chemicals	−68%(1,570 jobs)

Local decline of basic industries (contd.)

% of jobs (1966)		*Recent Job Loss*
Batley 39%		
1966-71	Textiles	−31%(1,700 jobs)
Benwell 37%		
1964-71	Mechanical Eng.	−39%(2,200 jobs)
	Gas	−95%(400 jobs)
North Shields 17%		
1966-71	Ship repair	−21%(469 jobs)
	Transport	
	(including Docks)	−40%(1,000 jobs)

Source: 1966-71 Census/Department of Employment Returns

WORKERS IN DECLINE

The costs of industrial change are borne by local working-class communities. These communities grew up in response to the demand for labour from new industries, yet over time changes in these industries have destroyed their original role. The decline of each area's traditional industrial structure sets off a chain reaction of economic and social consequences, undermining every aspect of life in the local community.

Over the last decade in particular there has been an accelerating rate of job loss from the traditional industries. Opportunities locally for relatively high-wage employment in these industries have diminished dramatically to be replaced in part by low-paid, unskilled jobs. These changes have fundamentally altered the function and life of the local community. It increasingly serves as a 'reservoir' of unemployed and underemployed workers to be tapped only in times of boom, and as a source of workers for low-paid service activities over a widening area of each conurbation.

LOCAL WORKPLACE JOBS 1966

	Total jobs	*% industrial*
Batley	14,260	74%(39% in traditional sectors)
Benwell	20,590	52%(37% traditional)
Canning Town	51,400	83% (75% traditional)
North Shields	26,360	62%(17% traditional)
Saltley	36,800	95%(80% traditional)

HIGH RATES OF CHANGE 1966-71

	Industrial jobs	*Resident population*	*Resident working population*
Batley	−20.4%	+ 2.9%	− 2.7%
Benwell	−14.0%	−23.6%	−23.1%
Canning Town	−24.0%	−11.8%	−17.5%
North Shields	−13.2%	− 1.0%	− 7.0%
Saltley	−13.9%	− 6.4%	−17.5%

Source: 1966-71 Census/Department of Employment Returns

As we saw in the last section, from the mid-sixties, each area experienced the particularly rapid and serious decline of its traditional employment structure. The local workforce has paid the costs of this decline in a variety of ways.

Fewer local jobs

RESIDENTS STILL WORKING IN THE LOCAL WORKPLACE: 1966

	%
Batley	52.0
Benwell	31.4
Canning Town	48.0
North Shields	58.8
Saltley (1961)	(36.0)

Source: 1966 Census

Up to the mid-sixties all five areas still had significant numbers of workers both living and working there. Manual jobs, in particular, were done by local residents, although the higher-paid managerial and supervisory jobs were performed usually by commuters from outside. In 1966, half the working population of Batley, Canning Town and North Shields still worked locally. Of the residents of Benwell and Saltley, traditionally more integrated into a wider employment network, rather fewer worked for local firms.

Since then, thousands of local jobs have been lost. Many firms have closed down altogether, and productivity drives in those remaining have meant the loss of many more jobs. As rationalisation brought widespread redundancies, workers with skills acquired over a lifetime, often with one employer, found they counted for nothing. With little comparable work available, they either remained unemployed or were forced into lower-paid, less-skilled work where that existed.

After 1966 unemployment rates in the five areas rose and remained consistently above the national average. At each slump the rate rose more rapidly, and at each boom it was slower to fall. In Canning Town, unemployment for nearly a decade has not fallen below 8%, four times the rate for the South East as a whole.

Unused skills

High though unemployment rates have been, they are still a poor indicator of the very serious problems affecting local working people. If it were not for the fact that many of those made redundant took jobs in the poorly paid but generally expanding activities of services and distribution, unemployment rates would have been even higher.

In most areas, the high proportion of residents working in higher wage industrial jobs in 1966 had fallen significantly by 1971; over the same period, the proportion of men working as skilled or semi-skilled workers fell, and the proportion of lower paid, unskilled workers rose. In Benwell, a survey of unemployed men classed by the employment exchange as unskilled showed that half of them did not consider themselves unskilled nor had their previous job been unskilled. What was happening was that more and more people were being turned into low-paid workers. Some of these have found work in the new activities which moved into the old factories or vacant sites of these areas. Warehousing, light manufacture, and local service industries provided some jobs. But the jobs lost have been replaced by far fewer new jobs, most of which are low paid by comparison.

Change in the skill structure of local residents: 1966-71

	% skilled		% semi-skilled		% unskilled	
	1966	1971	1966	1971	1966	1971
Batley	39.5	38.9	∠1.9	19.7	9.8	9.3
Benwell	42.6	42.2	19.6	15.4	14.8	17.1
Canning Town	34.4	32.4	21.7	18.9	25.0	24.0
North Shields	40.0	40.2	21.6	18.9	16.0	18.1
Saltley	44.5	37.4	26.6	28.7	16.0	20.3

Source: 1966-71 Census
Note: the trends reflect a significant overall loss of skilled and semi-skilled work opportunities for local residents and a growth of less skilled/low paid activities.

In Batley, Saltley, and to a lesser extent in Canning Town, the increasingly unskilled local workforce has been joined by black and Asian workers who had been encouraged to migrate to Britain when labour was short in the 1950s and early sixties. They constituted a hard-working, but unorganised and vulnerable workforce within older and newer sectors of industry. In Batley's textile firms, and large firms like Tate & Lyle and STC in Canning Town, they were employed on the nightshift equivalent of women's daytime jobs. Elsewhere, they were a major source of cheap labour; for example, in Batley's worst textile jobs and Southall's sanitary goods firm in Saltley.

Longer journeys

The workers of each community are forced into low
wage jobs over a wider and wider area. A survey of the
Tate & Lyle workers made redundant in Canning Town
in 1968 discovered that, by 1975, two thirds were
travelling much further to work, a similar proportion
were working for far less money (as caretakers, security
guards, postal sorters or hospital porters) than sugar
workers were then earning. Many Canning Town workers
travel 15 miles eastwards to the car works of Dagenham
or ten miles west into Central London. In Benwell, local
manufacturing offers fewer and fewer jobs for local
workers. Most of the available manufacturing jobs are
now located in places like the Team Valley Estate, or
further away still in the new towns like Killingworth,
which are difficult to reach from Benwell. So Benwell's
unemployed either remain out of work or find jobs in
the hospital services, distribution or other service work.
In Batley, textile workers travel to the more stable firms
in neighbouring Dewsbury, or all the way into the
larger centres of Leeds and Bradford. Workers from
Saltley also have to travel long distances to find work,
and this pattern of working-class commuting increasingly applies to North Shields also. Communities where
people once both lived and worked have now become
dormitories for those who do the poorest jobs elsewhere.

In 1966, in most of the five areas a third of all the
local resident workers had walked to work. By 1971,
with this figure halved, transport problems had become
acute. Less than one third of local households in 1971
owned a car, and local public transport is inadequate
to the changing employment patterns. These areas were
not built as middle-class dormitories, well linked by
bus or tube to their city centres. As a result, journeys
are long, expensive, and sometimes simply impossible.
Thus many people are forced to seek low-paid work

locally, or become long term unemployed or prematurely retired, in the absence of alternatives.

This widening 'journey to work' pattern has been institutionalised by the Department of Employment, which now advertises vacancies city wide. In East London, nine employment exchanges are now linked together to provide a computerised service over a huge area, and unemployed workers without recognised skills eventually have little choice but to take the advertised jobs, however low-paid and wherever they may be.

	% of households with a car		
Saltley	26%	Canning Town	33%
North Shields	30%	Batley	39%
National average	48%		

Source: 1971 Census

Services

So now it is the people who live in areas like these five who are the waitresses, porters and cleaners in the centres of London, Birmingham, Newcastle and Leeds. It is not just the private sector that uses them in such low-paid, unpleasant and low status jobs. State agencies have also taken advantage of their availability to provide services on the cheap. The expansion of government services in the fifties and sixties means that many residents in these areas are now employed in hospitals, local authority social services departments, schools and colleges and the DHSS – as cleaners, home helps, canteen workers and clerical workers. They provide an important source of work for people in Batley, Benwell and North Shields, and to a lesser extent in Canning Town and Saltley.

In Batley in 1929, less than 10% of the workforce worked in services (including construction) whereas 72% worked in textiles. By 1971, the respective figures were roughly 40% and 31%. But this growth in employ-

ment in services was mainly of low-grade, low-paid jobs,
mainly in the public services like the health service and
education. Other areas shared this pattern, Newcastle
General Hospital near Benwell, together with Newcastle's
other major hospital, employed 6,500 people in 1971. In
the same year, the local authority, as well as the local
hospital, was a major employer in North Shields.

Many of the workers drawn into these expanding
fields of work were women. Many had not previously
worked outside the home, but others – like Batley's
women textile workers whose numbers declined at a
rate of 3.4% a year between 1959-69 – had been
thrown out of jobs in the traditional industries. Without the growth of the service sector, local unemployment in such areas would have been much higher.
As it was, this growth disguised the full extent of job
loss without compensating the workers in any way
for their losses of skills and wages.

This 'safety net' is now fast disappearing as the
public sector is cut back. In Saltley, 230 workers,
mainly ancillary staff, will lose their jobs when
St Peters, the local teachers' training college, closes
in about two years time. The situation is getting worse
as the public sector bears the brunt of the attempt to
restructure the British economy through increased investment in manufacturing.

Shiftwork

Efforts by firms in the five areas to raise productivity
have meant the permanent loss of many better paid
jobs. They have also meant deteriorating working
conditions for many workers still employed locally.
Shift working has become widespread disrupting
peoples' lives with anti-social and often irregular
hours. For example, Tate & Lyle in Canning Town
and Formica in North Shields have introduced continuous shift work. In Batley's textile industry, shift

work was responsible for the loss of many jobs for women, as employers discovered they could use Asian men for nightshifts which women are not allowed by law to work. In some areas, part-time 'twilight' shifts for women have become commonplace.

Under assault

In the five areas, the process from the creation of a working-class community to 'deprived area' status has taken less than a century. The last decade in particular has seen marked changes in their local populations, accompanying the basic economic changes in each area.

The depression of the 1930s brought long-term unemployment to the areas, especially on Tyneside, and many workers left their homes and localities altogether in search of work in the midlands and south east. In recent years people have left in much greater numbers to escape the declining employment situation and generally deteriorating state of local housing. In spite of often high rates of in-migration, most of the areas show a net population decline since 1966. This is most marked in Benwell, which has lost a quarter of its population, and in Canning Town, which has lost over a fifth. In both areas major housing redevelopment programmes have exaggerated the fall of population, but the underlying trend is clear. The total population loss figures disguise the selective basis of population changes. Most of the loss has been of younger, more skilled workers.

The significance of these changes is shown by the fact that the present rate of population change in the older areas of Newcastle is at least as great as that which occurred during the Industrial Revolution when the working-class community of Benwell was created. These five areas were built during the Industrial Revo-

lution to provide labour for the new and growing local
industries. Now this role has been undermined by the
decline of these industries locally, and the older working class communities are left to carry the costs of
industrial change by companies in no way accountable
to the local people.

CONTROL OVER LOCAL INDUSTRIAL JOBS: 1973/74

Company		*Activity*	*Jobs*	*% of indus-trial jobs controlled*
Batley				
Fox's Biscuits		Biscuits	1425	↓
Bristall Carpets (Homfrays)		Carpets	1036	20%
Whitworth Hall (Homfrays)		Carpets	826	
J. Newsome		Textiles	620	
Thos. Carr		Textiles	258	
J.R. Burrows		Textiles	316	
J. Blackburn (English & Scottish)		Textiles	201	
Jessops		Clothing	215	↓
Joshua Shaw		Engineering	184	55%
Benwell — West Newcastle Riverside				
Vickers:	Elswick	Engineering	2297	
	Scotswood	Engineering	777	
	Michell		} 3531	↓
	Bearings	Engineering	457	55%
Glass Tubes & Components		Glass Tubes	708	
Anglo Great Lakes		Synthetic graphite electrodes	680	
Ever Ready		Batteries	c650	
Tress Engineering		Engineering	310	
Elswick lead works		Leadworks	c200	↓
Canning Town				
P.L.A.		Port	3500	↓
Tate & Lyle		Sugar refiners	3260	25%
I.T.T.*		Telecom-munications	2400	
Scruttons Maltby*		Stevedores	1840	
P&O Ltd		Ship repair	1680	↓

Company	Activity	Jobs	% of industrial jobs controlled
Canning Town (contd.)			
Overseas Mail Sorting Office	Post Office	1200	50%
Lamson Ind*	Printing	975	
Furness Withy	Stevedores	925	
Tube Investments	Metal foils	720	
Spillers	Flour milling	655	↓
North Shields			
Formica	Plastics	1000+	
Swan Hunter	Ship repair	1000+	
Dukes & Marcus	Gown manuf.	500+	
Universal Bedding	Bedding	250-500	↓
Spillers Tyne Brand	Fish Food	,,	10%
Torday Ltd			
Thor Tools	Power tools	,,	
Ronson Products	Lighter access.	,,	
Newalls Ind.	Thermal insul.	,,	
Levi Strauss UK	Clothing	,,	
General Foam Prod.	Plastics	,,	
AEI Ltd	Electrical eng.	,,	↓
Saltley			
B.L.M.C.	Car manuf.	9400	33%
Southalls	Sanitary towels	937	
Post Office	Storage/distribution of telephone equipment	1870	
Birmingham Co-op	Dairy	1500	
Metro-Cammell	Bus/railway carriages	1465	
W.M. Gas Board	Gas	1173	
British Rail	Goods/parcel/local sheds	1000	↓ 64%
Motor components	Car manuf.	745	↓

Source: Department of Employment Returns/Local Sources
Note: Since 1973/74 those firms marked* have partially or fully closed their plant.

Chapter VI

Ashfield - How Participation Turned Sour

Ken Coates

In the Autumn of 1976, I received a telephone call from a former student of mine, who informed me that he had learned of the existence of a complex plan for the phased closure of all the collieries in the Ashfield area of Nottinghamshire, together with a number of others which were scattered along the Western fringe of the County. This plan, he said, was revealed in data furnished by the National Coal Board to the Structure Planning Unit of the Nottinghamshire County Council. He wished to know whether it was possible to discover if the Miners' Union had been informed of this sweeping transformation, which would one day overtake them. Apparently the plan anticipated the exhaustion of coal reserves across a wide area, resulting in a serious concentration of shut-downs bunched towards the mid-1980's.

It quickly became plain that some sort of detailed plan did exist, and my local Labour councillor began to ask for it. After his enquiries had failed to produce the offending document, and after a couple of months of other investigations on my own part, we both decided that the proper course of action was to open the matter out to wider discussion. Accordingly I wrote an open letter to members of Ashfield Labour Party, and to branch and area officers of the NUM. This stimulated a stiff local controversy, which necessitated a series of further letters: the sequence of these is, once they are interspersed with the various rejoinders and denials which provoked them, self-explanatory.

In my first open letter on this topic, dated 10th December 1976, after explaining the brief history which is outlined above, I had written:

"Of course, the life of a colliery is not permanent. There may, for all I know, be a good case for some closures over a longer or shorter period of time. I am, however, convinced that some earlier closures in our broader area were profoundly mistaken. For this reason the fullest consultation is necessary from the very earliest stages, if the Board is to avoid such mistakes by profiting from the experience and advice of the mineworkers. So I asked leading members of the NUM whether they had been notified of the Ashfield proposals. They had not.

Further enquiries revealed that the document in question was "confidential", and was not even to be shown to County Councillors.

Now, I am not arguing that the document in question is without merit. I am saying that it is without *legitimacy*. Supposing the Coal Board wants to persuade Sutton miners to move, say to the Vale of Belvoir. That could be sensible, but it will be subject to negotiation. People might not want to go. They might prefer to stay where they are. They have, in any case, opinions of their own. They have a union which represents them. Shouldn't their opinions be asked, through the NUM, *before* anybody files a report with the structure planners? Supposing the county could be persuaded to commit funds to developing one area, and encouraged to promote changes in another, in order to fit one prognosis, offered by the Board. Wouldn't this nullify all future consultation? Shouldn't the workpeople's chosen delegates be involved in whatever argument is necessary about these questions, *from the beginning?* Here is a question which takes us to the very heart of the problem of industrial democracy.

Of course, there are things we can do about this. We can ask the County Council officers to divulge this plan to Councillors. We can ask the Board to divulge it to the Union. We could ask our own Councillors to issue instructions to all personnel that no plans submitted by any employer may be given any consideration at all unless they are previously initialled by the proper representative of the appropritate union or unions. Then employers will *have* to consult first, and form plans by agreement. I hope all three of these things will happen.

Sutton and Kirkby face serious changes in their industrial
prospects, and these will be very painful for well-established
and harmonious local communities unless they are consulted,
and involved in all important planning questions, from the
earliest possible moment."

During the next ten days a fairly fierce discussion
broke out, and this involved not only local people in
the threatened areas, but councillors and officials of the
planning department. Most of the rank-and-file councillors were no better informed than I was myself, and
it was plain that they had not been carefully briefed
on the industrial inputs to the structure plan. But the
staff of the planning department were unfailingly
courteous, and as helpful as they were allowed to be
within the terms of their agreement with the NCB to
respect the confidentiality of the information which it
had furnished to them. Accordingly, by 20th December
1976, I was able to send out a further open letter, which
said, on the question at issue:

"First, I should say that my statements have encouraged a
most helpful response from the County Council staffs and a
number of Councillors representing the mining community.
I am now in a position to state exactly what is the location of
the secret document which considers future pit-closures in
Sutton and elsewhere. This is listed in a publication called
Draft Report of Survey, available from the Nottinghamshire Structure Plan. On page 200, the document with which
we are concerned is listed as a *Draft Structure Plan Topic
Report on Coal Mining,* of November 1975, 'available in
summary form only'. The summary is, of course, rather
uninformative, since there is no point whatever in classifying
the Topic Report if all its contents are to feature in an
abbreviated form.

Secondly, I do not know in what form the NCB filed the
evidence from which the secret Topic Report was compiled,
and I am told that some Board Spokesmen have denied that
they have given any 'document' to the County Council. That
may be literally true: they may have given oral evidence to
the planners. The information in question seems to be bulky,
carefully considered, and technically highly competent.

Now let us come to the central issues. The published Structure Plan speaks of the loss of 13,500 jobs in mining in two decades. The formula of a 'double decade' can be very misleading. Why not say 'in twenty years' time'? I think the answer can only be that this would not be true. From now to 1986 is one decade. From to to 1996 is another. Let's guess that this massive closure programme could start in 1984 and finish in 1988. That would complete it within 'two decades'. It would also complete it within twelve years, which might seem to make it more urgent for us to think about it.

If the Board is going to sink not one, but four or three pits in the Vale of Belvoir, from where will come the miners to staff them? If they come from Ashfield, will they be asked to commute? If that happened, how long would the journey take? Or will they be invited to move? If so, will they be able to take gran and grandad, or will Teversall or Stanton Hill become old peoples' ghettoes? Will there be jobs for miners' wives in the Vale? Will the new houses be built as part of a self-contained mining settlement, of will they be scattered round existing rural villages and townships? I do not know the answers to these questions, but I expect the Board's planners must be worrying about them, even now. If this is so, why not ask miners, and their wives, and their aged relatives, and, yes, their children, what *they* think? The social consequences of such a migration would be enormous, and they are certainly not confined to problems of jobs and rehousing. We live in a *community,* where old people help younger ones, where each depends on the other. Most of the time we don't even notice it, it is so familiar. But it will hurt very much on the day it isn't there.

That is why we must insist on our right to know, and to talk things over *before* decisions are made.

New laws have come into force, or partly into force, since 1974. These include the Industry Act and the Employment Protection Act, both of which guarantee trade unionists 'the right to know'. Employers are bound to reveal information for collective bargaining purposes, and the Government recognises, in principle, the right of workers to bargain about investment decisions, questions affecting closures and a variety of other major economic matters. It could be argued that employers who compel an elected authority to conceal such information even from elected representatives are acting against the declared will of Parliament, and if they were pressed they would find this very difficult to justify."

After these broadsides, the issue quickly found its
way into the local newspapers. The first of these to
explore the ground was the *Mansfield Chronicle
Advertiser:*

> "An allegation that the National Coal Board has prepared a
> detailed plan outlining various time scales and options for the
> closure of all the pits in the Sutton . . . area claims that the
> plan suggests they might finish in the period ten years from
> now, and alleges secrecy on the part of the Board over the
> issue. Following this Nottinghamshire miners' leaders have
> instructed the Nottingham Area NUM Executive Committee
> to seek talks with both the North and South Nottinghamshire
> areas of the National Coal Board to discuss job security in the
> Notts. coalfield.
>
> Both Mr Len Clarke, Nottingham area president, and its
> general secretary, Mr Len Martin, are anxious for clarification
> over future Board plans, especially in view of the coal bonanza
> that might accrue from the Vale of Belvoir.
>
> A spokesman for the Board strongly refuted the existence
> of any detailed plan for such closures, and denied that secrecy
> was involved in what he states is a purely tentative assessment
> supplied in confidence to Nottinghamshire County Council's
> planning department.
>
> It is subject to change in the light of continuing exploration
> and newer technology, he stressed, adding that the Board is
> continually faced with the need to look at the exhaustion of
> coal reserves, and that regular discussions with all the interested
> parties keep everyone informed of the prospects.
>
> Mr Clarke told CHAD that, although he did not know of the
> the alleged plan to close all the Sutton pits, his area had always
> been satisfied that its consultations with the Board on these
> matters was all it should be."

(*30 December 1976*)

But according to the *Chronicle Advertiser,* the Coal
Board spokesman was emphatic that

> "although the assessment submitted to the county planners
> was confidential, full discussions on a regular basis take place
> at pit consultative meetings, colliery and area review meetings
> at which union representatives are kept fully in the picture.
>
> He stressed that any review can change drastically over a
> period of time.
>
> 'It is a fact that we consult with the county planning

authority on a confidential basis about the exhaustion of seams, but any assessments made are only on a purely tentative basis. They are a continuing process, and I can assure all concerned that no firm decisions have been made for any pit closures in the Sutton area or anywhere else', he said."

A less objective story was filed a week later in the rival journal, *Notts Free Press* which cited Mr Len Martin, the area secretary of the NUM, as dismissing the whole story. In my reply I was able to make two points:

"I did tell the *Free Press* newsman that the first and most crucial complaint I had raised was a constitutional one: that a key planning document was being withheld from our elected representatives, and that this must in any circumstances be unjustifiable. The reporter said he agreed with me that this was an unanswerable charge: but he did not even mention this central complaint in his story as it finally appeared.

Since then I have had the opportunity to discuss this matter with the Chairman of the County Council's Planning Committee, Frank Higgins. He unreservedly confirmed that the councillors have not been given sight of this document, and he strongly agreed that they must be entitled to see it. I believe he has informed the *Free Press* that this is his considered view. We shall all wait with keen interest to see how fairly they report his statement."

In fact Councillor Higgins did issue a series of statements, on 14th January, 20th January and 3rd February. In the first of these, the councillor forthrightly called for release of the topic report.

"Pressure on the National Coal Board and Notts. County Council planners to release a 'secret' document on the future of mining in the county mounted this week when Notts. Environment Committee chairman Coun. Frank Higgins revealed that he may go to the Department of Energy for support . . .

While not sharing Mr Coates' fears that the document contains information which miners and their unions are not aware of, Coun. Higgins is annoyed and puzzled that councillors have not been allowed to see it, even in confidence. He explained that the information required had been passed on by the Board on the understanding that it was purely on an

officer to officer basis. An attempt to persuade them to alter
their minds had since failed, and if another appeal met with
the same fate, he may ask the Department of Energy to
his request." (*Notts Free Press*, 14th January 1977)

The second report, in the *Chronicle Advertiser* the
following week, was more specific about how publication
was to be tackled:

"The National Coal Board is to be approached again next
Thursday by at least one county councillor in an effort to gain
publication of a detailed Board estimate of pit closures in
Nottinghamshire within the next 20 years.

Coun. Frank Higgins, chairman of the county Environment
Committee told CHAD that he will bring the issue up at major
seminar arranged with Board officials. He does not see why the
best interests of the community should not be served by
abandoning the cloak of secrecy.

Following pressure from Mansfield councillors at last
week's council meeting a letter has been sent to Nottinghamshire County Council demanding that the information given
to county planners be given also to Mansfield District Council.

The NCB has admitted that the report was given to top
officers of the county council as confidential, but has claimed
that it does not contain detailed plans for pit closures. Its
spokesman denied secrecy and stressed that it was a purely
tentative assessment subject to change in the light of continuing exploration and newer technology.

Coun. Higgins added that he could understand the Board's
problems in wishing to keep the document confidential.

The seminar next Thursday will include discussion on the
coal reserves discovered in the Vale of Belvoir, which recent
investigations have shown could be in the region of 1,200
million tons." *(20th January 1977)*

However, after the meeting in question, although the
embargo was not lifted, Councillor Higgins seemed to
have changed his view about matters. Now, he told the
Chronicle Advertiser,

"The information detailed estimates of pit closures in the
county over the next 20 years, given under a pledge of strict
confidence by the National Coal Board to Nottinghamshire
County Council officers only, would prove to be of no

importance if published, is the view of Coun. F. Higgins,
chairman of the county Environmental Committee.

The estimates were given to assist in the preparation of
the Draft Structure Plan for the county, but the information
is now completely out of date, is Coun. Higgins' view.

He admits that he has not read the report which was
prepared by County Council officers upon facts supplied by
the Coal Board." *(3rd February, 1977).*

As far as the newspaper-reader of Ashfield would
have known up to this time, then, this was the state of
affairs: allegations that a secret county council planning
report existed, and that it forecast widespread pit
closures in West Nottinghamshire, had first been denied,
and then confirmed, by a variety of public officials.
Having confirmed them, the chairman of the appropriate
council committee had first called for their publication,
and threatened to invoke the assistance of the Secretary
of State for Energy, and then later offered the view that
the Report in question was unimportant, outdated, and
inaccurate, even though, at the time in question, he
admitted he had still not seen in. Rightly or wrongly,
important union spokesmen had been quoted as dismissing the whole notion that there might possibly be
something to worry about in the scheduled Report. The
Coal Board had denied giving the County Council any
information which was not already openly available to
the miners, and had not answered the question "why,
then, enjoin the planners to respect as confidential
something which is already widely known?" It was in
this rather cloudy context that the leader of the County
Council said to me "why, you've stirred up a hornet's
nest, to be sure!"

2. *What the Structure Plan Said*

County planning authorities are obliged, under section
6 of the 1971 Town and Country Planning Act, to
prepare a detailed survey of the "matters which may be

expected to affect the development of its area, or the
planning of its development". The planning authorities
are enjoined to prepare a Structure Plan, which "must
be justified by the results of the survey, which will
accompany the submission of the Structure Plan to
the Secretary of State.

In England and Wales the planners work over a 20-
year period: in Scotland, under parallel legislation, the
forward plans are prepared to cover a period of eight
years. When the Nottinghamshire area found itself
brought into the reorganised system of local government, there had been no statutory report on the region
it covered for well over two decades. The structure
plan team which is responsible for the Nottinghamshire plan is part of the County Council's department
of Planning and Transportation. It is a highly qualified
and efficient group, and it set about its work with
considerable élan and some rigour. In 1976 the various
final drafts of the Plan were published. Before this, a
whole series of Topic Reports had been issued, covering
a range of specific issues, such as housing, employment,
leisure and recreation, population, public utilities and
so on. In all, twelve such reports were prepared. Eleven
were published, and made available to the public. The
remaining one, completed in November 1975, was the
Topic Report on Coalmining, "available in summary
form only".

This summary is not long, and it would not honour
the pledges of confidentiality given to the NCB, which
provided most of the information upon which it is
based, it it did not reduce most of this data to the
vaguest abstractions. However, since it is still all that is
publicly known about the scheduled report, it is worth
reproducing it:

"Coal Mining in Nottinghamshire — A Summary

1. The coal industry has declined substantially nationally since

the war, both in employment, from 780,000 in 1951 to
315,000 in 1973, and in output from 209m tons p.a. to 118m
tons p.a. over the same period. Nottinghamshire has one of the
most productive coalfields in the country, and while it has also
declined in employment and output mainly in the west of the
County it has been substantially insulated from the national
decline largely as the result of the low price of its pithead
coal, and particularly during the 1960s due to the construction of a number of coal-fired power stations in the Trent
Valley. Coal mining is still Nottinghamshire's major single
employer, with 45,000 employees in 1973.

2. The future prospects for employment in the coal industry
   are for greater stability, and are better now than at any
   time since the 1967 Fuel Policy White Paper (Cmnd. 3438).
   Based upon the 'Coal Industry Examination', a tri-partite
   report produced by the National Coal Board, the Mining
   Unions and the Government, the present output of the coal
   industry is planned to remain at its present level until 1985
   with declines through pit exhaustion being matched by
   increases from existing and new collieries. The main con-
   straints to achieving this target are stated as the availabilitv
   of finance, and the problem of labour mobility likely to
   arise through the depletion of useful economic reserves at
   some mines, while others are expanded.

3. Projections of future mining employment in Nottinghamshire have been made, based upon expected colliery life and
   the need to meet national output targets. It is anticipated
   that employment will continue falling from its 1974 level
   of 40,500 to 32,400 in 1986 and 25,700 in 1996. The
   likely diminution in employment would mean that for
   every 100 miners in 1974, only 63 would be required in
   1996. However, this anticipated fall in employment is misleading in relation to the real labour needs of the mining
   industry. The age structure of the mining workforce, is such
   that 63% of those presently employed are over 40 years of
   age, so only 37% would be available for work in 1996.
   Therefore even though total employment is likely to fall,
   recruitment into the industry needs to continue.

4. The practical planning problems resolve around the need to
   cater for the inevitable exhaustion of reserves at some
   collieries, coupled to the need to make good the potential
   labour deficits at those mines with substantial reserves.

   (i)   the greatest problem is the inability to state with any degree of certainty the likely date of exhaustion;

(ii)   the problems associated with mine exhaustion are concerned with the need to provide alternative job opportunities for those who neither wish to transfer to other collieries, nor are eligible for the Redundant Mineworkers Payment Scheme; many of these older miners will register as unemployed with little hope of re-employment, even given the availability of re-training opportunities;

(iii) the magnitude of the labour deficit at continuing mines will be reduced by the transfer of miners from collieries where reserves are likely to become exhausted, but it still likely to be about 7,800 over the 1974-86 period, and 10,100 between 1974 and 1996. It must be stressed that these are minimum figures, taking account only of natural wastage due to retirement; any wastage from within the workforce, for instance due to movement into other industries, will increase the likely deficit. Thus the main need for recruitment will come in the period up to 1986, and will be experienced most in those areas distant from the present concentrations of labour, and at those pits with an above average age of workforce.

5. The major policy implications of these issues relate to changes in the travel-to-work patterns of miners, and the provision of housing. The present travel-to-work pattern is characterised by the majority of miners travelling a very short distance and a small minority travelling a considerable distance; these latter have either transferred from collieries now shut, or are skilled men involved in increasing production at mines with substantial reserves. There is also a general west to east movement of miners reflecting the historical development of the coalfield. Future travel-to-work patterns will be closely related to housing policies, but two features are likely: firstly, a marked decline in commuting from Derbyshire, as the centre of mining shifts eastwards; secondly, an increase in the average length of journey-to-work as more miners transfer to work at collieries which are further from main towns.

6. The National Coal Board is a large property owner, mainly through the Coal Industry Housing Association, owning 5% of the total County housing stock (up to 80% in some communities). The main problems associated with the housing are:

    (i)   a large proportion of houses are occupied by retired
           or disabled miners and widows, termed 'benevolent
           provision';
   (ii) the problem under (i) occurs at a time and in areas
           where housing is required to attract skilled miners to
           the County;
  (iii) the 'tied' nature of NCB housing leads to dissatis-
           faction either when the miner wishes to leave the
           industry or when the house is sold to the Local
           Authority in the efficient management of their
           District's total housing stock.

The two issues of immediate concern are, firstly, the need
for additional housing (by Local Authorities) for incoming
miners, bearing in mind that a better use could be made of
the housing stock through the provision of dwellings for the
retired. Secondly, is the issue of the feasibility and appro-
priateness of extending the municipal control of housing in
the 'tied' sector.

7. The three areas which appear to be most suited to the
location of new housing for miners are, to the east of
Mansfield, at East Retford, and at Ollerton/Boughton.

8. The National Coal Board are studying the feasibility of
new mining operations in parts of the east and south of
the County, but have made no firm decisions as yet. If any
such operations are authorised during the plan period, the
position of coal mining in Nottinghamshire will need to be
reviewed.''

Somewhat more information can be dug out of the
overall documentation of the Structure Plan.

− 'a decline in mining employment over the County as a whole
of approximately 6,300 between 1976 and 1986 are of approximately 7,200 between 1986 and 1996 is expected'. (4.9
Consultative Draft Written Statement of the Nottinghamshire
Structure Plan, 1976)
    This is the basis for the statement that 13,500 jobs will
disappear. Subsequently the Planners have revised this estimated
decline for the second decade to 6,400.

− 'The decline in employment in the mining industry is expected
to continue, especially in the west of the Mining system *in the
early part of the plan period* (my emphasis) as a result of the
exhaustion of coal reserves, with the result that there is
likely to be a loss of approximately 5,500 jobs between 1976

and 1986, and and approximately 7,000 between 1986 and 1996'.
(Ibid, 4.21).
— These estimated losses have subsequently been corrected to
  read 6,300 and 6,400 respectively, a total of 12,700.
— The Structure Plan divides the "Mining System" into several
  zones. In the Erewash Zone we read:

> 'Employment in the coal industry is likely to decline from
> approximately 9,100 jobs in 1976 to 2,300 in 1996 due to
> the exhaustion of coal reserves. *Any significant decline is
> not expected until after 1980 and probably not until the
> mid 1980s* (my emphasis) beginning in the West of Zone
> but extending eastwards over the Plan period.' (4.29).

This confirms the suspicion that the closures are
likely to bunch near the middle of the time-span, rather
than disperse towards its end. 'Exhaustion of reserves'
is liable to occur with relative simultaneity in the
Westermost part of the area, unless something happens
to revalue the Board's estimates of which resources are
viable. There is a fair amount of Derbyshire coal still
ungot, as a result of Lord Robens' closure programme
earlier.

We all know that forecasts are uncertain and sometimes even misleading. Nonetheless, the inaccuracies
within them can often cancel each other out. One thing
is perfectly clear: if they are useful to the structure
planners they would be useful to the County Councillors
who are not allowed to see them.

To return to the published data, we must consider
the age-structure of the existing labour force. *The Draft
Report of the Survey,* still published by the structure
plan, gives aggregate figures as follows: over 40 years of
age in 1974 were 64% of miners in West Bassetlaw, 63%
in Central Notts., 67% in Mansfield-Ashfield, and 69%
in Erewash. (DR of S 6.60.) This means that the Board
will need massive and effective recruiting campaign,
coupled (unless this were preternaturally effective) with
a policy of concentration of the able-bodied labour

force into the most variable units of production. This, rather than depletion of resources, could well become the over-riding drive towards closures in the older areas. If this reasoning is accepted, it will be plain that the process would be accelerated by early retirement, and accelerated yet again if it were anticipated that any significant amount of labour for Belvoir might come from the old Notts. coalfield.

The Leicestershire County Council, whose chairman is the Duke of Rutland, has not prepared a confidential topic report on coal-mining, and all of its mining data (sadly out of date, Leicester's planners maintain) is freely available in the published Topic Report on Employment.

We can now forecast with some accuracy the contents of the secret report. It will contain pit-by-pit estimates of reserves, with possibly upper and lower expectations. It will contain pit-by-pit, or perhaps area-by-area, age-profiles of the labour force. It will locate the time-scales with greater precision than the statement of the estimated decade of possible closure. If it is to be at all useful to planners, it will have to narrow this focus to enable phased responses in the fields not only of employment, but also of relevant welfare provision. We may therefore anticipate shrewd guesses about the actual years of forthcoming closures, or at least about the time-scales within which closure becomes imminent likely.

No one who was in a position to know the contents of the offending Topic Report has ever denied these contentions about its scope and composition. However, there remained another important source of official information, derived from the Topic Report. This is the Employment Topic Report.

Not for the first time, this document raises some interesting questions of consistency. We have already been informed, in the published short version of the

Coal Mining Topic Report, that "It is anticipated that employment will continue falling from its 1974 level of 40,500 to 32,400 in 1986 and 25,700 in 1996", (paragraph 3, see above). Now we learn that "it will continue to fall . . . from its 1971 level of 32,000 to perhaps 25,600 in 1986 and 18,400 in 1996". (Employment Report, 5.8). Obviously such discrepancies as this imply that we are not considering the same populations, and that the Topic Reports for Derbyshire or other neighbouring areas must be considered alongside those we are currently investigating.

The Employment Report divides up the coalfield into four subsidiary zones. These are: Zone 1, Worksop and District; Zone 3, West of Newark, including Gedling and Edwinstowe; Zone 5, Mansfield-Ashfield; and Zone 7, Erewash. The Report continues:

"The age structure of the mining workforce is such that 65% of those presently employed are over 40 years of age so that only 35%, or 11,200, will be available for work in 1996. Therefore, even though total employment in the industry is likely to fall, recruitment will need to continue and will have to attract a substantial proportion of the growth in male working population, especially in Zones 1 and 3 (40).

The employment problems within the Mining System revolve around the need to cater for the inevitable exhaustion of reserves at some collieries, principally in the west of the System, whilst at the same time to make good the potential labour deficits at those mines with substantial reserves which tend to be in the east of the System. It should be noted that whilst the greatest reduction in the number of mining jobs is expected to be in Zone 5, the reduction in Zone 7, as a percentage of the total workforce, presents far more serious problems. The main problems are as follows:

a. the greatest is the inability to state with any degree of certainty the date at which reserves at any particular colliery are likely to be exhausted. The implications of new reserves possibly being exploited from Zones 1 and 3 should also be borne in mind;

b. with colliery exhaustion there is a need to provide alternative job opportunities for those who neither wish to transfer to other collieries nor are eligible for the Redundant Mineworkers Payments Scheme; many of these older miners will register as unemployed with little hope of re-employment even given the availability of retraining facilities;

c. the magnitude of the labour deficit will be reduced by the transfer of miners from collieries whose reserves are likely to become exhausted over the Plan period to existing or new workings where labour is required.

"It has been estimated that at least 27,000 new jobs will be required in the System over the Plan period, an increase of a quarter over existing employment, of which a large proportion will be required by 1986. This estimate is based on the projected fall in mining employment and an assumed growth in the working population equivalent to natural change."

"(40) Although precise figures may be misleading, the proportion of the population achieving working age (assuming no net migration) who would have to be recruited to mining, based upon the projected deficit 1974-1996 would be 31% in Zone 1, 58% in Zone 3, 8% in Zone 5 and 12% in Zone 7. This assumes no attraction of labour from elsewhere."

The Employment Report also lets some other interesting cats poke at least their whiskers out of the bag. In Zone 7, we are told "By 1996 employment in the industry will probably be limited to administrative personnel". (p.56). Why this Zone will need administrators once the mines have gone is not explained, but no doubt it has something to do with the great demand which may be perceived for admirals in a rapidly-shrinking Navy.

When we examine what is reported on the Ashfield Zone, we find confirmation that mining employment is expected to decline by 9,000 (5.95); we also find more elaborate information about the age of the mining labour force: "41% are currently over 50 and will retire before 1986, while a further 26% will retire between 1986 and 1996. This is only loss by natural wastage. It is likely to be a minimum figure inasmuch as wastage

. . . can be considerable". This reinforces the likelihood that the structure planners have, in the scheduled topic report, a detailed grid giving age structures colliery by colliery. It also reinforces the supposition that estimates about the life of available reserves will have much smaller weight than those of the residual working-life of an ageing work-force: the first kind of estimates may be variable and contingent, while the second constitute extremely inflexible hard facts, which rigorously imply that pit-closures will become necessary in order to re-deploy a shrinking manpower, unless remarkable success were to be achieved in colliery recruitment. We shall return to this matter.

3. *How the County Council "Consulted"*

Before a planning authority can finalise its structure plans, it is obliged by law to undertake a thorough programme of public consultation, in which the general public, other local authorities which may be affected, and special interest groups may discuss the implications of the proposals which are made, and offer suggestions about suitable modifications of them. The structure planners will then consider these proposals, and any objections which may be raised, before finalising their draft and submitting it for approval by the Department of the Environment.

In the abstract, the Nottinghamshire authority took this duty very seriously. Some £60,000 were allocated to finance a whole programme of meetings and lectures, copies of most of the key documents (although not, of course, of the Secret Topic Report) were made available in all branch libraries, and a most effective visual aid kit was prepared in order to highlight some of the main issues in a very imaginative way. There is a good deal of evidence that the responsible officers of the structure plan staff regarded this part of the process of planning as an important one. Certainly they worked at it, and worked hard.

Yet mining remains the basic industry for a crucial part of the area, and the existence of a scheduled statement dealing with it, which had been withheld from councillors, was inevitably bound to impede this process. This was still further affected by the fact that many councillors were to say the least of it, inadequately briefed even on the contents of the published documents, and most councillors were apparently unaware of the very existence of the classified topic report. Although this document was listed in a published bibliography attached to the Draft Report of Survey, it is clear that its significance had not been explained to the majority of councillors before the time when the public discussion of the matter broke out.

Soon after the news became generally known, the Labour Group of members on the County Council met, and according to the information which I received, resolved to approach the National Coal Board in order to request their permission to release the Topic Report to Council members. But permission was obviously not forthcoming, and once this became understood, leading members of the Labour Group changed their public position on the question. However, some rank-and-file councillors continued to insist that the Report should be released.

Meantime, the Mansfield District Council officially resolved to ask for access to the Report, and the Ashfield Constituency Labour Party unanimously agreed to approach the Secretary of State for Energy, Tony Benn, to secure its release to councillors. In spite of this, it soon began to look as if the leaders of the Labour Group were anxious not to press too hard in order to allow their council members permission to unlock the filing cabinets of their planning department. Four councillors had been given the duty of approaching

the NCB in order to secure the raising of the embargo
on the circulation of the Topic Report. On 24 January
1977, the following memorandum was sent by Councillor Cattermole, the secretary of the Labour Group
of County Council members, to the Group Leader,
Councillor Wilson, and to Councillors Higgins and
Cowan:

"At the last Group Meeting it was agreed that Councillors
Wilson, Simms, Higgins and myself should see the Coal Board
with regard to the so-called 'Secret Document' which was in
the hands of the Environment Committee in conjunction with
the compilation of the County Council Structure Plan. I
obtained convenient dates from the Councillors concerned
and approached the Coal Board with a view to arranging a
meeting.

The County is covered by two area boards and it was
proposed that a joint meeting should be arranged. After a
number of telephone calls it has not been possible to arrange
a meeting and it will certainly not be possible to arrange one
before the next Group Meeting as the Coal Board are reluctant
to agree to such a meeting.

The events which had led to the press publicity on the
'Secret Document' are as follows:

'In mid 1975 the Coal Board were approached by the
County Council for information that would enable the
County Council to prepare its Structure Plan. Certain information was given to Council Officials on a confidential basis
to enable this Plan to be prepared. No document was, however, prepared by the National Coal Board itself and I have the
assurance of the National Coal Board that no information that
was given to the Council has not been given to the National
Union of Mineworkers Nottinghamshire Area. Indeed I have
been assured that the Union are in possession of much more
information than has ever been given to the Nottingham
County Council. In conversation with National Coal Board
Officials, they have said that the information given to the
Council was given before they had completed their trial
borings in the Vale of Belvoir, which will have a great
impact on the Coal Board's future developments . . . '"

The statement went on to say that the NCB, following

the release of information which I had passed to Tony
Benn, would not agree to meet councillors until a new
procedure for dealing with planning matters had been
devised.

A few comments upon this revealing text are called
for. First, the slight complexity involved in arranging
a meeting between two area Boards and the four councillors was not a necessary precondition for solving the
problem. Many of the threatened collieries were in the
South Nottinghamshire Area of the NCB, and it would
have been a quite sufficient beginning to fix a meeting
with the Area Director of South Nottinghamshire alone.
Further, it was subsequently made clear, at a meeting
between both North and South Nottinghamshire Area
Directors and the Nottinghamshire NUM Executive, that
the Topic Report did indeed contain information which
had not previously been given to the union, even though
the reliability of this information was put into serious
doubt. Whilst this fact would probably give comfort to
the NCB's staff, it was not convenient to the County
Council, since, if its plans were based upon seriously
unreliable evidence they were scarcely worthy of official
ratification by the Department of the Environment.

What Mr Cattermole refrained from explaining was
far more important. Who was it that authorised the
collection of information from a prominent industrial
interest under conditions of secrecy which prevented
even elected councillors from access to it? Was this
remarkable authorisation obtained solely from the
senior employed officials? It so, how could it bind
councillors, and what was to prevent them simply
issuing an instruction that the Topic Report on Coal-
mining be circulated? If not, which councillors authorised so dubious a procedure, and why did they not
consult their colleagues about it? Where was the decision
to permit such an intrigue minuted? If it was not
minuted, what was its validity? On all such urgent

constitutional matters, Mr Cattermole's memorandum
preserves an eloquent silence. Also not discussed in the
memorandum is the obvious question, why did not Mr
Cattermole's committee of four address themselves
directly to Mr Benn, in order to seek his help in resol-
ving the difficulty? They did not, and in fact it was not
until late April 1977 that members of another Council, in
West Yorkshire, appealed to the Secretary of State to
intervene in order to secure proper consultation
between the planning authority and the Board. Had
Nottinghamshire reacted promptly, it might be thought,
valuable time could have been saved, and improvements
in these obviously inadequate mechanisms could have
been initiated from the beginning of the year.

Informed local observers did not miss the point of
this argument. Writing in the *Mansfield Chronicle
Advertiser,* Harry Whitehouse insisted:

> "It is all too easy to seek hidden motives for the release of
> the information that the National Coal Board has supplied
> confidential to Nottinghamshire County Council planners
> which casts doubt on the future viability of many North
> Nottinghamshire pits . . .
>
> At the moment the confidentiality of the report is being
> maintained against allcomers, and therefore it is impossible
> to judge just what are the precise effects of its information.
>
> The industrial implications are obvious, the local govern-
> ment ones perhaps less so.
>
> First and foremost is the rather disturbing situation that, as
> far as County Hall is concerned, the contents of the com-
> munications from the NCB, and indeed the existence of the
> communications itself, were known only to certain senior
> members of the planning staff, not to any councillors.
>
> Moreover, according to my information, not only were
> these elected members kept in the dark, they were by-passed.
> Several copies of the NCB report have gone to Government
> departments as part of the procedure for keeping them
> informed of planning developments.
>
> To be fair to the officers, the report was necessary for them
> to compile the draft structure plan for the country which is
> now undergoing public discussion. They received it under the

pledge of confidentiality, the NCB apparently being under the fear that publicity might cause unnecessary alarm, and feel themselves still bound by that pledge. The impression I have gained is that they now wish they could be relieved of it.

One other aspect is also causing some concern, and the £60,000 public participation exercise now being carried out by the County Council on the draft structure plan is seen in some quarters as a farce.

The public, local authorities and other organisations and bodies are being asked to make their comments on the proposals in the plan.

What, it is being asked, is the use of bothering to make these comments if they will be ignored because those who have made the proposals have not revealed the true reason for making them? Anything which is said, possibly after a great deal of research and trouble, would be a waste of time because the planners have unrevealed information to use against them."
(27th January, 1977)

Mr Whitehouse was not aware of the revision of the structure plan which reduced the estimated job-shrinkage to 12,700, and he speaks of "North Nottinghamshire" meaning a geographical expression, and *not* "The North Nottinghamshire Area of the NCB". Such ambiguities are necessary in any journalistic coverage, since journalists are trying to simplify their reports to achieve wide understanding.

Of course, the legal position of a council employee who withholds information from an elected councillor could be difficult. Awareness of a complex history of cases on this matter obviously put Nottinghamshire's planning staffs on their toes. On February 1st 1977, Mr Howard Jackson, acting for the Director of Planning and Transportation, sent me a short letter insisting that the officials of the planning department had received no requests from councillors to see a copy of the scheduled report. The pre-occupation of the planners with legal technicalities revealed itself in the last clause of this letter which concluded: "So actual denial of access to the report has not occurred".

4. *What they told the Union*

As has already been explained, early in 1977 the NUM Area Council requested an early meeting with the two Area NCB directors in order to discuss "future employment prospects". On the 15 March, the NCB issued a press release on this meeting. Two days later this was circulated to the County Council Labour Group by Mr Cattermole.

> "The Executive Committee of the Nottinghamshire Area of the NUM and the Directors and supporting staff of the two Nottinghamshire Areas of the NCB met recently to discuss anxieties about future employment prospects in the mining industry.
>
> The Chairman, NUM President Mr Len Clark, explained that the meeting had been called as a result of questions about security of employment arising from comment on the Nottinghamshire Draft Structure Plan and references to a report allegedly forecasting a large reduction in local mining jobs.
>
> Mr Ian Dowson, South Notts. Deputy Director explained that the report referred to − a 'Topic Report' on the mining industry − was prepared by County Council officers as one element of the build up to the Draft Structure Plan. He said the mining manpower estimates provided by the Board reflected the situation as it then appeared two years earlier. Similar estimates provided for an earlier planning study had proved to be about 50 per cent wrong as a result of changed circumstances, such as oil price increases and improved mining methods.
>
> On this occasion projections up to 20 years into the future had been requested but the published Draft Plan had, in fairness, noted that the figures were only projections and were subjected to continuous review.
>
> In fact, they were now already out of date.
>
> Mr Merrik Spanton, North Notts. Area Director, pointed out that developments resulting from Government approval of 'Plan for Coal' were only just being formulated when the figures were being prepared.
>
> Executive member Mr Vic Lloyd said the County Council had to try to anticipate replacement job requirements so it was important that their information was regularly brought up to date.

This was agreed and the meeting also felt it might be beneficial for Union and Board representatives to jointly meet County Council members prior to the Council meeting to approve the Structure Plan.

Mr George Cheshire said it was important to allay fears, particularly in the Sutton-in-Ashfield area, that there were going to be wholesale pit closures.

Dr Alan Griffin, North Notts. Industrial Relations Officer, said the request for 20 year forecasts had meant that the Board had had 'to peer right into the future, outside their own normal planning timescale, and in these circumstances accuracy was impossible'.

He was supported by Mr Joe Whelan, the Union's Financial Secretary, who asked who would have forecast the large increases in oil prices and who could forecast relative prices in the future? Mr Whelan said he was satisfied that local NCB management were not keeping secrets from the Union and saw no point in getting alarmed about long term predictions which were bound to be unreliable.

The Union Vice President, Mr Neville Hawkins, agreed, pointing out that fears of the closure of Harworth Colliery a few years ago had proved groundless.

Mr John Longdon, Senior Mining Engineer, reviewed the Board's current view of the prospects for North Nottingham-shire, saying that apart from the exhaustion of Teversal Colliery — and it was recognised that this was not necessarily accepted by the Union — no closures were expected before 1986. In the following ten years another colliery was likely to exhaust its reserves but there would be larger numbers of men needed elsewhere, for example at Silverhill, Bevercotes and Harworth.

We do not envisage any significant reduction in the total number of jobs in the North Nottinghamshire coalfield for as far afield as we can reasonably foresee, Mr Spanton said.

Mr Dowson said no South Notts. Area mines were expected to close before 1986 but in the following ten years some pit closures were likely due to exhaustion.

South Notts. Area Director Mr Donald Davies, stressed that no pit in the county would be closed to develop mining in the Vale of Belvoir. No decision had been taken about mining there but if any projects did receive approval of would doubt-less be the Board's objective to keep pits nearing exhaustion open as long as possible to maintain coal supplies and to be able to offer alternative jobs when they eventually had to close.

Mr J. DeLacy, an Executive member, said the two NCB
Area reviews showed that the 1986 predictions in the mining
Topic Report were already wrong and anything beyond that
date was 'guesswork'.

Summing up, Mr Clarke said the meeting had confirmed
that there was unlikely to be any serious contraction in the
period up to 1986 but it was accepted that the following
decade could see some exhaustion of reserves although this
was likely to be offset by expansion at existing long-life
collieries and the possible development of new ones.

The meeting agreed to the issue of this joint press release
summarising the discussion."

Various things are missing from this report. First,
although the Topic Report was handed to the NUM
chairman, it was not circulated to members of the
Executive. Some of these members have still not seen
the full report. What the Board spokesmen did at the
meeting was to project various slides onto a screen,
illustrating some matters which had been covered in
the Report and some which had not. When Jack
Grainger tried to raise the vexed question of the
social consequences of closures, he was ruled out of
order by the union chairman, on the grounds that the
meeting was called to consider employment prospects,
not social consequences. Other members of the NUM
team found apparent errors in the arithmetic of the
evidence which was furnished to them. Vic Lloyd
pointed out that if the figures were "out of date" this
would invalidate parts of the structure plan. One member asked that the final decision be not minuted as
unanimous. The joint press release, therefore, is not
quite as informative as it might have been, and it does
some of the members of the union side less credit than
they deserve.

The fact remains that the document is painfully
obscure at precisely the points where it needs to explain.
Which figures, we must ask, are "out of date"? It has
always been understood that figures about reserves are

subject to serious fluctuation. But are the figures about
the age-structure of the work-force also so subject?
Of course not. For the existing labour-force, these
figures are entirely accurate. Estimates of recruitment
can be wrong, but they are distinctly unlikely to err on
the bright side. The NCB's *Report and Accounts* for
1975/76 give the following picture of national
recruitment:

"The number of men at collieries fell by 5,100 during 1975/76
to 243,656 at the end of the year. Both wastage and recruitment were lower than in 1974/75, with juvenile recruitment
virtually stable and a substantial reduction in voluntary
wastage.

	1975/76	*1974/75*
Recruitment Newly Employed		
Under 18s	5,268	5,948
Others	3,842	8,442
Re-entrants	7,874	16,413
Total Recruitment	16,984	30,803
Involuntary wastage		
Death and retirement	4, 199	4,435
Medical reasons	2,031	2,596
Dismissals and redundancies	8,589	7.024
Voluntary wastage	7,297	10,495
Total wastage	22,116	24,550
Net change in manpower	−5,132	+6,253

"The low voluntary wastage and the substantial recruitment of
ex-mine-workers in the last two years mean that this source of
already trained manpower is now much smaller and recruitment in future will increasingly require to be from men and
boys new to the industry. It is to be expected that recruitment
will become more difficult as the economy recovers from the
recession of 1975. Virtually all the men made redundant were
over 60, and benefitted from the provisions of the Redundant
Mineworkers Payments Scheme. The number redundant as a
result of colliery closures was less than in 1974/75: the increase
in other redundancies, which were carried out with the agreement of the men concerned, allowed an improvement in the

age balance of the mining labour force, which had worsened
considerably in the 1960s. The average age of mineworkers
fell for the second year in succession, from 43.6 at the end of
December 1974 to 43.2 at the end of December 1975, the
lowest since 1964."

The failure to keep up with "natural wastage" is more
likely to accelerate than decline, with the gradual
introduction of early retirement. Writing on this matter
in the *Sunday Times,* Roger Eglin pointed out at the
time of the miners' ballot on this question that
"Implementing the initial stage of the miners' bid to
reduce retirement to 55 by 1980 would mean 80,000,
a third of the labour force, retiring in the next three and
a half years. With the older men going, wastage would
obviously fall but would still be there to some extent.
NCB officials pale at the Herculean prospect of
recruiting some 40,000 to 50,000 men a year to maintain the labour force. Some regions would be hit harder
than others. While only 35% or so of the labour force in
Barnsley, South Yorkshire, North Derbyshire and South
Midlands would retire between now and 1980 under the
NUM's proposals, South Wales — hence the fears about
its ability to keep working — would lose 40.4% of its
men.

Such regional figures disguise even greater local
variations. Three of the above regions have pits where
more than half the men would go by the end of the
decade."

When Mr Dowson told the NUM Executive that
"similar estimates" to the "man-power estimates
provided by the Board" "had proved to be about 50%
wrong", what exactly was he saying? The structure
plan is a direct consequence of local government
reorganisation, which is a recent event. Nottinghamshire has sought no "similar estimates" in a very long
time.

"The report of Survey is the first statutory report on

the geographic county for almost 30 years" claims the *Summary of Draft Report of Survey* (para 1.2). A very dissimilar enquiry was undertaken in the Nottingham-shire-Derbyshire sub-regional study, at a time when an insane shrinkage of mining capacity was taking place. Is it this enquiry to which Mr Dowson is referring? If so, why did he not say as much? Surely such an admission would have put his audience on their guard?

Whenever the Board makes press statements on these matters, they invariably highlight the problem of geo-logical reserves. But *has* the County Report got the *manpower* potential wildly wrong? This is gravely to be doubted, as anyone who consults the published Employment Topic Report, cited above will readily see. No plan is mistake-proof. But if the Board now has dif-ferent figures from those published in the County's Reports, is it not crucially urgent to publish them, and soon? Should not the NUM demand a careful break-down of all recruitment figures, revealing annually what proportion of the "31% in zone 1, 58% in zone 3, 8% in zone 5 and 12% in zone 7" have in fact been attracted to mining upon reaching working age, and what propor-tion of outside recruitment has taken place?

Mr Dowson would have been far more persuasive if he had given these figures instead of vaguely querying the validity of those already furnished by his own colleagues to the structure planners. Even then, the $64,000 question would remain: what guarantees are to be given to this intake of new, predominantly young, workers, that they have any real or acceptable security in an industry which can apparently plan major up-heavals in its structure without prior consultation with its employees?

It seems entirely clear that this is a national problem. As Michael Walsh pointed out in *Tribune:*

"Pit manpower will be cut by up to one-third over the next decade if productivity targets mapped out by the National

Coal Board are met. As many as 80,000 mineworkers' jobs
will go, perhaps even more.

This prospect − so far kept under wraps by the NCB for
obvious reasons − emerges from the latest progress report on
the long-term *Plan for Coal* agreed by the board, the unions
and the Government. Though not necessarily meaning redun-
dances, it is certain to worry the mineworkers just as the board
is stepping up its calls for increased productivity.

The progress report, released last week, avoids setting down
future manpower targets. But other figures make the picture
clear: if the board is right about how much coal it will be
getting from new and existing pits by the end of the century,
and if its productivity predictions prove even partially correct,
then we will need fewer than 200,000 miners by the year 2000.

At present, the pit workforce stands at around 247,000. If
the NCB targets are met the number looks like having to be
slashed to between 165,000 and 195,000.

The key projections are on productivity in the new generation of ultra-modern pits planned or likely, for example,
Selby, and in those existing pits that will still be operating in
20 years' time. The plan's figures suggest that:

> In the new generation of pits, fewer than 80,000 miners
> will be required. In those still not worked out by the end of
> the century a maximum of 109,000 miners will be required,
> even if there is no productivity improvement whatsoever
> between now and then − an unlikely event.

The target originally laid down three years ago, and re-
affirmed last week in the latest report, is 150 million tons of
deep mined coal annually by the end of the century. Two
thirds of it is to be from new mines like Selby, the rest from
existing long-life pits. At present, annual production −
excluding open cast coal − is running at about 112 million
tons. The hope is 120 million tons by 1985, rising by another
30 million tons annually over the next 15 years.

According to the report, productivity in the new pits will
be at least three times as high per man as it is now. On that
basis, output per man shift, will be more than seven tons, or
between 1,200 and 1,300 tons a year. With that kind of
output, the new generation of pits will need between 75,000
and 89,000 workers. And some of the new generation will
have even higher productivity. In Selby the prediction is that
it will need only 4,000 men to mine 10 million tons of coal
a year.

As for the existing pits, if there were no increase in productivity whatsoever, the total manpower requirement at the end of the century to produce 50 million tons of coal would be just under 110,000.

In fact, it will be regarded as a disaster if productivity in existing pits does not rise dramatically, which of course would mean that manpower requirements in 20 years' time would be that much lower. The NCB aim is a 4 per cent increase in productivity a year, and the board has been pouring so much new investment into existing coalfields that some improvement must be expected.

As a result, the manpower requirements of the existing long-life pits could well turn out to be nearer 90,000 giving a total in Britain's pits of some 170,000 miners with a couple of decades.

Shoud the productivity projections come true, redundancies could presumably be avoided by 'natural wastage' and early retirement. Indeed the figures put the fears expressed about the manpower consequences of early retirement into something of a new light.

But, redundancies or not, the mineworkers aren't likely to be complacent over the implications of another sweeping reduction in their numbers. The suspicion that 'productivity' arrangements lead to premature pit closures is deep in the mind of most pitworkers who recall all too bitterly the closures of the sixties . . ."

The need for a new style of open consultation remains, and remains a burning one. This could not have been more clearly spelt out than it was when Tony Benn spoke to the Nottingham Area NUM durings its Annual Two-day Conference in Sutton-in Ashfield during February 1977. The *Chronicle Advertiser* reported:

"A call to the National Union of Mineworkers to press for an end to secrecy over official proposals that affect the future of the industry and the lives of the mining families, who depend upon it was made by Mr Tony Benn . . .

He called it bringing to an end the 'obsessive secrecy' of some official bodies and local authorities . . .

Attentively heard by the 280 delegates present, Mr Benn criticised local authorities, central government and other

organisations for what he alleged was the inclination to keep
important information from the public it vitally concerned.

'Knowledge is power. If they know something you don't
know they have the advantage, but if you know what they
know they realise you can argue with them'."

5. *What They Did Next*

The argument up to this point was presented rather
more fully in a pamphlet *Ashfield — What's Going
Wrong?* published in mid-1977.[1] After that, a variety
of new responses were to come from the relevant
authorities. In the Spring elections, the Conservatives
gained control of the Nottinghamshire County Council,
and all the senior councillors (who had presumably
licensed officers to negotiate privately with the NCB for
planning information) were defeated. The leader and
secretary of the Labour Group, together with the chairman of the planning committee, all lost their seats. The
Labour financial spokesman, Michael Cowan, had
previously retired in order to fight the Ashfield Parliamentary by-election, which he, too, had lost. A new
leadership emerged in the Labour opposition group, and
several members agreed to formally request access to the
classified Topic Report. Up to February 1978 these
requests had not borne fruit.

Meantime, although the councillors had still not seen
the original Topic Report, the revision of the Structure
Plan produced remarkable variations in the mining
estimates. Now, we were told "employment in the
industry could fall from 41,500 jobs in 1976 to 40,900
jobs in 1986 and 33,600 jobs in 1996". At the same
time, specific reference was now made to the Belvoir
coal reserves and an inevitable "increase in the number
of miners and their families in the Rushcliffe zone". In
Mansfield-Ashfield, it was newly calculated, "mining is
expected to decline by approximately 4,800 jobs . . .
to which should be added probably reductions in

mining employment in surrounding areas . . ."

The revision in these figures is marked, and so I queried it with the planners. I was informed that the only new figures in it were based "upon a Coal Board press release". Meantime, a public controversy had broken out between Mr Tim Smith, the Conservative MP for Ashfield, and the NCB, in which doubt was cast on whether the Board stood by these estimates. Still further enquiries revealed that the NCB had given no new information whatever to the County Council beyond the press release already cited above, after receipt of which the planners had reworked their estimates to take account of the institution of early retirement. Numerous difficulties afflict such extrapolations, not least because of the complication of migration over County boundaries. Be that as it may, the plans, if not the figures, do reflect a shift in policy: while the 1975 plans were based on relocation of smaller number of miners in productive pits on the eastern fringes of the coalfield, the 1977 projections assume some contingency preparation for the exploitation of Belvoir.

This assumption was supported when the figures printed overleaf were produced by the Calverton Branch of the NUM (apparently from NCB sources) during the Nottinghamshire Miners' Annual Conference in February 1978.

How reliable such estimates may prove to be depends on a number of imponderables. Will the demand for coal hold up? Will productivity remain close to 1977 levels, or will the new wage structure unleash vast new output? Assuming the NCB can maintain production unaffected by slump and competition from other energy sources, will the timing of Belvoir development fit its schedules, or will the public enquiries throw a spanner in the works? How will recruitment match up to the "wastage", increased by early retirement, which is a constant preoccupation of manpower planners?

Actual and Estimated tonnages at South Notts Area Collieries, 1976-2000

	Actual 1976/77 tons	June Proj. 1977/78 000 tons	1978/79 000 tons	1985/86 000 tons	1990/91 000 tons	2000 000 tons
Annesley	511,513	560	560	600	—	—
Babbington	580,171	620	620	630	—	—
Bentinck	1,232,134	1,350	1,400	1,300	1,300	—
Calverton	731,130	895	900	960	960	500
Cotgrave	1,012,280	1,060	1,100	1,200	1,200	1,200
Gedling	618,201	700	700	850	850	850
Hucknall	923,097	1,000	1,000	1,000	1,000	800
Linby	443,810	470	600	630	630	—
Moorgreen	637,767	610	700	700	—	—
New Hucknall	355,230	330	300	330	—	—
Newstead	886,040	675	750	900	900	—
Pye Hill	982,414	930	850	520	—	—
Total Collieries	8,913,787	9,200	9,480	9,590	6,840	3,350
Relaxation	—	400	480	490	240	150
Area Total	8,913,787	8,800	9,000	9,100	6,600	3,200
NEW MINES						
Hone	—	—	—	—	3,000	3,000
Saltby	—	—	—	—	450	2,000
TOTAL	8,913,787	8,800	9,000	9,100	10,050	8,200

Source: document published from NCB sources by Calverton Branch, NUM.

If the Board has got its sums right, and if the County
Council accurately understands the Board's intentions,
we still have all the crucial questions to face. New
housing is still scheduled at Boughton, the centre of one
of the major areas of social deprivation in the Central
Nottinghamshire region, according to a specially com-
missioned survey by the County Council itself. Other
new housing will be created East of Mansfield and at
East Retford, as well as the Rushcliffe provision for
settlers around the anticipated Belvoir pits. Will all this
be built according to the precepts of the Robens era,
which sometimes unloaded resettled miners and their
wives and children into neat packages of houses in a
rural desert, without even rudimentary community
supports, or will miners and their families be invited
to help in its planning? Will there be work for women,
or accommodation for ageing relatives who wish to stay
near their grandchildren; will there be shopping and
recreational amenities, and nursery provision?

Even if the doomed mining settlements can be
given adequate financial inducements to move, they
will ignore these problems at great peril. Perhaps people
are ready, even keen, to change their lifestyles in order
to follow alluring modern trends: but before they make
that choice, they need to contemplate very carefully
what organised substitutions are offered to compensate
for the loss of community and the disruption of family
networks. In Nottinghamshire the old mining villages
have a most interesting juvenile crime pattern, in which
quite high in the league table of charges is "unauthorised
possession of firearms". The new complex at Boughton
seems to be rich, by contrast, in cases involving personal
affrays. The difference could easily be explained: in
the old country, grandfather teaches the boys to go
shooting, and each generation supports the other.
Poaching may be criminal in some eyes, but it is in others
a convivial and educational pastime. In the new villages,

however, grandpa may be a couple of hundred miles away, and social nature may come to appear lonely, if not red in tooth and claw. On a related, if different, plane, if your husband works three shifts, all designed to do maximum damage to family and social life, then you desperately need the extended kin network which has for generations given help with the children, advice and moral support. Even more do you need this if there is no work for you yourself to do, so that you are isolated in a double sense. Hundreds of working women catch the buses from the village of Cotgrave to Nottingham, every day. Other villages are just too far away to permit such wholescale commuting. These conditions can be mitigated by luck or by force of personality, and it would be wildly unjust to say they applied equally irksomely to everyone in post-Robens colliery settlements. But it would pay all who may be affected by the new dispensation to take a close look at townships such as Boughton, or the new colliery settlements near Tuxford, before forming any judgement about what to do.

6. *To Sum Up*

In this story, the industrial relations problems of consultation have necessarily been highlighted, and the procedures of the National Coal Board are bound to be faulted.

Faulty, too, have been the consultative procedures of the County Council, because, in spite of a real attempt to discuss general planning questions, councillors themselves have been denied access to a key source of information.

Some leading trade unionists have now given the impression that they are satisfied with this state of affairs. Some councillors, too, seem to agree that it is all quite tolerable. Why, then, should the rest of us complain? The truth is, in a nutshell, that about one-third of the miners of the large condemned area are young enough to be compelled, within a relatively short time, either to uproot themselves, or to commute for considerable distances, in order to be able to carry on in their chosen jobs. Firstly, they have a right to know what to expect. Secondly, they need to know in time to be able to put up any alternative proposals which seem sensible to them. Thirdly, and critically important, they have a right to insist that any new-mining developments will avoid the dreadful and callous mistakes of the Robens era, and that redevelopment will be planned for and with *communities,* rather than concerning itself simply with the adjustment of a pay-roll.

This means that we need to develop democratic pressures to ensure that miners, and miners' wives, and all the senior and junior members of their families, all have a real say in what is to happen, how investments are made, and to what use the industry's resources are put.

REFERENCE
1. IWC Pamphlet No. 53

Chapter VII

Alternative Energy Plans

Socialist Environment and Resources Association

Among the bodies giving evidence to the Windscale Enquiry,
which was called in order to examine the arguments for and
against the granting of planning permission for a huge new plant
for reprocessing nuclear waste from Britain and other countries,
was the Socialist Environment and Resources Association (SERA).
In these excerpts we feature some of the main arguments pre-
sented to the Enquiry, many of which have implications which
are wider than the immediate issue under consideration.

The question of whether or not to expand reprocessing facilities at Windscale cannot be separated from the
much wider energy policy issues, and indeed from the
nation's overall industrial strategy.

In particular there is a need for a comprehensive
assessment of the employment implications of nuclear
power and of the alternatives. In this submission we
suggest that nuclear power technology in general, and
the Windscale expansion in particular, represent a very
poor investment in terms of creating jobs, as compared
with viable alternative energy generating and conserving
technologies.

The expenditure of £600 million or so at Windscale
will create approximately 1000 permanent jobs which
means that each job will cost around £600,000. Clearly
this investment will also stimulate the local economy
to some extent and through the multiplier effect,
create demand in other parts of the economy. But, even

so investment in less capital intensive alternatives — for example energy conservation and alternative technology development — could create more jobs both locally and nationally. Moreover these jobs would involve a much wider range of skills. For example, if we embarked on a major national programme of energy conservation through domestic insulation (at a cost of say £6000 per job) we would create many more jobs in urban areas which would alleviate the widespread unemployment in the building construction and materials supply industries. At the same time, according to Building Research Establishment figures, such a programme could reduce our primary energy consumption in the domestic sector by approximately 50% — that is — a 15% reduction in overall primary energy consumption.

Similarly the development of alternative energy technologies — wind, wave and solar power — would create many jobs in various industries. For example, the types of skill required for solar panel production and installation include: plumbers, glaziers, sheet metal fabricators and installers, welders, pipefitters, bricklayers, carpenters, concrete finishers, painters, cement masons, iron and insulation workers, electrical and mechanical engineers, electricians, crane operators, surveyors, heating technicians and refrigeration technians. For wind system construction, skills required include: sheet metal and structural steel fabricators, generator manufacturers, electrical component manufacturers, cement producers, wire producers, electricians, engineers, heavy equipment operators and other construction workers. Comparing these with skills required in the nuclear industry shows that the job mix for the two technologies is different and that the skills required by solar panel and wind power technologies are much more basic and widely applicable than those required by nuclear. Indeed there is potential with windpower system construction to utilise

skills and industrial facilities which already exist, for
example motor companies which make gears, aircraft
companies making blades, electrical companies making
generators. There is considerable potential for product
diversification in many high technology industries,
for example the Aerospace industry.

Unfortunately few detailed assessments of the short
and long term employment implications of the various
energy options at national level have been carried out
in the UK. This should be rectified as a matter of extreme
urgency. In the absence of detailed analyses of the employment implications at national level for the UK we are
presenting in our submission a brief report of assessments
made in the USA, together with some necessarily general
comments.

Energy and Industrial Strategy

One of the basic assumptions informing Britain's
present industrial strategy is that advanced technologies
of various kinds should be introduced in order to increase productivity and competitiveness, thus leading
to economic growth and full employment. This is not
the place to develop a detailed critique of this policy.
Suffice it to say that it can equally well be argued that
investment in capital and energy intensive technologies
will, unless the economy continues to expand at an
ever increasing rate, lead to more structural unemployment, as machines replace people. The problem of
structural unemployment has assumed increasing importance in the UK during a period of low growth.
It is of course difficult to separate cyclical (temporary)
unemployment due to recession, from structural (permanent) unemployment, due to the introduction of
labour saving or skill eliminating technologies. However the past decade has seen the establishment in
most advanced technological countries (USA, Germany,

UK etc.) of an apparently permanent pool of unemployed workers.

In pointing to the problems that can be generated
by technologies which substitute energy and capital
intensive machines for labour, SERA is *not* advocating
a return to pre-industrial labour intensive methods.
Rather, we are calling for the development of technologies which enhance rather than eliminate workers'
skills. In some circumstances it will be highly appropriate to automate out unskilled and repetitive jobs,
even though this may involve the use of capital and
energy intensive techniques. But the tendency at
present is precisely the reverse — to use automation
to eliminate skilled, interesting jobs.

The same argument applies to the energy supply
industry itself. It is not surprising therefore that
workers in the industry — and in particular in the
associated equipment manufacturing firms — have
begun to question the logic of continued emphasis on
large scale capital intensive plant, faced as they are
with job security problems as a result of the current
overcapacity in the generating capability. Shop stewards
at GEC, Parsons and elsewhere have been discussing
alternative technology options in an attempt to fight
redundancies. One possibility is a national programme
of construction (or re-commissioning) of small coal-
fired city based combined heat and power units, linked
to district heating networks. Such systems would increase the overall efficiency of energy conversion which
would rise from its current 30% to 60 or 70% or more,
and create employment in a wide range of industries.
Researchers at the Open University's Energy Research
Group have pointed out that we should use the current
period of over-capacity and energy glut to upgrade the
efficiency of our energy generating system in preparation for any subsequent rise in electricity demand.

A wide ranging assessment of alternative energy

options has also been carried out by shop stewards
(AUEW-TASS) at AEI Trafford Park, who have produced a report which discusses, amongst other options,
windpower, wavepower and energy storage techniques.

In January 1976 the Lucas Aerospace Combine
Shop Stewards Committee published a detailed Corporate Plan outlining a number of alternative energy
products on which their members could be employed.

Support for programmes of product diversification
of this sort has come from the Transport and General
Workers' Union and from the Labour Party.

SERA's aim in reporting on these various trends in
Trade Union thinking is to indicate that there is a growing awareness in the movement that job security cannot
automatically be guaranteed through investment in
advanced technologies and that social needs may be
better satisfied through alternative, less environmentally
problematic, technologies.

Although there have been a number of ad hoc assessments for specific industries, so far in the UK there has
been no systematic attempt to analyse the overall employment implications of the various alternatives. The
task is a large one — requiring considerable financial
and technical resources. For the present we feel that at
the very least we can say that it is not proven that the
nuclear power option is the best or wisest in terms of
job creation and that it may turn out to be the worst.
Given this situation we feel that it would be foolish to
commit ourselves to a nuclear future until extensive
analyses of the employment implications have been
conducted.

The US Evidence

A number of studies of comparative manpower requirements have been carried out in the USA. For example
in a paper presented to a conference on Energy Efficien-

cy in May 1976, Laitner indicated that per unit energy a solar power programme would create approximately 2.5 times as much employment as a nuclear power programme. In a report issued in February 1977 Frank Mills of the Sheet Metal and Air Conditioning Contractors' Association in the USA estimates that fitting 3 million homes for 60% reliance on solar heating and cooling would create 12.2 million hours work per year, for ten years. A report to the New York State Legislative Committee on Energy Systems in May 1975 indicated that the operation and maintenance of large wind power systems would require 2-4 times the labour force on a continuous basis compared with nuclear or coal-fired systems: the combined continuous labour requirements for construction and operation of wind systems was calculated to be 7,000 person years more than for an equivalent rated nuclear plant, and when storage facilities were included, this rose to 19,000 more person years.

Dubin, reported in the *Environmentalists for Full Employment Newsletter* of March 1977, has argued that a combined energy conservation and solar power programme would create four times as many jobs than if the money were spent on nuclear power.

The Federal Energy Authority's "Project Independence" estimates that whereas nuclear energy production utilises two tradespeople to every professional scientist or technician, solar energy production uses nine to one, so that a broader array of skills are necessary for building and maintaining solar systems than for building and maintaining nuclear plants.

Support for alternative technology development has come from the United States Labour Unions. For example the President of the Labourers' International Union (AFL-CIO) has pointed out that:

"the annual market for installing solar systems has a potential of $77 million alone . . . not including maintenance . . . that translates to a goodly number of jobs for construction workers in our jurisdiction."

Also the President of the International Association of Machinists and Aerospace Workers (AFL-CLO) has commented that to equip each home in America with roof top solar heaters would mean that:

"scores of factories would be retooled and re-opened. Thousands of jobs would be created for unemployed machinists and autoworkers."

Similarly the United Auto Workers have supported solar power, together with other environmentally oriented technologies as being likely sources of employment for the future.

A detailed account on the situation in the US is included in the report by the Environmentalists for Full Employment, entitled 'Jobs and Energy'.

The object of recording these various assertions and estimates is to illustrate that, far from being the preserve of eccentrics or romantics, alternative technology is rapidly becoming of major importance in the US. Current US expenditure on solar power is £170 million per year and the US intends to meet 24% of its total (projected) energy demand from solar and windpower by 2020 (i.e. 58% of its current demand).

Alternatives in the UK

As the evidence provided by other contributors to this Inquiry will have indicated, Britain is in an excellent position to develop a strong domestic and export industry based on wind, wave and solar power. The British section of the International Solar Energy Society have pointed out that solar power could meet 14% of our present net energy consumption, while Musgrove and Ryle's work indicates that windpower could supply 25% of our electricity needs. An even larger contribution could be expected from wavepower, and the potential of the various bio-synthesis techniques is as yet untapped.

The document produced by the National Centre for Alternative Technology entitled 'An Alternative Energy Strategy for the United Kingdom' outlines an approach with which SERA is broadly in agreement — although SERA would emphasize that a move to less energy and capital intensive technology would initially at least create many new jobs. Although the move to a low growth economy prescribed in the NCAT report clearly would reduce employment ultimately SERA believes that this could and should be orchestrated in a way that minimizes social dislocation, and in any case need not be implemented rapidly. In this regard SERA believes that we should investigate the viability of a non-nuclear programme based on coal, utilised efficiently in combined Heat and Power plants with fluidised-bed coal combustion. At the same time we should improve pollution control and develop less hazardous mining methods using remote control equipment and ultimately, if possible, in situ coal gassification techniques. This programme, coupled with energy conservation programmes in industry and the domestic sector, would extend the current 'breathing space' and allow us to fully develop the renewable solar, wind, wave, tidal and biological sources of power. It is worth pointing out that these technologies are inherently less technically complex than nuclear power and could be rapidly developed given sufficient funding. As Ryle has pointed out: "by 1985 wind energy could be providing 10 GJ annually."

Diversification into these alternative technologies would also open up an immense new market for Britain. So far however both the industry and the government seem to be ignoring this potential. As Dr A. Strub, chairman of the EEC technical committee on solar energy has pointed out:

> "It is not a case of Britain needing a national policy in solar
> development in order to keep pace. She is already so far
> behind that a major policy change will be needed to give
> her industry a chance."

We have not developed a detailed analysis of contributions that the alternative technologies could make or outline a strategy for their implementation. SERA feels that before these arguments can be developed further it is imperative for government sponsored research to be carried out, not only in regard to the alternative energy sources but also to investigate the employment implications of these technologies.

However, despite this, SERA feels that there is sufficient evidence to show that nuclear energy gives a small number of jobs for a large capital investment, and that there are viable, less capital intensive alternatives. We therefore call for a moratorium on further expansion at Windscale and the nuclear industry in general until research has been done and its findings fully appraised.

Trade Union and Employment Rights

Environmental safety and national security, which are issues of central importance to this Inquiry, may have a decisive influence on industrial relations and the practical operation of labour laws. In our view, the projected Windscale development would impose a severe constraint on the conduct of industrial relations and the exercise of employment rights. From this we draw implications to support our more specific objections to BNFL's application. These objections concern:

1. The Conspiracy and Protection of Property Act 1875, section 5.
2. The Emergency Powers Act 1964.
3. The general restriction on the freedom to engage in

industrial action and the possible consequences thereof.
4. National security as it affects labour recruitment, the right of employees not to be dismissed unfairly, disclosure of information and industrial safety.

Voluntary collective bargaining is the primary method of regulating relations between management and labour, and of determining the terms and conditions of employment. The possibility of resort to direct economic sanctions is an essential ingredient of the bargaining process. We believe that if BNFL's application were granted, these freedoms and the laws which support them would be curtailed unreasonably. In order to develop this proposition we now describe a strike which took place recently at Windscale. This account is based on the research of Mr M. George, the secretary of SERA, who undertook a series of interviews with the workers involved in the dispute.

There are numerous issues which lie at the root of the dispute, but the ones which appear most relevant to us are the following. There is a widespread feeling amongst the workforce that the BNFL management is and has been unnecessarily secretive over a wide range of issues which are of concern to employees; this has fostered suspicion and mistrust. Secondly, there have been attempts to install incentive schemes at Windscale which were not favourably regarded by the workforce; such incentive schemes have had deleterious effects on plant safety according to some employees, and such schemes have been subsequently withdrawn, but an element of suspicion remains about management plans of this nature. Third, there are numerous pay problems; overall the workforce favours improvements in pay, plus other terms and conditions of employment, which would bring them in line with workers in the petro-chemical industry. In addition, there is a demand for increased special pay for certain types of work, especially that carried out in accepted 'high risk' areas. These pay problems have not been adequately resolved in the past. There is also a feeling amongst the workforce that all radiation-induced sickness should be regarded and classified as an industrial disease which would enable compensation and other payments to accrue to workers affected in this way. Finally, we are told that fuel rods commonly remain in reactors for six months more than the design specifications allow; this renders the cladding fragile and highly irradiated, and consequently safety conditions for workers operating in and around the cooling ponds are not regarded as satisfactory by many workers.

Within this scenario a dispute among Locker Room workers in February of this year developed over a pay issue. These workers, being unable to obtain a satisfactory solution to their pay problems eventually left the plant after spending four hours 'making safe' their area, which time was unpaid. One thousand workers were then immediately laid off by BNFL – this was regarded as an act of extreme provocation by the workforce as it was not deemed necessary to engage in such a rapid lay-off; a strike was called shortly after this lay-off by manual workers. There was a feeling, fuelled by a decision to lay off white collar workers as well, but on a paid basis, that BNFL was attempting to cause a division in the workforce. During the strike, fears began to be raised about the continuing safety of the installation and attempts were made to pass safety equipment through the picket line. Fears about the safety of the installation increased in the fifth and sixth weeks of the strike and pressures on the workforce and on union officials to end the strike became more pronounced. The Health and Safety Executive, the TUC and the Secretary of State for Energy were involved in risk assessment and consequent persuasion to resolve the strike.

The workforce was aware of moves to use troops to bring safety equipment into the installation, and the use of the 1875 Conspiracy and Protection of Property Act was mentioned to at least one shop steward. At length the picket line was broken by the delivery of materials, though in the event troops were not used for that purpose. Shortly afterwards the strike was terminated. The final settlement in no way met the original demands of the workforce, despite the exceptionally long duration of the strike. It is clear that great pressure was placed on the parties in the last week of the strike.

The SERA evidence in this section goes on to argue that the proposed development poses a serious threat to trade union rights in that it would:

1. *Bring another area of employment within the potential ambit of Section 5 of the Conspiracy and Protection of Property Act, 1875 (prohibition of breaking contracts when life etc. might be endangered).*

2. *Make probable the invocation of the Emergency Powers Act, 1920 (use of troops in industrial disputes).*

3. *Encourage the intense security-vetting of employees and the limitation of their political rights.*

4. *Involve the limitation of the right of appeal against unfair dismissal under the Trade Union and Labour Relations Act, 1974 and 1976 by the use of the provision that debars legal remedies where dismissal is 'for the purpose of national security'.*

5. *Limit the rights of information under the Employment Protection Act, 1975.*

6. *Limit the rights of safety representatives under the Health and Safety at Work Act, 1974.*

The Case for Alternatives

History of Employment in West Cumbria

The narrowness of the economic base in West Cumbria
has been documented by others both outside and
within this Inquiry. It is well known that earlier
dependence on coal and iron ore mining resulting
from 19th century exploitation of mineral resources
in an otherwise rural area has been replaced, since
the mid 1930s, by an equally marked dependence on
a small number of large employers – in particular
British Nuclear Fuels, Marchon Chemicals and Local
Government. These, together with various light industries attracted into the area as a result of central
government incentives, have not managed to completely offset the unemployment caused by the
gradual rundown of mining and metal working in
the 20th century. Gordon Fanstone of Cumbria
County Council refers in his evidence to Department
of Employment figures which show that between
1961 and 1971 over 3000 jobs were lost net in the
Whitehaven, Cleator Moor and Millom employment
office areas where much mineral and metal working had
been concentrated, and that between 1971 and 1976
only 2000 net jobs were created in the whole of West
Cumbria in compensation by new firms moving in.

Unemployment Today

Department of Employment figures show that unemployment has increased in the post war period both for
men and women and that the present (July 1977 figures)
average unemployment rate of 7% in the County is
exceeded by Whitehaven (9.4%), Millom (15.2%), and
Workington (9.2%). It has been established in cross-
examination (29 June p.61 F - p.62 F transcripts) that
of the unemployed in the BNFL catchment area
20-40% are female and that of the male unemployed

60-70% are unskilled, 30-40% have been unemployed for over one year and 30-40% are over 50. Furthermore it has been shown by the CDP team (working in the Cleator Moor/Frizington area between 1969 and 1975) in their report 'Unemployed and Unskilled in West Cumbria' that many of the unemployed live in dispersed settlements and suffer as a result from a low level of access to jobs offered due to their relatively high dependence on public transport which is considered far from adequate in the West Cumbria area. The response to this employment situation has already been remarked on during the Inquiry – there is a high level of out-migration of the young and able tending to deplete the area of its most productive reserves of manpower and weaken its potential further.

Employment Impact of the Proposed Development

The major attraction of the proposed reprocessing plant to West Cumbria is that, in this situation of economic decline it will provide jobs for local people. However, a certain amount of doubt has already been cast on the exact proportion of jobs offered which will prove suitable for locals, and it seems necessary to look more closely at the extent to which the development will provide for local needs and contribute to a solution for the problems just outlined.

Construction and operation of the proposed plant will create some 1000 permanent jobs and 600 temporary jobs over a period of 10 years up to 1987 of which BNFL claim that 550 permanent jobs will go to local people within the next five years. These jobs involve industrial craft and non craft skills, attractive to men from an area with a tradition of heavy industry, while the scientific and professional jobs will be filled from outside the County. However, CPRE have demonstrated that, due to the nature of the available pool of local labour only 350 at most can be expected to be

drawn from the present BNFL catchment area. Both
Copeland District and Cumbria County Councils admit
that attempts should be made to increase the suitability
of local people for employment at Windscale in order
that the proposed project gives a reasonable degree of
benefit to West Cumbria, and that skilled and hard to
replace labour should not be attracted away from
existing firms in the area to BNFL, thus draining the
remainder of the economy. The main suggestions involve
extending the BNFL catchment area to Workington
by provision of works buses and increasing the capacity
of training schemes at the works for local people. The
former will merely add to road congestion already a
problem on certain routes in the area, while the latter
will certainly increase the numbers of skilled workers,
but the skills acquired will be very specialised and of
little relevance to any industry outside the nuclear field,
particularly to those represented at present in West
Cumbria. Given that there is an annual turnover of
staff at Windscale of 11.3%, and assuming this rate
applies equally to trained and non trained staff, there
will be a significant number leaving each year whose
training will fit them for little else in the area. BNFL
training schemes cannot then be said to necessarily
be of long term value to the trainee or to help increase
the general level of skilled labour in West Cumbria.

Finally, there is the question of the numbers of
people who must come into the area from other parts
of Britain to fill the professional and white collar jobs
and possibly some of the industrial jobs. It is claimed
that this influx will boost the local economy by increasing demand for goods and services. Although
retailers and the service sector will benefit, little will
accrue to manufacturers as so few goods on sale in the
area are actually locally produced. The major effect
of the increase in population will be to create pressures
on services provided out of public funds – housing,

roads, sewage systems etc. As James Bailey, Copeland's
Planning Officer, states in his evidence funds will have
to come from BNFL or central government to meet
infrastructure improvements necessitated by the expansion as the local authorities are hard pressed to meet
even present commitments.

The evidence then seems to suggest that a major
extension to the plant at Windscale is likely to make
a relatively small impact on local employment levels,
will create some strains on infrastructure and will
contribute little to the diversification of the local
economy, in fact helping to reinforce its unbalanced
nature. It will be useful now to look at the attempts
which have been made to restructure ailing economies
like that of West Cumbria in order to point towards
a more relevant form of investment to meet the needs
of such areas.

Regional Development Policy and West Cumbria

Since the depression of the 1930s central government
has been empowered to allocate aid to regions of Britain
suffering economic dislocation due to structural shifts
in the national economy. The emphasis has been on
attracting industry from South East Britain and the
West Midlands whose economies have generally been
thriving, into the depressed regions – with a range of
incentives such as rent free periods in ready built
factories on industrial estates, grants for capital equipment, tax concessions and recently, employment sub-
sidies, all administered by a variety of government
agencies. Cumbria, with Special Development Area
status has 11 central government bodies, 5 county
bodies, and six other bodies based either in or outside
the County, advising and administering the various aids.
The Manpower Services Commission has set up a
Skill Centre at Maryport to augment the training facilities
of the West Cumbria Technical College, and the Depart-

ment of Industry, as well as the County and Districts, has developed factory sites, mainly concentrated on the Lilleyhall and Glasson industrial estates.

However, these Regional Development policies have been far from completely successful as the present rates of unemployment in West Cumbria indicate, and people involved in the area's development feel that a vicious circle has set in, which is proving very hard to break. First of all, the emphasis in Regional policy has been to attract enterprise in from outside the area with the main result being that branch plants of existing firms have been set up on the industrial estates with their own training schemes. They tend to be serviced from other parts of the firm thereby failing to stimulate the growth of local servicing industry. They also tend to close down after a few years production when the various financial aids have been exhausted. Secondly, the local workforce has been reluctant to undertake training courses due to the lack of opportunity to use the skills afterwards, so that this has both kept the scope of training courses offered limited and has deterred a good many employers from coming into the area due to the continuing un-skilled nature of the workforce. Those who do take training courses, especially young people at the West Cumbria Technical College, frequently leave the area in order to seek better opportunities elsewhere. Finally, there is a distinct lack of risk capital made available to local enterprise starting up from scratch. Despite the large amounts of finance available as Regional aid, very little of this filters through to firms – particularly local firms – which have no credibility i.e. no private back-ing, and it is this wastage of local potential which is perhaps the most serious factor of all in limiting the area's growth.

Local Government in West Cumbria — changing Planning Policies

The general syndrome has been noted by the Local Authorities who are beginning to reorient their development policies. Copeland District Council have stated that it will be their policy in future to steer job creating development (both indigenous and from outside) to those places where unemployment is acute due not only to the overall shortfall of jobs in the County but also to the lack of access to the present concentrations of job opportunities. Cumbria County Council also state in their Structure Plan report of Survey 'Choices for Cumbria' that an important policy option to be considered amongst the emerging alternatives is one which promotes manufacturing and service activity and takes it to the available labour force by providing new or converted sites in towns and villages lacking employment opportunities. This results from a disenchantment with the regional growth point philosophy which has been dominant until now, whereby industrial investment has been concentrated in a small number of favoured sites on the assumption that the potential labour force is prepared or able to travel to work. It has been realised that a result of the policy has been to increase unemployment levels in certain localities remote from the growth points and particularly badly served by public transport. The County Council suggest that any policy on industry and employment should aim to reduce the narrowness of the economic base and should encourage the development of a wider range of small scale manufacturing and service activities dispersed more equitably over the County area. The Small Business Advisory Unit was set up in Whitehaven three years ago by the County in order to promote just this kind of development, but it has been prevented from having any positive effect due to its lack of funds and reliance on unforthcoming Regional Authorities for finance. It is to be hoped that the recent NEB initiative to back small firms employing 100 to 200 people with an annual turnover of £500,000 to £2 million will go some way towards channelling a new source of risk capital to those who need it.

The total estimated allocation of money for Regional Development in Britain between 1978 and 1981 is £1,650 million according to the latest government White Paper on Public Expenditure, and now it is proposed that £600 million should be spent on only one development in just one area which, as evidence to this inquiry has shown, is of questionable need to the British economy. It is true that the money is to be provided by the foreign customers making use of the plant, but the British government has underwritten the entire investment in the event of the failure of the plant, thereby implying its priorities – it would rather risk wasting £600 million of public money on one plant, well over a third of the total funds allocated to the entire Regional Programme for the next four years, than use it to boost this programme and deal more satisfactorily, in ways now being indicated, with the economic problems suffered by West Cumbria and many other parts of the UK.

An Alternative Strategy

The policy context then that should be pursued involves encouragement of small and medium sized enterprises by provision of risk capital and allocation of suitable sites and premises in areas where unemployment is particularly acute. However, this by itself is not enough if the vicious circle described previously is to be broken and a healthy economy generated. Coordinated planning by the Regional County and Local Authorities, training authorities and potential industries is required so that training facilities and markets are organised and assured for the firm by the time it is set up for operation. At the same time, individual enterprises should be developed wherever possible which service others in the area, therefore contributing to a network of linkages which give a more solid foundation to the local economy. In addition, where skills and processes introduced are of fairly wide application a good basis has been laid for future diversification and growth.

Using Existing Resources

It remains to consider the types of economic activity that would be most suitable for the area. Although there must be countless activities that local people could set up successfully in West Cumbria, and there are examples of successes to draw on, SERA would like to suggest one approach that could be useful — that is, that the unused or under used resources of the area be put to work in ways that will help meet some of the needs of the area and thus bring double benefit.

Some of the more obvious unused and under used resources include *the unemployed,* currently (July 1977 figures) 2,688 men and 1,822 women out of work in West Cumbria; *empty factories and workshops,* currently 13 government advance factories in West Cumbria plus, for example in Copeland District alone a further 10 smaller sites totalling 120 acres and 12 premises totalling 83,000 sq.ft: *blast furnace slag* — 27 million tons of slag are available at the Old Barrow and Millom iron works, the former still blighting the surrounding landscape; large quantities of waste paper, for example 700 tons are produced each year in Copeland District alone; *under-used training facilities* — for example each of six basic engineering courses is short of 3 or 4 trainees this session at the TSA Skill Centre in Maryport.

Possible Activities

One example of a viable activity employing some of these resources is the use of the blast furnace slag mentioned to make a range of industrial ceramics. Materials of this kind are extensively used elsewhere in the world — especially in the USSR — for a wide range of applications including building products, and in the civil, chemical and electrical engineering industries. A typical use of the ceramic is as a lining in plant which has to deal with the movement of large quantities of heavy, abrasive material, and is particularly suitable for lining pipes and shutes in coal fired power stations where it can replace the less durable products used at present, at much lower cost. The Central Electricity Generating Board have shown great interest in the ceramic, and would assure it a market, so it only remains now for the process to be developed on a commercial basis. Several firms already established in related fields have been approached by the developers of the process with a view to setting up production in West Cumbria, and feasibility studies are now being undertaken. It seems vital to the interests of West Cumbria that a local enterprise to be set up to obtain full benefit from this potentially valuable local resource before outside firms move in to monopolise production. In this way, not only would local employment levels be boosted, but profits accruing would also remain in the area and therefore be available for future investment.

The capital cost of a commercially viable plant is approximately £2 million and the process would employ around 200 people on both production and administration. An exercise in coordinated planning on the part of the local, County and Regional Authorities as previously outlined, could be effective in setting up such a plant. The county and local authorities could negotiate for the use of the slag with the owners and could initiate a feasibility study using money allocated for economic development, or that from other legal sources. For example, money derived from the rates under Section 137 of the 1972 Local Government Act for activities promoting the general good of the area, is currently being used by Wandsworth council in London to fund the development of local worker cooperatives in a bid to offset unemployment in the Borough. It could be used for a similar purpose in West Cumbria.

When the negotiations for use of the slag and feasibility study are successfully completed the Department of Industry or National Enterprise Board could be approached for the £2 million capital. Then the Authorities could begin planning the recruitment of staff. The technical expertise is available within the country, while skills in furnace work exist within West Cumbria, so that staff, including construction workers, could easily be recruited locally. At this stage, provision of any training schemes necessary can be planned and implemented by liaison between the local authorities and the skill centre and technical college. Once the plant has been constructed and the workforce adequately trained, the organisation can be set up ready for production.

Another possible product which would both create employment and help meet a need in the area, is the Road Rail vehicle developed by the Lucas Aerospace Combine Committee. The vehicle has pneumatic tyres and is able to ride on road or rail. A prototype version has already been tested. There is a potential market for such a vehicle in predominantly rural areas such as West Cumbria where the local public transport system is poor. These rural areas with relatively low, dispersed populations have problems maintaining an adequate public transport service as return on fares does not meet overheads and maintenance of vehicles. In general, buses and trams cannot make as many trips per day as is necessary to cover their costs, and, for example, the bus service in West Cumbria ran at a loss of £750,000 in 1976-7. A road-rail/vehicle is able to double up on British Rail and bus routes and this flexibility means that, in an integrated service, fewer vehicles are required overall and each one is able to make more trips per day thus increasing efficiency of operation. Such a vehicle introduced into West Cumbria and the many other areas of Great Britain suffering from inadequate public transport facilities could go a long way towards improving local communications.

Should definite markets be arranged with Transport Authorities both locally and elsewhere, and should negotiations with the Lucas Aerospace combine to adopt the design prove successful, production could be set up in West Cumbria under the auspices of the Local Authorities, with Regional Development or NEB money as outlined previously. The various empty factories available could house production of the components as well as the final assembly of the vehicle, while training in the necessary engineering skills could be carried out at the TSA skill centre which, as mentioned, has spare capacity to expand the range of courses where sufficient demand exists. The importance of such an activity to West Cumbria lies in the fact that it introduces into the area an integrated vehicles engineering sector, hardly represented at present — as well as a whole range of general purpose engineering skills. This lays the foundation for growth and diversification of that sector with all the implications for the development of a strong economic base as well as for future job creation.

Contribution of these activities to the local community

The organisational form these suggested activities take could be one of several. It could be that of a conventional private firm, a cooperative, or a municipal enterprise. In any event SERA would like to suggest that provisions are made to ensure a fair proportion of the profits are given back to the West Cumbrian community via, for example, an Investment Fund administered by the Local Authorities, set up in order to accumulate local capital that can be used for the creation of future community enterprise and the jobs the area needs so much.

In conclusion then, we would like to express the hope that the foregoing has done something to indicate the potential already existing in the area — both in terms of financial and material resources — for investment and job creation independent of the expansion plans of existing employers usually relied on. All that is required is that risk capital be made available by central government, and that resources are effectively channelled by coordinated planning on the part of the Local Authorities concerned. Such Community planning would not only mean that activities more beneficial to the area could be developed, but also that greater opportunity would exist to promote smaller scale industry dispersed to the areas most needing employment. Such a strategy, as we hope has been demonstrated, would do more to promote the creation of a strong diversified economic base in West Cumbria than continued investment in highly expensive, specialised projects such as the BNFL proposal under consideration at this Inquiry.

Part Three

SHOP STEWARDS' ALTERNATIVE INDUSTRIAL PLANS

Mike Cooley admirably sets forth the basic principles of Alternative Planning in his introductory essay. The two cases which follow, concerning plans at Lucas Aerospace and Vickers, are among the first to have appeared, although others have been prepared, such as the draft by workers at Chrysler. All this evidence should be considered alongside that which is posed by the new workers' co-operatives, most of which, in the course of their evolution, had to prepare similar strategic plans, albeit for enterprises of smaller scale.

Chapter VIII

Design, Technology and Production for Social Needs

Mike Cooley

There are many contradictions which highlight the problems of our so-called technologically advanced society. Four of these contradictions are particularly relevant to what I shall have to say.

Firstly, there is the appalling gap which now exists between that which technology could provide for society and that which it actually does provide. We have a level of technological sophistication such that we can design and produce Concorde, yet in the same society we cannot provide enough simple heating systems to protect old age pensioners from hypothermia. In the winter of 1975-76, 980 died of the cold in the London area alone. We have senior automotive engineers who sit in front of computerised visual display units 'working interactively to optimize the configuration' of car bodies such that they are aerodynamically stable at 120 miles an hour when the average speed of traffic through New York is 6.2 miles an hour. It was in fact 11 miles per hour at the turn of the century when the vehicles were horse-drawn. In London at certain times of the day it is about 8.5 miles an hour. We have sophisticated communication systems such that we can send messages round the world in nano seconds, yet it now takes longer to send a letter from Washington to New York than it did in the days of the stagecoach. Hence we find the linear drive forward of complex esoteric

technology in the interests of the multinational corporations and on the other hand the growing deprivation of communities and the mass of people as a
whole.

The second contradiction is the tragic wastage our
society makes of its most precious asset — that is the
skill, ingenuity, energy, creativity and enthusiasm of
its ordinary people. We now have in Britain 1.6 million
people out of work. There are thousands of engineers
suffering the degradation of the dole queue when we
urgently need cheap, effective and safe transport systems
for our cities. There are thousands of electricians
robbed by society of the right to work when we
urgently need economic urban heating systems. We have
I believe, 180,000 building workers out of a job when
by the government's own statistics it is admitted that
about 7 million people live in semi-slums in this
country. In the London area we have about 20 per
cent of the schools without an indoor toilet, when
the people who could be making these things are rot-
ting away in the dole queue.

The third contradiction is the myth that computer-
isation, automation and the use of robotic equipment
will automatically free human beings from soul-
destroying, back-breaking tasks and leave them free
to engage in more creative work. The perception of
my members and that of millions of workers in the
industrial nations is that in most instances the reverse
is actually the case.

Fourthly, there is the growing hostility of society
at large to science and technology as at present
practised. If you go to gatherings where there are
artists, journalists and writers and you admit to being
a technologist, they treat you as some latter day
Yahoo, to misquote Swift. They really seem to believe that you specified that rust should be sprayed on
car bodies before the paint is applied, that all commodi-

ties should be enclosed in non-recycleable containers and that every large-scale plant you design is produced specifically to pollute the air and the rivers. There seems to be no understanding of the manner in which scientists and technologists are used as mere messenger boys of the multinational corporations whose sole concern is the maximisation of profits. It is therefore not surprising that some of our most able and sensitive sixth formers will now not study science and technology because they correctly perceive it to be such a dehumanized activity in our society.

All these four contradictions – and indeed many others – have impacted themselves upon us in Lucas Aerospace over the past five years. We do work on equipment for Concorde, we have experienced structural unemployment and we know day by day of the growing hostility of the public to science and technology.

Lucas Aerospace was formed in the late 1960s when parts of the Lucas Industries took over sections of GEC, AEI and a number of other small companies. It was clear that the company would engage in a rationalisation programme along the lines already established by Arnold Weinstock in GEC. This, it will be recalled, was the time of Harold Wilson's 'white heat of technological change'. The taxpayer's money was being used through the Industrial Reorganization Corporation to facilitate this rationalization programme. No account at all was taken of the social cost: Arnold Weinstock subsequently sacked 60,000 highly skilled workers. This may have made GEC look efficient but the taxpayer had to pick up the tab firstly for the payment of social services and secondly the nation state as a whole suffered the loss of the productive capacity of these talented workers.

We in Lucas Aerospace were fortunate in the sense that this happened about one year before our company embarked on its rationalisation programme. We were

therefore able to build up a combined committee which
would prevent the company setting one site against the
other in the manner Weinstock had done. This body —
the combined committee — is unique in the British
trade union movement in that it links together the
highest level technologists and the semi-skilled workers
on the shop floor. There is therefore a creative cross-
fertilisation between the analytical power of the scientist and the technologist on the one hand, and, perhaps
what is much more important, the direct class sense and
understanding of those on the shop floor. As structural
unemployment began to affect us, we looked around
at the manner in which other groups of workers were
attempting to resist it. We had in Lucas already been
engaged in partial sit-ins, in preventing the transfer
of work from one site to another and a host of other
industrial tactics which had been developed over the past
five years. But we realised that the morale of a workforce very quickly declines if they can see that society,
for whatever reason, does not want the products that
they make. *We therefore evolved the idea of a campaign
for the right to work on socially useful products.*

The Lucas proposals

It seemed absurd to us that we had all this skill and
knowledge and facilities and that society urgently
needed equipment and services which we could provide,
and yet the market economy seemed incapable of
linking these two. What happened next provides an important object lesson for those who wish to analyse
how society can be changed.

We prepared 180 letters which described in great
detail the nature of the workforce, its skills, its age, its
training, the machine tools, equipment and laboratories
that were available to us and the types of scientific
staff, together with the design capabilities which they

had. We wrote to 180 leading authorities, institutions, universities, organizations and trade unions, all of which in the past had one way or another suggested that there was a need for the humanisation of technology and the use of technology in a socially responsible fashion. What happened really was a revelation to us: all of these people who had made great speeches up and down the country, in some instances written voluminous books about these matters, were smitten into silence by the specificity of our request. We had asked them very directly what could a workforce with these facilities be making that would be in the interest of the community at large — and they were silent with the exception of four individuals, Dr Elliott at the Open University, Professor Thring at Queen Mary College, and Richard Fletcher and Clive Latimer at the North East London Polytechnic.

We then did what we should have done in the first instance: we asked our own members what they thought they should be making. I have never doubted the ability of ordinary people to cope with these problems, but not doubting it is one thing, having concrete evidence is something different. That concrete evidence began to pour into us within three or four weeks. In a short time we had 150 ideas of products which we could make and build with the existing machine tools and skills we had in Lucas Aerospace. We elicited this information through our shop stewards' committees via a questionnaire. I should explain that this questionnaire was very different from those which the soap powder companies produce where the respondent is treated as some kind of passive cretin. In our case, the questionnaire was dialectically designed. By that I mean that in filling it in the respondent was caused to think about his or her skill and ability, the environment in which he or she worked and the facilities which they had available to them. We also deliberately composed it so that they would think of themselves in their dual role in society, that is both as producers and as consumers. We therefore quite deliberately transcended the absurd division which our society imposes on us, which seems to suggest that there are two nations, one that works in factories and offices and an entirely different nation that lives in houses and communities. We pointed out that what we do during the day at work should be meaningful in relation to the communities in which we live. We also deliberately designed the questionnaire to cause the respondents to think of products not merely for their exchange value but for their use value.

When we collected all these proposals we refined them into six major product ranges which are now embodied in six volumes, each of approximately 200 pages. They contain specific technical details, economic calculations and even engineering drawings. We quite deliberately sought a mix of products which on the one hand included those which could be designed and built in the very short term and those which would require long-term development; those which could be used in metropolitan Britain mixed with those which would be suitable for use in the third world, products incidentally which could be sold in a mutually non-exploitative fashion. Finally we sought a mix of products which would be profitable by the present criteria of the market economy and those which would not necessarily be profitable but would be highly socially useful.

Products for the community

I shall explain briefly some of the products we are proposing.

In the medical field Lucas already makes pacemakers and kidney machines. About three years ago the company attempted to sell off its kidney machine division to an international company operating from Switzerland. We were able to prevent them doing so at that time both

by threats of action and the involvement of some MPs.
When we checked on the requirements for kidney
machines in Britain we were horrified to learn that 3,000
people die each year because they cannot get a kidney
machine. If you are under 25 and over 55 it is almost
impossible in many areas to get one. The doctors involved
sit like judge and juries with the governors of hospitals
deciding who will be allowed, as they so nicely put it,
'to go into decline'. One doctor said to us how distressed
he was by this situation and admitted that sometimes he
did not tell the families of the patients that this was
happening because they would otherwise be distressed.
We regard it as outrageous that the skilled workers who
design and make this equipment face the prospect of the
dole queue where they will be paid about £40 a week
(which when administered by the bureaucrats is approximately £70 a week), when with a little commonsense if they were paid £70 a week to stay in industry
they could at least be producing artefacts which will be
required by society. Indeed, if the social contract meant
anything and if there were such a thing as a social wage,
surely this is precisely the sort of thing which it should
imply, namely having foregone-wage increases in order
that we could expand the services to the community at
large we should have the opportunity of producing
medical equipment which they require.

Before we even started the corporate plan our members at the Wolverhampton plant visited a centre for
children with Spina Bifida and were horrified to see
that the only way they could propel themselves about
was literally by crawling on the floor. So they designed
a vehicle which subsequently became known as Hobcart
— it was highly successful and the Spina Bifida Association of Australia wanted to order 2,000 of these.
Lucas would not agree to manufacture these because
they said it was incompatible with their product range
and at that time the corporate plan was not developed

and we were not able to press for this. But the design
and development of this product were significant in
another sense: Mike Parry Evans, its designer, said that
it was one of the most enriching experiences of his life
when he actually took the Hobcart down and saw the
pleasure on the child's face — it meant more to him,
he said, than all the design activity he had been involved
in up to then. For the first time in his career *he actually
saw the person who was going to use the product that
he had designed*. It was enriching also in another sense
because he was intimately in contact with a social
human problem. He literally had to make a clay mould
of the child's back so that the seat would support it
properly. It was also fulfilling in that for the first time
he was working in the multi-disciplinary team together
with a medical type doctor, a physiotherapist and a
health visitor. I mention this because it illustrates very
graphically that it is untrue to suggest that aerospace
technologists are only interested in complex esoteric
technical problems. It can be far more enriching for
them if they are allowed to relate their technology to
really human and social problems.

Some of our members at another plant realised that a
significant percentage of the people who die of heart
attacks die between the point at which the attack occurs
and the stage at which they are located in the intensive
care unit in the hospital. So they designed a light, simple,
portable life support system which can be taken in an
ambulance or at the side of a stretcher to keep the
patient 'ticking over' until they are linked to the main
life support system in the hospital. They also learned
that many patients die under critical operations because
of the problem of maintaining the blood at a constant
optimum temperature and flow. This, it seemed to
them, was a simple technical problem if one were able
to get behind the feudal mysticism of the medical pro-
fession. So they designed a fairly simple heat exchanger

and pumping system and they built this in prototype. I understand that when the assistant chief designer at one of our plants had to have a critical operation they were able to convince the local hospital to use it and it was highly successful.

In the field of alternative energy sources we have come up with a very imaginative range of proposals. It seemed to us absurd that it takes more energy to keep New York cool during the summer than it does to heat it during the winter. If therefore there were systems which could conserve this energy at a time when it is not required and use it at a time when it is, this would make a lot of sense. One of the proposals for storing energy in this way was to produce gaseous hydrogen fuel cells. These would require considerable funding from the government but would produce means of conserving energy which would be ecologically desirable and socially responsible. We also designed a range of solar collecting equipment which could be used in low energy houses and we worked in conjunction with Clive Latimer and his colleagues at the North East London Polytechnic in producing components for a low energy house. I should add that this house was specifically designed so that it could be constructed on a self-build basis. In fact some of the students working on the Communications Design Degree course at that polytechnic are now writing an instruction manual which would enable people without any particular skills to go through a learning process and at the same time to produce very ecologically desirable forms of housing. One can now see that if this concept were linked to imaginative government community funding it would be possible in areas of high unemployment where there are acute housing problems to provide funds to employ those in that area to build their own housing.

We have made a number of contacts with county councils as we are very keen to see that these products

are used in communities at large. We are unhappy about
the present tendency of alternative technology for
products to be provided which are little more than play-
things for the middle class in their architect-built houses.
Hence we have already made links via the Open University with the Milton Keynes Corporation and have
designed and are currently building in conjunction with
the OU prototype heat pumps which will use natural
gas and will increase the actual coefficient of performance (COP) by 2.8 times.

Drawing on our aerodynamics knowhow, we have
proposed a range of wind generators. In some instances
these would have a unique rotor control in which the
liquid which is used as the media for transmitting the
heat is actually used to achieve the breaking and is
thereby heated in the process itself. We have proposed
a range of products which would be useful in Third
World countries. We feel, incidentally, that we should be
very humble about suggesting that our kind of technology would be appropriate in these countries; if one
looks at the incredible mess we have made of technology
in our society probably one of the most important
things the Third World countries could learn from us
is what not to do rather than what to do! It is also a
very arrogant assumption to believe that the only form
of technology is that which we have in the West. I can
see no reason why there should not be technologies
which are compatible with the cultural and social structures of these other countries. At the moment our
trade with these countries is essentially neo-colonialist.
We seek to introduce forms of technology which will
make them dependent upon us. When the 'gin and
tonic brigade' go out to sell a power pack, for example,
they always seek to sell a dedicated power pack for
each application, that is one power pack for generating
electricity, another power pack for pumping water and
so on. We have proposed a unique power pack which

could operate on a range of indigenous fuels and methane and which, by means of a variable speed gearbox, would be capable of alteratively pumping water, compressing air, providing high pressure hydraulics and generating electricity. This would, therefore, be a sort of universal power pack which could provide a small village or community with a range of services. This is quite contrary to the present design methodology which seeks to do actually the reverse.

Time and space does not permit a detailed account of the rest of the 150 products. Three further ones, however, are worth describing.

We are proposing a hybrid power pack which could be used in cars, coaches, lorries or trains. There is now a growth in the use of battery driven vehicles. This is clearly ecologically desirable but has the great disadvantage that in a stop-start situation they have to be charged every 40 miles and on a flat terrain about every hundred miles. We are proposing a power pack in which we have a small internal combustion engine running at its constant optimum revs: this will mean that all the energy which is lost as one accelerates, decelerates, idles at traffic lights, starts cold and so on, is put in as useful energy through a generator which charges a stack of batteries which then operates an electric motor. Our initial calculations (which have subsequently been supported by work done in Germany), suggest that this would improve specific fuel consumption by 50 per cent; it would reduce toxic emissions, since the unburned gases are not going out into the atmosphere, to about 80 per cent. Further, since the whole system would be running at constant revs one could calculate all the resonance of the system and effectively silence it: our calculations suggest that a power pack of this kind would be inaudible against a background noise of about 60 or 70 decibels at 10 metres.

It may be asked, of course, why such a power pack

had not been designed and developed before. The simple answer, it seems to us, is that such a power pack would have to last for about ten or fifteen years and this is absolutely contrary to the whole ethos of automotive design which has as its basis the notion of a throw-away product with all the terrible waste of energy and materials which that implies. We are convinced that Western society cannot carry on, in this wasteful and arrogant fashion much longer.

This work has caused us to question very fundamentally the underlying assumptions of industries such as the automotive industry. We have had long discussions with our colleagues at Chryslers and British Leyland. In fact the workers at Chryslers now see that the choice facing them two or three years ago was not to continue producing rubbishy cars or to face the dole queue. There were a whole series of other options open to them if the political and social infrastructure were there to allow them to do so. We have been working with Richard Fletcher and his colleagues at the North East London Polytechnic on a unique road-rail vehicle which is capable or driving through a city as a coach and then running on the national railway network. It could provide the basis for a truly integrated, cheap, effective public transport system in this country. It uses pneumatic tyres and is therefore capable of going up an incline of 1:6 − normal railway rolling stock can only go up an incline of 1:80. This meant in the past that when a new railway line was laid down it was necessary literally to flatten the mountains and fill up the valleys or put tunnels through them. This costs about £1 million per track mile − this was the approximate cost of the railway in Tanzania which the Chinese put down. With our system a track can be put down at about £20,000 per track mile since it follows the natural contours of the countryside. This vehicle would therefore not only be of enormous use in metropolitan Britain but would also be of great interest in

developing countries and even in areas such as Scotland
and some of the less densely populated areas in Europe.

The last range of equipment I would like to mention
is what we call telearchic devices. This literally means
hands or control at a distance. If we examine the present
development of technology we will see that machines
and systems are designed in such a fashion as to objectivise human skill and thereby diminish or totally replace the human being. This means in practice that
industries are becoming capital intensive rather than
labour intensive. These are also invariably energy intensive. This is now giving rise to massive structural unemployment in all of the technologically advanced nations.
There have been about five million permanent unemployed in the United States over the past ten years; in
Britain we have now got 1.6 million. Even in West
Germany, that most optimistic of technologically advanced nations, they now have one million people out
of work and 700,000 on short time working. In 1974
they increased the number of process computers by
50.3 per cent and in 1975 by 33.8 per cent. They will
have 60 times as many microprocessors by 1984 and they
reckon that in 1982 60 per cent of all measuring and
control equipment will include these microprocessors.
It is clear that this is going to give rise to a massive
dislocation of the workforce and these concerns are
now being expressed by the West German trade union
movement, in particular by Ulrich Briefs of the DGB
(German TUC). Gradually they too are learning that
the more we invest in industry in its present form, the
more people we put out of work. When we were considering the design of robotic equipment to maintain
North Sea oil piplines, the more we thought about this
the more it became clear the terrible waste we are
making of the great human intelligence which is available to us. If you try to design a robot to recognize
which way a hexagon nut is about, much less to select

the correct spanner to use on it and then to apply the correct torque, it is an incredible programming job and you realize how intelligent people are in the sense that they can do this without really 'even thinking about it'. In fact comparisons we have made show that the most complicated robotic equipment with pattern recognition intelligence has intelligence units of 10^3, whereas human beings have synaptic connections of 10^{14}. There is therefore no comparison even at a theoretical level between the intelligence of human beings and the intelligence of these artificial devices. Yet with the linear drive forward of science and technology we deliberately design equipment to eliminate all that vast human knowledge.

So we are proposing these telearchic devices which reverse the historical tendency to diminish or objectivise human skill. Basically they are a range of equipment which will mimic in real time the motions of a human being. This would mean that in the case of mining, the skill of the miner would still be used but the miner could go through the mining process remotely in a safe environment whilst the telearchic device actually did the mining for him. Thus we human beings would continue to be involved in that precious learning process, which comes about through actually working on the physical world about us and it would also mean that we would be countering structural unemployment. We would, in a word, be very creatively linking a relatively labour-intensive form of work with a reasonably advanced and responsible technology. We would not therefore be proposing a return to the so-called 'good old days' in which some romantics seem to believe that the populace spent its time dancing round maypoles in unspoiled meadows. We are deeply conscious of the squalor, the disease, the filth which existed in the past and the contribution science and technology has made in overcoming these. What we believe is necessary is to draw on that which is best from our past and link it with that which is best in our science and technology.

Harnessing technology to human needs

The Lucas workers' corporate plan has the distinct
advantage that it is a very concrete proposal put forward
by a group of well organised industrial workers who
have demonstrated in the past, by the products they
have designed and built, that they are no daydreamers.
It is proving to be a unique vehicle with which to test
the boundaries of the system both in a technological,
political and economic sense.

We have of course approached the government and
we have had every sympathy short of actual help. We
have been enormously impressed at the ability of the
various ministries to pass the buck; indeed we have
experienced at first hand the white heat of bureaucracy.
Although the company has centrally rejected the corporate plan and is now refusing to meet the combined
committee to discuss it, no Minister has been prepared
to insist that the company should meet us to do so. In
fact junior ministers, like Les Huckfield continually
write to us saying 'In my considered view those best
suited to deal with this question are the company and
the trade unions involved'. It is absolutely clear that
the company will not and has not met us to discuss
the plan. However, support from the trade union movement is growing – large shop stewards' committees at
Chryslers, Vickers, Rolls Royce and elsewhere are now
discussing corporate plans of this kind. One of our
colleagues from Burnley, Terry Moran, has made a tour
of trades councils in Scotland discussing these matters.
The combined committee is now itself organising a
series of meetings in the towns in which Lucas Aerospace has sites. We think it is arrogant for aerospace
technologists to believe that they should be defining
what communities should have. We are seeking through

the local trade unions, political parties and other organisations in each area to help us to define what they
need and to begin to create a climate of public opinion
where we can force the government and the company
to act. At the national level the TUC has produced a
half an hour television programme on BBC2 dealing
with our corporate plan: this is part of its TN training
programme for shop stewards. The Transport & General
Workers Union has just come out with a statement indicating that its shop stewards throughout the country
should press for corporate plans of this kind. At an
international level the interest has been truly enormous.
In Sweden, for example, they have produced six half-
hour radio programmes dealing exclusively with the
corporate plan and have made cassettes which are now
being discussed in factories throughout Sweden. They
have also made a half-hour television programme and a
paperback book has been produced dealing with the
corporate plan. Similar developments are taking place
in Australia and elsewhere and the interest centres not
merely on the fact that a group of workers for the first
time are demanding the right to work on socially useful
products, but that they are proposing a whole series of
new methods of production, where workers by hand
and brain can really contribute to the design and development of products and where they can work in a non-
alienated fashion in a labour process which enhances
human beings rather than diminishes them.

Our society in the past has been very good at technical invention but very slow at social innovation. We
have made incredible strides technologically but our
social organizations are virtually those which existed
several hundred years ago. One of the Swedish television
interviews said 'when one looks at Britain in the past it
has been great at *scientific and technological invention*
and frequently has not really developed or exploited
that. The Lucas workers corporate plan shows *great*

social invention but it probably is also the case that they will not develop or extend that in Britain' (my italics). If this were true it would be very sad indeed.

The concluding point I would make is this. Science and technology are not given. It is not like the sun or the moon or the stars. It is man-made and if it does not do what we want then we have a right to change it. It is interesting to look at some of the adverts for tranquillizers: one I have here shows a woman dominated by what technology has done to her — high-rise flats, she is suffering from high-rise blues and it says very subtly, 'she cannot change her environment but you can change her mood with Serenid D' — which incidentally is a tranquillizer. We in Lucas Aerospace are trying to say that it is not pills and tranquillizers we need but a very clear political and ideological view of what we want technology to do for us and the courage and determination to fight for its implementation. We hope that in that fight we will be supported by widespread sections of the community because we will not be able to create an island of responsibility in Lucas Aerospace in a sea of depravity.

Chapter IX

The Lucas Plan[*]

Lucas Aerospace Combine Shop Stewards' Committee

This Corporate Plan was prepared by the Lucas Aerospace
Combine Shop Stewards' Committee for that section of
Joseph Lucas Industries which is known as Lucas Aerospace.

If a brief description of Lucas Industries is provided this
gives an economic, technical and company background
against which the performance and potential of its wholly
owned subsidiary, Lucas Aerospace, can be viewed. It was
also felt desirable to do so as some of the alternative products
proposed elsewhere in this report, although emanating from
aerospace technology, could more appropriately be handled,
at the manufacturing stage, by production techniques and
facilities available elsewhere in the Lucas organisations.

Lucas Industries Ltd.
Lucas Industries is a vast and complex organisation with
design, development, manufacturing, sales and services
activities in the automotive, aerospace and industrial sectors
of the economy.

The Company which was formed in 1877 now has some
80,000 employees and an annual turnover of approximately
£300,000,000 and capital investment of £110,000,000.

A discernable feature of the Company's mode of operation during the past few years has been to shift large quantities of capital, resources and technological know-how into
overseas activities. This raises a whole host of fundamental,
political, economic and industrial questions, as is the case

*A more complete summary of this plan is available in IWC Pamphlet No.
55, from the Institute for Workers' Control.

with the operation of any Multi-National Corporation. It is
not the purpose of the Corporate Plan to analyse these.
Suffice to say that this tendency is causing deep rooted concern amongst large sections of Lucas employees and they
will clearly have to consider appropriate means of defending
themselves from the likely repercussions of these developments. These views and anxieties are reflected in the Aerospace division.

Lucas Industries hold a monopoly, or near monopoly
position, in respect of a number of product ranges both in
the United Kingdom and in Europe. However the present
economic crisis, itself a reflection of the inherent contradictions of the market economy, is having serious repercussions
within Lucas Industries. At the time of preparing this report
the Company is attempting to shed large sections of labour
in some of its plants. There has also been a serious cut in
the living standards of all Lucas workers both by hand and
brain since 1972. The attitude of the Company to its employees and society at large is however no worse than that
of its international competitors and it is certainly better
than some of them. However, a sophisticated industrial
relations set up and a relatively elaborate network of consultative devices simply provide a thin veneer of concern,
beneath which is concealed all the inevitable ruthlessness
of a large corporation involved in the frantic international
competition of the 1970s.

The Combine Committee

The five years from 1964 to 1969 saw a very rapid mono-
polisation of large sections of British Industry and the emergence of massive corporations such as British Leyland and
GEC. This process was actively supported by the government, which, in many instances, was providing the tax
payers money to lubricate this process. Within Mr Wilson's
philosophical framework of 'the white heat of technological change' many thousands of highly skilled workers
found that the consequence of the 'White Heat' market

economy was that it simply burned up their jobs and gave
rise to large scale structural unemployment. The 'logic'
of the market economies and rationalisation programmes
in these vast corporations resulted in the illogical growth
of the dole, queue with all the degradation and suffering
and loss of economic activity of hundreds of thousands
of highly skilled men and women.

The Weinstock empire, that is GEC, was the pacemaker in
this development. The work force was reduced from 260,000
to 200,000 whilst during the same period the profits went
up from £75,000,000 to £108,000,000 per annum. Thus
whilst it was profitable for Weinstock to cut his work force,
society at large had to pay the price, firstly in social security
payments for those involved and secondly in the loss of
productive capacity which these people could have made
available to the economy of the nation as a whole. Wein-
stocks's attitude to the work force, summed up by one of
his managers in a statement to the *Sunday Times* "he takes
people and squeezes them until the pips squeak" was seen
as some kind of virtue. Indeed it is a measure of the deep
rooted economic and political sickness of our society that
a person like Weinstock was then, and is still, held up as the
pinnacle of managerial competence.

When Lucas acquired parts of English Electric in the
process described above, the lessons of the Weinstock esca-
pade were not lost on Lucas workers. It was clear that Lucas
Aerospace, if it were permitted, would embark on a similar
rationalisation programme. Strangely enough it was recognition that this attack would be made upon the work force
that provided the objective circumstances in which the
Combine Committee was formed.

Its formation resulted in the first instance from fear of
redundancy, and the recognition of the need to provide an
organisation which could fight and protect the right to
work. It was realised from the onset that the Combine Committee could itself become another bureaucracy and that
there were real dangers in centralising activities of all fac-

tories through one body. Accordingly a constitution was carefully worked out and widely discussed at all sites which provided adequate safeguards.

Development of the Combine Committee, now known as the Lucas Aerospace and Defence Systems Combine Shop Stewards Committee, took approximately 4½ years. In its early stages it lacked cohesion and strength. The Company was, as a result of this, able to embark on a rationalisation programme in which the work force was reduced from 18,000 to the present 13,000.

Gradually the Combine Committee set up a series of advisory services for its members. These include a pensions advisory service which has recently negotiated a complex pension structure for manual workers[2] and the campaign for the election of trustees for the staff pension fund in order that information could be available as to where this pension fund money is being invested. The importance of this development may be judged by the fact that the staff pension fund has a market value of something like £80,000,000 and the works one £40,000,000 at a time when the capitalisation value of Lucas as a whole on the stock market has been as low as £36,000,000.

Other services included a Science and Technology Advisory Service which provided technical information on the safeguards to be campaigned for when new equipment was being introduced[3] or when health hazards were possibly involved.[4]

The Combine Committee is also a reflection of the growing awareness, of those who work at the point of production, that the traditional trade union structures based on geographical divisions and organised on a craft basis are incapable of coping with the new and complex problems of these large monopolies. However the Combine Committee should not be seen as an alternative to the traditional trade union movement rather it is a logical development from it, and complementary to its aims.

The Combine Committee produces its own four page

illustrated newspaper approximately bi-monthly, 10,000 copies of this are circulated amongst the 13,000 manual and staff workers.

In practice the Combine Committee has become the voice on a number of subjects for the 13,000 manual and staff workers who now work throughout Lucas Aerospace in the United Kingdom. It has also taken a series of steps to establish close links with those employed by Lucas Aerospace abroad. The significance of its development has been included in lectures at the TUC[5] on the training courses for shop stewards and for full time TU education officers.

Employee Development Programme

The prosperity of Britain as a manufacturing nation depends to a very large extent upon the skill and ability of its people and the opportunity to use that skill and ability to produce commodities.

During the past five years the Lucas Aerospace work force has been reduced approximately 25%. This has come about either by direct sackings or by a deliberate policy of so-called natural wastage, i.e. not replacing those who leave, or encouraging early retirement. The net result has been that highly skilled teams of manual workers and design staff have been seriously diminished and disrupted; we cannot accept that such a development is in the long term national interest.

Coupled with this development has been one inside the Company in which attempts have been made to replace human intelligence by machine intelligence, in particular the introduction of numerically controlled machine tools. This has, in a number of cases, proved to have been quite disastrous and the quality of the products have suffered in consequence.

In many instances the Company has fallen victim of the high pressure salesmanship of those who would have us believe that all our problems can be solved by high capital equipment. We have allowed our regard for human talents to be bludgeoned into silence by the mystique of advanced equipment and technology, and so forget that our most precious asset is the creative and productive power of our people.

When we reviewed the work force we now have, our concern centres on four points. Firstly, very little is being done to extend and develop the very considerable skills and ability still to be found within the work force. Secondly, the age group in some of the factories is very high, typically around 46-50 years average. Thirdly, there is little indication that the Company is embarking on any real programme of apprenticeships and the intake of young people. (It is in fact sacking apprentices as they finish their time.) Fourthly, the Company is making no attempt to employ women in technical jobs, and apart from recruitment of these from outside, there are many women doing routine jobs well below their existing capabilities. Quite apart from the desirability of countering these discriminatory practices, the employment of women in the male dominated areas would have an important 'humanising' effect on science and technology.

In that section of the report dealing with specific recommendations we propose a number of steps which should be taken in this direction. The section of this report is concerned with development and retraining facilities for the existing workforce, this we regard as important at two levels, firstly retraining and re-education would mean that we were developing the capabilities of our people to meet the technological and sociological challenges which will come during the next few years. Secondly, in the event of work shortage occurring before alternative products have been introduced the potential redundancy could be transformed into a positive breathing space during which re-education could act as a form of enlightened work sharing.

During the past ten years a number of social, political and economic factors have become clearly discernible which suggests that the traditional pattern of education/

work/retirement will grow increasingly inappropriate in
the fourth quarter of the 20th century. For the purpose
of the Corporate Plan the most important of these factors
are:

1. The exponential nature of technological change.[6]
2. The rate of knowledge obsolescence and break up of
   skills associated with 1 above.[7]
3. Structural changes in manpower requirements.[8]
4. The movement towards equal employment and education
   opportunities for women.[9]
5. The political and social unacceptability of structural
   unemployment as a feature of advanced industrial
   society.[10]

There are some indications that the trade union movement,
educational institutes, and even some managements are
beginning to respond to this new situation. The growing interest in adult and recurrent education and retraining is an
indication of this.[11] It is also encouraging to see international bodies, such as the OECDs Centre of Educational
Research and Innovation, proposed recurrent education
which permits 'educational opportunities to spread out over
the individual's life time'.[12]

Some countries have already well established and coordinated retraining and educational programmes. In
Sweden for example, apart from all training within industry,
and the individuals own initiative, the state recognises an
annual training need of 1% of the total work force.[13]
Even in the United States, where the short sightedness of
private enterprise is at its worst, some large corporations
now include training and education as part of the corporate
social responsibility activities.[14]

In general, however, the tendency is to discard older
employees and engage younger ones 'with new knowledge'.
This, unfortunately, is likely to remain the predominant
business attitude for some time to come. It is an attitude
which we cannot and will not accept. In our view there is

a need for a blending of the dynamism and drive of the young people, to be counterbalanced by the experience and knowledge of older workers, who should also have the opportunity of having their knowledge updated.

More attention is now being given to the importance of 'human assets', although the terminology used reveals the real motives of many of the companies, for example reference is made to 'human capital'.[15] However, there are some indications that the value of re-training employees 'who know the company system' is beginning to be recognised. The growing pressure from the international trade union movement for retraining and re-education of older workers (which can frequently mean a little over 40 in some fields) is likely to be a significant factor during the next decade.[16]

It is to be anticipated that these international tendencies will be reflected in the United Kingdom, although to date the emphasis has been on compensation and unemployment payments rather than re-education as an occupational form of 'work-sharing'.

Unemployment is a social evil which need not occur in advanced industrial society and should not be tolerated. It represents a tragic wastage of the nations greatest asset, its people's creative and productive power. Whilst it may seem feasible from an accountant's viewpoint to balance his books by sacking a few hundred workers the loss to the nation as a whole can be very considerable. This loss arises firstly be-cause the individuals involved are denied the right to produce hence the commodities that they would have created are no longer available. Secondly, the state is involved in vast sums of money which are paid as earnings-related unemployment benefit and in compensation to the individuals who lost their jobs.

For the individuals involved there is the indignity and degradation of the dole queue; for the tax payer there is the expenditure on these social benefits. It is our view, therefore, that even in a narrow economic sense it would be feasible to propose that part of the money that would have been available had these people been redundant, should be provided as a basis for part time education, thereby protecting the individual from the dole queue whilst at the same time investing in the nation's future manpower . . .

It should be emphasised that we are not, in this context, talking about retraining for white collar and technical staff only. It is our view that the entire work force including semi-skilled and skilled workers are capable of retraining for jobs which would greatly extend the range of work they could undertake. This would provide opportunities which they may have been denied, for a number of reasons, at an earlier stage in their lives.

Such courses could best be organised in local technical colleges and polytechnics. It is our view that universities are too rigid in both their entrance requirements and teaching methods. The courses would have to take into account that many of those involved would not have had traditional forms of education and paper qualifications, but could bring to the course a wealth of experience through actual work in industry.

It would further mean that those teaching on these courses would have to develop new teaching methods and have a real respect for people who had industrial experience. Such an arrangement would not be without its advantages for the polytechnic and technical colleges involved, as such trainees could bring to these institutions a much more mature and balanced view about productive processes in general, but also about wider political, social and economic matters.

Featured below are outlines of the Lucas Shop Stewards' proposals in two particular areas. Information about other alternative products is included in the preceding chapter, by M. Cooley, and a summary of all the main proposals is to be found at the end of this chapter.

Oceanics- A Brief Review

The ocean beds cover over 70% of the earth's surface. It is clear that during the coming years there will be an ever increasing use made of this vast area. Judging by the irresponsible manner in which human beings have used the first 30% of the earth's surface the prospect is one which we view with considerable trepidation.

The exploitation of the ocean bed is likely to take at least three forms:

1. Exploration and extraction of oil and natural gas.
2. Collection of mineral bearing nodules.
3. Submarine agriculture.

Oil

It has been estimated that 15% of the world's oil is already drawn from coastal waters and this figure will be increased to 33% by 1980. The significance of this in the United Kingdom has of course been underlined by the work on North Sea Oil.[17] The scale of this activity may be judged by the fact that the total capital expenditure on process industries is forecast to amount to £8.6 billion pounds in the three years up to the end of 1977. Of this some 40% is likely to go on North Sea Oil production development.[18]

Five years ago, efforts to interest Mr Rivett and Mr Clifton-Mogg in the possibility of using existing Lucas Aerospace valve technology, and the manufacturing facilities of the ballscrews to provide a complete valve operating and controlled system were ignored. It is perhaps not surprising therefore that Sir Fredrick Warner, Chairman of the NEDC process plant working committee maintains that process plant and equipment manufacturers are missing out to overseas companies on much of the North Sea Oil work. He stated in presenting the NEDC report on the 9 June 1975 'I wish we were getting half the business'.[19]

Although such valve work would represent only a minor part of the capital investment in such installations it would have been of major significance to Lucas Aerospace. However the real growth area would be in a whole range of automatic and electronically controlled remote equipment. 'It is easy to envisage a time when all facilities now used in processing and distributing oil are put in the sea bed in vast plants manned by men living in atmospheric conditions, or handled by robots and automatic systems electronically controlled from the shore.'[20]

It is significant that Westinghouse and Lockheed are both actively engaged in these fields, and Lockheed are concentrating their efforts on developing sub sea working chambers which can be approached by diving bells.[21]

These activities will require a wide range of submersible vehicles which in turn will need generating and actuating systems on board. Lucas Aerospace should be entering into working agreements with the manufacturers of these in particular with Vickers Oceanics. In fact they should consider entering into an agreement with Vickers which would establish the same relationship which they have in the aerospace field with Hawker Siddeley or BAC.

Metal Bearing Nodules

One of the richest sources of mineral resources is the metal bearing nodules to be found on the sea bed. They exist virtually everywhere and are usually 20mm to 40mm in size and average 17% manganese and 11% iron. They also contain considerable quantities of trace elements of nickel, copper, cobalt and zinc, together with lead and phosphates. By the year 2000 the land sources of some of these metals will have been exhausted, whilst the marine reserves are enormous. The quantity of copper in nodule form for example is 150 times greater than the terrestial reserves.[22]

Although this field of activity is only in its infancy three large companies in the United States, including Hughes Tool, has already put $100 million into the project to exploit the seas off California. In Europe both France and Germany have carried out initial experiments of deep sea retrievers. The initial investment of projects of this kind is likely to be enormous and as a consequence international co-operation is likely to be the pattern. In fact a spokesman for the German company said 'the technical development is so expensive that exploitation of these metal bearing nodules is out of the question for one firm alone, or even a national group of companies. It can only be done by inter-national co-operation as through cross frontier consortia'.

Marine Agriculture

During the coming ten years there is likely to be a growing interest in marine agriculture. Products of the sub acqua farms are likely to range from directly consumable vege-tables to those producing by products which can be pro-cessed on land. This type of farming will require a whole range of special purpose small vehicles to take the 'farmers' down to the work areas. There are also likely to be require-ments for a range of submersible vehicles and telechiric machines which could carry out both the sowing and reap-ing by remote control. It is our view that oceanics provides very important long term outlet for Lucas Aerospace as manufacturers of complete aircraft systems. We are in a unique position to provide total systems for the vehicles and equipment which will be required in this field. It would also be a logical point of entry for Lucas Aerospace into the wider and developing field of control systems as a whole. This is likely to be one of the leading growth areas during the coming years and a very considerable use of mini computers and micro-processors are likely to be involved. The predictions are that this will have a profound effect upon the whole nature of our technology during the coming years.[23] This field would also provide a logical framework in which Lucas Aerospace could get involved in micro-processing systems. It is significant that some of Lucas' leading competitors such as Plessey are already making con-siderable advances in the micro-processor field.

Braking Systems

The increased speed of both road and rail vehicles and the larger payloads which they will carry, both of passengers and goods, will give rise to stringent braking regulations during the coming years. This tendency will be further increased by Britain's membership of the EEC. The EEC is now introducing a range of new braking regulations. These specify, not only stopping distances, but calls for minimum standards of braking endurance over a continuous period. In addition, the regulations lay down conditions for 'braking balance' between axles in order to prevent a dangerous sequence of wheel locking.

Many individual EEC countries have, in addition, their own national braking requirements. In France for example, since the mid 1950s auxiliary braking systems have been compulsory for coaches operating in mountainous terrain.

A fundamental weakness of normal mechanical brakes is that when subjected to long braking periods they overheat and the braking linings, at elevated temperatures, tend to temporarily lose their 'gripping qualities'. This problem can be greatly reduced, if not totally overcome, by using a retarder. A retarder is basically an electro magnetic dynamometer which is fitted usually to the prop shaft between the engine and the back axle. To reduce speed its coils are excited by an electrical supply direct for the vehicle battery, thereby inducing a braking force as the disc rotates in the magnetic field.

At the Willesden plant some 25 years design experience exists in this field of dynamometry. Attempts by the design staff some 10 years ago to get the Company to develop and simplify these eddycurrent dynamometers for mass production as retarders failed. It is felt, however, that the time is now opportune to reconsider this whole project.

In Britain public attention has been dramatically focused on the weaknesses of existing braking systems by the Yorkshire Coach disaster which claimed 32 lives in May 1975. The *Sunday Times* (1.6.75) stated "last week's crash might have been avoided if the coach had been equipped with an extra braking device, such as an electro-magnetic retarder which is being fitted to an increasing number of coaches

in this country". In fact it would appear that only 10% of
Britain's 75,000 buses and coaches actually have retarders
fitted to them. There is, therefore, clearly a vast market
available to Lucas if it adopts an imaginative approach to
this problem. It is not suggested that Lucas should simply
produce dynamometers, rather what is proposed is that
they should analyse the whole nature of braking systems
through a wide range of vehicles, including buses, coaches,
articulated lorries, underground and overhead trains as used
by British Rail.

It is proposed that a braking system analysis and development team should be set up to take an overview of this
problem. The team should make an analysis of the actual
requirements for the different applications, and at the
same should analyse any patent problems which might
arise with respect of the French Labinal retarder which is
marketed in this country as 'Telma'. Simultaneously a
development team should develop an existing Lucas Aerospace dynamometer, using a unit capable of being fitted
in the conventional position, i.e. in the prop shaft between
the engine and the back axle, capable of absorbing 600
brake horse power and the weight approx. 200 kgs. Once
this unit has been designed and developed, discussions
should take place with Girlings to arrange for its mass
production under a licensing arrangement from Lucas
Aerospace. Although a vast potential market exists for
dynamometers of this kind this unit should be seen only
as the first step in evolving a total braking system capability.

The second stage would be a combined electro magnetic
braking system coupled directly to a traditional mechanical brake based on a Girling disc. The control system
would have to be designed such that by moving the brake
pedal the dynamometer would initially operate.and the
further depression of the pedal will gradually increase the
current and hence the braking load until finally the mechanical brake could be applied if necessary. Use of the dynamometer between the prop shaft and the back axle clearly

limits its range of application. To overcome this, discussion should take place with manufacturers of gear boxes to arrange to have them fitted on the output side of the gear-box such that they could be used on the tractors of articu-lated vehicles.

A further development would be to design and produce units which could be fitted to each individual axle. Work in this field is already being carried out in France, but based on traditional dynamometer units.

An elaborate control system would be necessary to ensure that as each of the individual axles is braked it still meets the new EEC requirements concerning the sequence and the effects on individual axles and their proper synchronisation to remove the risk of unstable skidding or 'jack knifing'. This work would dove tail in conveniently with existing work being undertaken by Girlings on anti-skid systems. It is im-portant that this programme should not be carried out in the usual piece-meal short term manner. A long term overall plan should be worked out, and each stage of the develop-ment programme should be a tactical step towards a long term strategy.

Part of that long term strategy should be the provision of radar applied braking systems. All the necessary components should be designed to produce a flexible range of system options. Dynamometers lend themselves ideally to this as the load is applied electrically. The 1975 Society of Automotive Engineers Congress held in Detroit, reported that the National Highway Safety Association's 71 statistics showed that 8% of the vehicles on the road were involved in rear end accidents. They represented 25% of accidents or 8½ million vehicles. The medium to long term aim should be to provide radar applied braking systems particularly for use on motor-ways.

The *Financial Times* (7.5.1975) stated

"in the longer run electronic station keeping devices which use a form of radar to apply brakes automatically to cars travelling along motorways when they approach too close to a slowly

moving vehicle ahead may be adopted. If they were introduced
compulsorily for traffic they would certainly lead to a substantial reduction in the number of lives lost through motorway
accidents in fog."

R.A. Chandler and L.E. Woods of the US Department of
Commerce Institute for Telecommunication Sciences have
said at the conference quoted above "while significant problems exist in the development of generally acceptable radar
sensors for automobile braking, no insurmountable difficulties are evident". Applications more complex than mere
station keeping should also be considered, but these give
rise to a series of technological problems which, although
they could be overcome, may only be soluble with very
expensive equipment. However both Chandler and Woods
had the following to say "both pedestrians and the cyclists
are detectable, radiation hazards are minimal, small radius
corners give a problem in false alarms, inter-system blind-
ing is a problem and that the effect of rain scattering
are serious". Spokesmen for the National Highway Traffic
Safety Association have stated that research in radar braking
fields warrants continuation, but the decision to implement such devices should be made only after cost benefit
studies and acceptable hardware performance had been
verified. It is clear that now is the stage for Lucas to become
involved in these developments.

It is proposed that a similar long term overview should be
taken of braking requirements for rolling stock railways
and underground. Already British Rail has introduced, on
an experimental basis, velocity monitoring systems, which
indicate to the driver if he is travelling at a velocity considered to be dangerous for an oncoming curve, junction or
other impediment. With these velocity sensing devices already
installed, it would be a logical step to use this information
to feed into braking systems such that the train was automatically slowed down to meet the travelling requirements
already determined for other sections of the track if the
driver fails to respond due to illness or whatever. Such over-

all braking systems would require many computers and micro processors. The use of these would fit in with suggestions made elsewhere in the Corporate Plan.

Summary of Proposals

This is a summary of proposals made specifically in sections of the Corporate Plan or those arising from a review of alternatives.

1. *Components for low energy housing*

a. Solar heating, in particular switching circuits and pumping components. The provision of materials and prototype components for research and development in the Essex County Council experimental house. The appointment or seconding of a research fellow to the Group working on this research project at North East London Polytechnic for the Sussex County Council.

b. An examination of the feasibility of the Luton site producing solar heating panels for such housing.

c. An investigation of the feasibility of applying advanced aerospace technology to wind power sources in particular 'windmills', with special emphasis upon rotor speed regulation systems.

d. The building of a prototype and the testing of it at the test house at Sibton Green, Sussex.

2. *Fuel Cells Technology*

A research and development programme to keep Lucas abreast of the technology in this field. Specifically, consideration to be given to the feasibility of building a prototype 30kW fuel cell power plant, using gaseous hydrogen and oxygen.

3. *Braking Systems*

Set up analysis and development team to adapt eddycurrent dynamometer technology to the requirements of retarders for coaches.

Analyse markets for such retarders and investigate patent complications in connection with the 'Telma' retarder. Establish relationship with British Leyland and with Girlings to produce an overall system for Leyland buses and coaches.

Initial staff required 2 R&D personnel, 1 prototype fitter over a 3-month period expand the team to cater for the following work:

a. The design of a 600 brake horse power unit weighing. approximately 200 kgs.
b. An integrated braking system incorporating both mechanical disc brakes and dynamometers.
c. Anti-skid systems.
d. Automatic braking systems incorporating station keeping capabilities.
e. Complete braking systems for railways.

4. *Transport Systems*

a. The design and development of a prototype hybrid power package incorporating internal combustion engine, generator, batteries electric motor.
b. Airship vectoring systems.
   Arrange meetings with Dr Edward Mowforth of the University of Surrey.
c. Combined road/rail vehicle. Establish transport systems design and development team.
   Establish working relationship with R. Fletcher of the North East London Polytechnic whose work in this area is supported by the Science Research Council.
   Examine feasibility of providing integrated braking system for this vehicle together with micro-processors, suspension systems using Girling know-how and the hybrid power package outlined above. Contact Scottish Development Board, and Derbyshire County Council through R. Fletcher with a view to establishing a test section of existing track.

Re-examine the Rotax railway van actuator in light of
current requirements.

5. *Oceanics*

Establish working relationship with Vickers Oceanics.
Consider feasibility of providing complete systems for sub-
mersibles.
Examine the feasibility of designing, developing and manufacturing, either independently or with Vickers, telecheiric
devices for metal bearing nodule collection and marine
agriculture.

6. *Micro-processors*

Marston Green Electronic Group to consider the provision
of micro-processors for the systems outlined above.
Particular attention to be paid to the development at
Plesseys.

7. *Medical*

Establish a medical division at G&E Bradleys, initially increas
ing the production of kidney machines thereby approximately 40%.
In conjunction with Ministry of Health build up a 'design
for the disabled' unit.
Investigate the feasibility of applying aerospace technology
to provide 'sight' to the blind.

8. *Power Units*

Examine the requirements of the computer industry for
standby power units using automatic sensing and starting
systems, to be developed by Marston Green.
Carry out market survey of requirements of Middle East
Oil producing countries and newly emergent nations for
power packs built on a module basis to meet alternatively
the requirement for pumping facilities, hydraulic power
pack facilities, electricity generation and compressed air.

9. Industrial Ball Screws

Analyse the application of ballscrews to valve control systems, machine tool control systems, telecheiric machines and submersible vehicles.

10. Telecheiric Machines

Augument existing systems and actuator know-how with specialists in remote control field.
Examine application for fire fighting telecheiric devices, mining machines and underwater devices.

11. Employee Development Programme

Arrange Union/Management negotiations on employee retraining.
In the event of immediate redundancies negotiate full time education as a form of work sharing backed by government grants.
Unions to have discussions with the Department of Employment and Manpower Services commission.

12. Integrated Product Teams

Union/Management negotiations on the establishment of integrated product teams incorporating design, development production engineering and manufacturing in one group.
Negotiations on the redesign of jobs.
Union to meet Dr Gilbert Jessop of the Work Research Unit of the Department of Employment to discuss job satisfaction schemes.

13. Other Products Under Consideration for Enlarged Corporate Plan

a. Linear motors operating pumps and compressors.
b. Range of applications for the '60 and 90 Gas Turbine'
c. Robot helicopter using Lucas gas turbine for crop spraying.
d. High speed motors.

REFERENCES

1.   Lucas Aerospace, Publicity Document No. ASD. SP. 213/74.
2.   *Economist,* May 3, 1975, p.113.
3.   *New Scientist,* March 21, 1974, p.732.
4.   Sheridan, Geoffrey, *The Guardian,* June 27, 1974.
5.   *Combine News,* March 19, 1975, p.1.
6.   Dr Herbert E. Stringer's evidence, Senate Hearing before the
     Clark Sub Committee, May 1963-1964. Published as *The
     Manpower Revolution,* Anchor Books, New York, 1966,
     pp.65-76.
7.   Sir Fredrick Warner in *Technology Today,* Routledge and
     Kegan Paul, 1971, pp.51-52.
8.   OECD, *Reveiew of National Science Policy (US),* Paris 1968,
     pp. 43, 45, 52, 54 and 56.
9.   Christine O'Connor, "Social Report", *The Engineer,* August 1,
     1974, pp.35-41.
10. "Positive Plans to tackle Unemployment", *Financial Times,*
     January 21, 1975, p.15.
11. Russel Committee Report: *Adult Education for Development,*
     paras. 3 and 5.
12. Ceri, *Recurrent Education,* OECD' 1973, p.5.
13. Senate Hearings, op.cit., p.84.
14. "The Current Status of Corporate Social Responsibility",
     Business Horizons, August 1973, pp.5-15.
15. "A Framework for Measuring Human Assets", *California
     Management Review,* Vol.XVI, No.4, 1974, pp.5-17.
16. I.L.O. 7th Session, September 1974. "Problems and opportu-
     nities of Employment and Re-employment of Older
     Employees in Commerce and Offices", paras 10, 16, 20-23.
17. Civeyrel, Francoise, *Vision,* February 1975, p.41.
18. N.E.D.O. Report on Process Plant, *Financial Times,* June 10,
     1975, p.9.
19. N.E.D.O. Report, op.cit.
20. Subsea Technology, *Financial Times,* April 23, 1975, p.27.
21. Subsea Technology, op.cit.
22. Civeyrel, Francoise, op.cit.
23. Rosenbrock H, "Future of Control", U.M.I.S.T. Report,
     August 1975.

*The complete report on the Alternative Plan takes up more than one
thousand pages. Enquiries should be directed to the Secretary, Lucas
Aerospace Combine Shop Steward's Committee, 86 Mellow Lane
East, Hayes, Middlesex.*

Chapter X

Building a Chieftain Tank and The Alternative

Vickers' National Combine Committee of Shop Stewards

The mechanical engineering industry is the largest in the UK. It accounts for nearly 5% of all civilian employment, 20% of all UK exports and 40% of all UK plant and machinery. Since the war, the industry has stagnated; the British share of the world market has declined, fixed investment has been low, employment has fallen since the early 1970s and the value per ton of British engineering exports, a measure of their technical content, is lower than the value per ton of the engineering exports or imports of any of Britain's main competitors. A recent NEDC report concluded that a major requirement of the British mechanical engineering industry was improvement in the quality of detailed design.[1]

In contrast, the export of tanks has risen substantially in recent years and the value per ton of the Chieftain Tank is higher than most of its main competitors — the American M-60, the West German Leopard, the French AMX-30, or the Soviet T-54.[2] Some of the finest engineering skills and talents are involved in building tanks and guns. While ordnance represents a rather small proportion of the total output of the mechanical engineering industry, 60% of the design engineers and scientists working in the industry are engaged in military work. It is evident that if those skills and talents were devoted to civilian work, to improvements in the quality of engineering

exports as well as the plant and machinery needed to
manufacture a wide range of civilian products, this
could not only improve Britain's economic position
but it could also contribute to the fulfilment of many
basic needs in British society today.

This is particularly relevant for West Newcastle,
where the Chieftain Tank is built. However, competitive
British armaments may be, the market is, by its
nature, erratic and unpredictable. It depends on wars
and arms races and shifting political allegiances. In
peacetime, it can never be expected to grow as fast
as civilian markets. For a hundred years, Vickers, or
its predecessor Armstrong's, has dominated employment in West Newcastle. The arms busuiness was built
upon the experience of two world wars. Older people
remember the days when 'tides of men' trudged up the
streets from the Elswick Works at the end of their
shifts.[3] Since then, employment has dwindled; from
12,250 at Elswick in 1939, to 5,700 in 1963, to
1,850 in October 1977. And this, despite the growth
of arms exports and the success of the Chieftain tank,
Elswick's staple, in the Middle East.

This was the reason why the Vickers Combine Committee undertook to examine the resources involved
in the construction of a Chieftain Tank and the alternative uses to which they could be put. But there was
also another more general reason. If unions are to
challenge the widespread redundancies now occurring
in the engineering industry and if victories won in wage
struggles are not to be overtaken by unemployment and
inflation, it is important that they be able to demonstrate at the level of the individual plant, the concrete
alternative strategies which could ensure future work
and social well being.

This chapter is divided into four sections. The first
section examines the market for tanks and the future
prospects for employment. The second section describes

the process of building a tank. The third section is about the past experience of Vickers' Elswick Works in the manufacture of commercial products and tries to explain the failures. The last section considers the principles on which an alternative strategy should be based and the suggestions that have been made for alternative products.

The Future of Tanks

The Chieftain Tank that the Elswick workers are building for Iran is the most advanced in the world. It is protected by the new Chobham plastic reinforced armour, described by the Ministry of Defence as "the single most significant development in the design of tanks since World War II".[4] Its 120mm gun is the most powerful tank gun in the world. The 105mm gun on Centurion, Chieftain's predecessor which was also built at Elswick, was widely reported to have proved superior to Soviet guns in the Arab/Israeli war of October 1973; the Chieftain gun is said to be even better. Moreover, it uses an extremely sophisticated and efficient fire control system, including infrared devices for night-time operations and a laser range finder. The main weakness of earlier Chieftains, their lack of power and speed, is said to have been corrected by the new Rolls Royce engine which will replace the problematic Leyland L.60. The Chieftain also has various little extras, like a collapsible fabric screen on which it can float and facilities to enable men to remain under the hatch for 48 hours in the event of nuclear, chemical or biological attack. Its main disadvantage stems from its very sophistication – the fact that complexity may entail a loss of ruggedness and reliability. According to the latest Annual Report, "prospective orders" for this splendid weapon of war should "ensure continuity of production . . . well into the 1980s".[5]

Beyond the 1980s, however, the future for tank orders is uncertain. First of all, by that date the Americans and Germans will have developed competing tanks, both using Chobham armour. The German tank is likely to have an advantage in speed and mobility. The American tank has been designed, at least in part, to operate in desert conditions and some versions may have a missile in place of a gun. The British Government has made it clear that there will not be a new British Battle Tank before the late 1980s. Secondly, the current market for tanks largely consists of oil-rich regimes in the Middle East (despite continued Israeli interest, the British Government has vetoed the supply of Chieftains to direct participants in the Arab/Israeli war). The repressive nature of these regimes is associated with political instability. Quite apart from the risks of British involvement in a war in the area, it is quite possible that such regimes may be overthrown by people who would not look kindly upon the arms suppliers of their oppressive predecessors. Thirdly, and perhaps most importantly, it is widely believed that tanks are obsolete. Lord Robens, for instance, considers that the future of armaments lies in electronics and not mechanical engineering and that tanks are unlikely to be used for much other than policing in the future. The electronics revolution has led to a vast improvement in the accuracy of guided weapons so that all tanks, even those protected by Chobham armour, have become much more vulnerable. Except in the desert, where concealment is difficult anyway, the case for these big sophisticated vehicles which are hard to hide and expensive to replace is questionable. A British Government, operating under severe financial restraint, will have to take this argument seriously when deciding upon a replacement for Chieftain. Its logic has already been accepted, at least implicitly, by Vickers management when the tank design team was disbanded.

But even if it were possible to anticipate continued growth in tank orders, this would not provide any kind of employment guarantee. Contrary to the popular impression employment in defence work is very insecure. Because individual plants are dependent on one or two major contracts, fluctuations in sales and jobs can be extreme. At Elswick, such fluctuations have been much greater on the military side than on the civil side. There have been major gaps in contracts which led to heavy redundancies; for example, in the early 1960s when work had ended on Centurion and not begun on Chieftain and in the late 1960s when the British Army's order for Chieftain had been completed and before export orders were received. This is shown in Table 1.

TABLE I: ELSWICK PRODUCTS, 1950-78

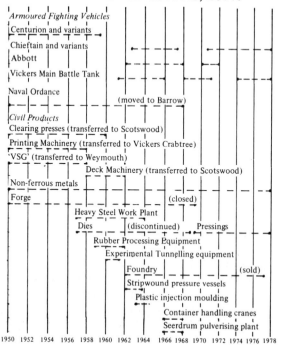

Moreover, despite the real increase in the volume of arms sales, employment has steadily declined. In 1939, tank orders amounted to £8m. In 1951, Centurion orders were £11m. The latest Chieftain order for Iran, which is to be shared with the Royal Ordnance Factory Leeds, is worth more than £500m. And yet, as we saw above, the labour force has fallen dramatically. On the last order, Elswick were producing four vehicles a month with 570 productive workers. On the new order, production is to be stepped up to 14 vehicles a month with only 520 productive workers. There are several reasons for this. One reason, probably the most important, is the utilisation of spare capcity. As we shall see below, the organisation of tank production tends towards underutilisation of people and space. The bigger the contract, the easier it is to organise production in such a way as to minimise this underutilisation. Another reason is the introduction of numerically controlled (NC) machines, which can do several operations that were once undertaken by a number of different individual machinists. There is one NC machine at Elswick which does 48 operations and it only requires a setter and an operator. On the new Chieftain order, for example, painters will be replaced by aerospray guns. Very often, the effect of new NC machines is not immediately apparent in redundancies. This is partly because there is currently an acute shortage of machinists and partly because the redundancies occur on the run down of a previous order before the machines are introduced. Thus the painters were declared redundant on the rundown of the last vehicle order. In fact, they demanded short time instead of redundancy and organised a stoppage. But in the end there was work going on in the shipyards and so they accepted redundancy.

Finally, reduced employment can be explained by an increase in outside jobs. This may take the form of an increase in "free issue", parts supplied by ROF

Leeds, the prime contractor for Chieftain, or of an increase in subcontracting from Vickers. While it is true that an increase in the sophistication of "free issue" or bought-in parts, such as the engine or fire control equipment, account for some but probably not all of the increase in the value of tanks, it is thought that outside jobs have not increased substantially. Moreover, such increase as there has been is partly offset by the increased complexity of successive tanks. Chieftain, for example, has many more individual parts than the Centurion.

In the future, one can expect the introduction of more machines, and more improvements in capacity utilisation. It is probable that, given the very low levels of employment at Elswick, the decline in jobs, assuming continued arms orders, is likely to be slower than before. But it is also most unlikely that a new Middle Eastern war or similar event is going to stem the gradual decay of West Newcastle.

Building the Chieftain Tank

As of October 1977, there were 1,846 people employed at Elswick, in the three divisions – Defence Systems, which used to be known as armaments, Pressings, and Non-ferrous Metals. The foundry, which employed about 200 people, was recently sold. Defence systems is the heart of the factory. It employs 1517 people of which 608 are white collar workers. The proportion of overhead workers is higher than for any other division. Formerly, Elswick used to build naval armaments. Today, the entire workforce of defence system division is engaged in the construction of armoured fighting vehicles: the Chieftain Tank, the Vickers Main Battle Tank, developed by Vickers for export, an Armoured Recovery Vehicle, based on the

Chieftain, and an armoured vehicle launched bridge
(the Mexi Bridge based on Centurion suspension).
A list of these is contained in Table 2. On the
current order, Vickers expects to produce 14 tanks
a month, although work is already somewhat behind schedule because of delays on the engine.

TABLE 2: VICKERS ARMOURED FIGHTING VEHICLES SINCE 1940

Valentine: Specifications drawn up 1934.
Abandoned 1937.
Revived in 1939 with order for 100.
Total of 2,515 were delivered.
Mid 1943: Elswick were producing sixty a month.
Had eleven marks. There was a bridge laying version
and a seagoing version.

Archer: Valentine chassis with 17 pounder gun. 800
ordered.
Deliveries began in 1944.

Centurion: Design began in 1943. Designed at Chobham but
Vickers were responsible for coordinating design
and production. Production began at end of war
and was Elswick staple until 1959.
About 1,000 were produced. Stockholm International Peace Research Institute (SIPRI) value
is about $100,000. Went through 13 marks with
numerous variants, including ARV, bridge layer,
Dozer tank, Engineer vehicle, artillery obser-
vation tank, Beach Armoured Recovery Vehicle.
"Most versatile and successful tank design ever
developed" (Jane's Weapon Systems 74- 5).
Sold to India, Egypt, Iraq, Israel, Jordon, Libya,
S. Africa, Switzerland, Sweden, Netherlands,
Kuwait.

Chieftain: Designed during 1950s. Production began in 1963,
by Vickers and ROF Leeds: 800 for British Army.
SIPRI Cost: $300,000. Bridge layer and ARV
versions. Seven marks. 1,500 sold to Iran. 165
sold to Kuwait.

Vickers Main   Developed between 1958-63 as a private venture.
Battle Tank: Sold to India, Kuwait and Kenya. Produced
under licence in India as Vijayanta. 50 for Kuwait;
Cost £7m. Prototype production began in 1961.

105mm SP   Vickers is sole manufacturer. Developed a simpli-
Gun Abbott: fied version for export. Export orders 1970-72.

SP 30mm AA Uses Abbott chassis and has Hispano-Suiza gun.
System
Falcon:

Building a tank is rather similar to building a
ship. Armstrongs, as the Elswick plant was known
before the merger with Vickers in 1927, built a
reputation on its ability to construct a complete
warship in the latter years of the last century. Many
of the concepts of tank manufacture were drawn
from the experience of warship building. The
chassis is known as the "hull" and the early tanks
were clasified as "cruisers" and "battle tanks".

Formerly, Vickers was at the forefront in the
design of tanks. Indeed, during the interwar period,
the tank department at Elswick was the only institution in Britain which maintained facilities for
the design and development of tanks and the
Vickers tanks provided a model for tank developments in many countries.[6] The official historian
of British war production commended the Vickers-
Armstrong designers for their "solitary and pioneering efforts".[7] During the Second World War, the
Government began to take a much more important
role in design and development and it was then
that the establishment at Chobham, now known
as Military Vehicles and Engineering Establishment
(MVEE), was set up. Both the Centurion and the
Chieftain were designed at Chobham, although in
the case of Centurion, Vickers took over responsibility for coordinating design and production.
Nevertheless, after the war, Vickers maintained
a considerable design team. They designed the
Vickers Main Battle Tank, which is cheaper and
lighter and, in Lord Robens' words, "nippier"
than the Chieftain, especially for export. It has

been sold to Kuwait and Kenya and is built under
licence in India. They also designed a version of the
Abbott self-propelled gun, the Falcon anti-aircraft
system consisting of an Abbott chassis and Hispano
Suiza 30mm anti-aircraft guns, and a "retro-fit"
package to bring old Centurions up to modern tank
standards.[8] There was close cooperation with the
Ministry of Defence and, at one time in the early
1960s, there were as many as 90 people from MOD
working on quality control. But following the
armoured fighting vehicles lull in the late 1960s,
the design team was run down. Many of the designers
were made redundant. Many of those who stayed
were hived off into International Research and
Development Company Ltd., formed jointly by
Vickers and Parsons in 1973. There is still a small
research laboratory but the two empty floors of
Head Office bear testimony to the disappearance
of design.

The production of tanks was streamlined during
World War II. To the experience of shipbuilding
was added the new example of automobile manufacture. A new tank shop was built on the site of
the old shipyard in 1937 and on the outbreak of
war, new methods of production were introduced.
According to J.D. Scott, the official historian of
Vickers:

"Production started in one corner of the large shop, where
plates were placed together and secured in position by a
few bolts through rivet holes in order to form a skeleton
of the hull. This fabrication was then rivetted. Then, stage
by stage, the hulls advanced down the shop until they were
ready to receive the suspension and the wheels. In the
early days this took place in the same shop, but as production grew it became necessary to take them into an ajdacent
shop for 'suspension' and 'wheeling'. After getting its suspension unit and wheels, the hulls went back to the erecting
shop to receive engines, transmission, fuel tanks and elec-

trical and other equipments. Meanwhile, construction of
the turrets had been going forward and the turrets and hulls
met and were fitted together. Some of the units involved
weighed several tons and mass production on this scale had
never even been attempted before."[9]

These were number 32 and 36 shops; at the height of
World War II, they were producing 60 tanks a month.

Next to the tank shops were the naval armament
shops. They were huge shops with nooks and
crannies where you could hide an army. No.24 shop
was purpose built for the 14 inch guns of George V
and other big ships and it was said to be the best
shop in the North East. It had lifting gear and gun
pits and, later, they installed handling gear for
missiles. People from Barrow who saw it were very
impressed. But when naval armaments moved to
Barrow in 1968 the big shops were knocked and a
year or so later, the tank shops were sold to Parsons.

Today, the methods of flow production have been
abandoned and production is dispersed in several different shops. The tanks or parts are moved backwards
and forwards on tank transporters from shop to shop.
There are three main stages in tank production. The first
stage is fabrication, which takes place in No.18W, No.19
and No.17 shops. Armour plate is purchased from the
old Vickers plant at Sheffield which is now part of
British steel and the turret casting is received from one
of the Royal Ordnance Factories. The steel is cut and
shaped and then fitted, tacked and finally welded together to make the hull. The skills involved are Burners,
Sheet Metal Workers, Whitesmiths,[10] Platers, Welders
and Grinders.

The second stage is machining, which takes place in
Nos. 11, 27 and 29 shops. This consists of big machining on the hull and turret (making holes, etc., in which
to fit various parts and apparatus) and small machining
on parts. The skills are related to the machines. There

are borers — vertical and horizontal — millers, plane-millers, slotters, turners — including combination turret lathe operators, grinders, drillers capstain operators etc. As mentioned above Vickers has introduced a number of NC machines and these have replaced much labour. Because machining work has increased, the number of machinists has not fallen by much. The unions at Elswick have a policy that a skilled man should operate the machines if they replace jobs that were previously skilled or a mix of skilled and semi-skilled. On NC machines, heavy machining takes about 40 hours per operation. There are 8 operations on the turret, 3 on the hull, and 3 on the glacis or panniers (protected storage space above the tracks). Then there are numerous smaller items where the machining times vary from 5 minutes to 40 hours. There are hundreds, perhaps thousands, of parts and as tanks grow more sophisticated, the number of parts increases. Some machining is subcontracted to other Vickers plants at Scotswood, Crayford, Team Valley and occasionally Thetford.

The last stage is fitting and final erection. This takes place in No.60, No.17, No.29 and No.21 shop. All the tanks pass through No.29 and No.21 shop. This stage involves final assembly of the hull and turret with the various machined parts, the gun and the engine, and the electrical equipment, finishing — i.e. painting etc. and testing. Nearly all the electrical equipment is provided by the Ministry of Defence as "free issue". The gun comes from ROF Nottingham and the engine comes from British Leyland or Rolls Royce. Some of the people who have fabricated or machined equipment are involved at this stage. In addition, there are fitters, coppersmiths, joiners, electricians, painters and rough painters, and leather workers. Some of the fitting jobs have also been affected by NC machines.

In all three manufacturing sections, there are also ancillary workers — handymen, craners, slingers and labourers — who do odd jobs such as carrying parts from one section to another and so on. There are also "hangers on", overhead workers, without whom, many believe, the work might proceed much faster. These include the progress people, who are supposed to make sure that equipment is in the right place at the right time which usually means that a worker asks for the equipment and a progress person goes and finds it, the store people, the rate fixers, the inspectors, the foremen, and, of course, the management.

The production process takes about 18 months; testing starts at 12-14 months. But these times are subject to great variations. There are enormous problems in programming the work and because these problems are not overcome, the process involves a good deal of waste — waste of space, capital equipment and above all people. It is not just the inefficiency resulting from the dispersal of shops, though this presumably adds to the problems. Workers are always waiting around. Sometimes it's waiting for orders. Sometimes it's waiting for work from other sections; or new orders, the fabrication shops may be working flat out while the finishing trades are on short time. Sometimes it is waiting for parts, like the engine, from outside. Sometimes, big delays can be caused by minor events; for example, two slingers off work can prevent the cranes from operating and halt production in an entire shop. The problems are easier to manage if the contract is big. Then there is enough work for all sections and subcontracting can be used to smooth the schedule. Subcontracting can also be used to undermine the unions, as when work is subcontracted to firms employing cheap non-unionised labour. This happened with the petrol tank for the Chieftain and, for a time, the tank was blacked.

Nevertheless, the primary problem is planning and this is all the more difficult if management doesn't under

stand the production process and workers are excluded
from management. Given the current framework of
capital/labour relations, increased efficiency in management terms tends to mean increased control over
workers. If workers are to ensure a certain degree of
autonomy over their work and an adequate rate of
pay, they need to maintain a monopoly on the information they possess. A skilled craftsman has considerable autonomy in determining the rate for a job. On
average, machinists at Elswick earn £12 less than other
skilled workers because their jobs are easier to time.
At Elswick, there is a method of batch costing, whereby each piece worker books his time, together with
his rate, against an order number. Theoretically, this
ought to facilitate costing and scheduling. In practice,
the workers often book against different contracts in
order to spread the work. The matter is complicated
by the hierarchical nature of management so that
the line management has an interest in confusing
the higher-ups since it does not wish to be seen to be
far behind on any one contract. The consequence is
that it is very difficult to obtain correct information
on the work involved in any particular product, so
that there is no reliable basis for efficient planning.

Apart from the boredom, the waste may not matter.
The alternative is increased output of tanks for the
repressive Iranian regime. It was different in World
War II when the tanks were needed for the war against
fascism. But when one considers how the time could
be spent, the socially useful work that could be
done, then this waiting around, the antagonistic
social organisation that impedes cooperative production,
is unacceptable.

Commercial Experience at Vickers

Since the war, Vickers Elswick has undertaken the
production of a wide range of commercial products.

Apart from non-ferrous metals, Vickers never established a basis for sustained production in any of these products and none of them served to stem the decline in employment. In 1939, the two main armament plants in West Newcastle, Elswick and Scotswood, employed 18,000 people. In 1963, they employed 7,000 people and in 1976, they employed 2,800 people. There used to be 50 pubs along the Scotswood road, with names like the Rifle, the Gun, or the Ordnance Arms. Today, there are only six.

The commercial products that have been manufactured at Elswick include moulds for prefabricated houses, electric furnaces and other equipment and plant for British steel, car presses, car dies, cranes, deck machinery, printing presses, newspaper presses, mining machinery, the variable speed gears and delivery pumps, rubber processing equipment, pulverising plant, stripwound pressure vessels, experimental tunnelling equipment and subcontract work on the Sulzer engine. These are shown in Table 1.* Most of them were undertaken under licence from other companies or under subcontract to other plants in Vickers. The great engineering works in the North East are widely regarded by management as jobbing shops. Commercial products tended to be treated as "filler-ins" to employ spare capacity between armament orders. Those products that proved successful were generally hived off to other parts of the Vickers empire. Thus printing presses were transferred to the old Crabtree Plant at Leeds while the Variable Speed Gear, a highly successful gear system based on hydraulic pressures, was transferred eventually to the Hydraulic Division at South Marston. The car presses and marine equipment were transferred to Scotswood.

Vickers also had a forge and a foundry at Elswick.

---

* see above page 237

Originally the forge and the foundry formed a single division. The foundry had a heat treatment plant which made a profit. It also had iron casting and pattern making facilities. The forge was situated on the riverside between the old tank shops and the old naval armament shops; it was where the bombs had been forged and it was the only forge in the North East. When the old tank shops were taken over by Parsons, the forge had to be moved to higher level. It needed stronger foundations to take the heavy hammers. The management decided instead to close the forge and modernise the foundry. But they made mistakes in the modernisation and, without the forge, the foundry could not make a profit. The plan for modernisation had depended on the demand for printing machinery; but the new printing venture at Crabtree failed and other markets had to be found. They sold the foundry in 1977 for a song; it might have been because of the expenditure needed to bring poor health and safety conditions up to standard.

There were two examples, during this period, of attempts by Vickers to build up an indigenous capability in a new commercial product in the North East. One was the die shop at Elswick. This was a spin-off from the Clearing presses. The die shop, which began about 1957, employed about 250 people and supplied dies to Vauxhall, Saab, Volvo, the Polish State Car Company, Renault and Volkswagen. It also supplied dies for other products, like fridges and baths, and research was undertaken at Vickers into a new kind of explosive forming die. But the shop was very dependent on Ford and when in the late 1960s Ford opened a new tool making plant outside Cologne, the die-shop was closed down. Some of the men went south to join Hall Brothers in Rugby.

The second example was the tractor scheme at Scotswood. Immediately after the war, Vickers were engaged in converting Sherman tanks for use as tractors

known as "Shervik". In order to break into the tractor
market which was then an American monopoly, Vickers
went into partnership with Jack Olding and Company,
who were the agents for selling the American Caterpillar
tractor in Britain, and Rolls Royce, who were to
manufacture the engine. With the aid of a designer from
Ferguson, Vickers developed a heavy earth moving
tractor, which had a Centurion suspension. There were
two main versions, the VR 180, named Vigor, with a
200 hp Rolls Royce engine, and the VR.X, with a 150
hp Rolls Royce engine, named Vikon. Vigor went
into production in 1952. Among other things, it was
used in the construction of the M.1 motorway, for clearing and deep ploughing large areas of land in the south of
Yugoslavia and by the British and Pakistani armies. It
was said to cost about £10,000, of which labour costs
at Scotswood were only £700. And it had a larger
work capacity than its main competitor, the Caterpillar.
At its peak it employed about a thousand people. It is
said that Jack Olding pushed the tractor into the market
place before it was properly proved and tested and also
that the engineering was too fine and complex –
there were many people who felt that it was wrong to
have higher engineering standards for machines to kill
people than for machines designed to benefit people.
In any case, after the tractor had been sold to a rather
large number of customers at home and overseas, snags
began to develop. In particular, the powerful engine
proved too much strain for the gearbox. Even though
the gear box was hardened and most of the snags ironed
out, the tractor gained a reputation for unreliability.
The scheme finally folded in 1960.

Right up to 1959, the company appears to have been
optimistic about the future of the tractors. In 1957,
a special tractor divison was established, combining
the tractor production at Scotswood with Onions and
Sons (Leveller) Ltd., which produced large scrapers and

had been acquired by Vickers. The distribution of
tractors was taken over from Jack Olding, additional
space was made available at Scotswood, and subsidiary
companies were set up in Canada and Australia. There
were plans for an ultimate turnover of £10m and for
mass production at Long Benton. As late as 1959, the
company was reporting hopefully on export prospects,
particularly in South America. The following year,
tractor production was discontinued because "markets
for the crawler type tractor narrowed and the future
did not hold sufficient promise to justify continuing
production".[11] It was around this time that Caterpillar
established a plant at Birtley.

The failure of the tractors and other commercial
products is often attributed to the nature of Vickers
as an armaments company — the lack of cost and market
consciousness, the view of itself as a "national institution" which can always survive. The interwar experience,
when Vickers attempted to enter the electricity and
automobile industries, is often cited as an example.
Vickers motor car company, Wolseley, for instance, was
very good at producing luxury cars, including "high
speed" cars for staff officers and scouting duties. But
it was not so good at marketing or mass production.
According to J.D. Scott:

> "Wolseley had built costly showrooms in Piccadilly before
> finding that the police would not let them bring cars across
> the pavement, and the incident was not unrepresentative."[12]

Likewise, Armstrongs turned down a plan to mass
produce automobiles in 1906 because the profit was
less, according to the Directors than on a single river
gunboat.[13]

But today, Vickers has succeeded in moving into
civilian industries outside the North East. After the
successive waves of nationalisation — steel in 1965,
aircraft and shipbuilding in 1977 — armaments account

for a small proportion of Vickers total output. The hiving off of successful commercial products from Elswick was part of a policy of streamlining and rationalisation, in which various spheres of production were concentrated in different locations. It also involved the separation of design, production and distribution so that in the development of products like the tractors, the designers were often remote from the customer and unfamiliar with the production process. It was a policy of financial diversification, in which Vickers entered new fields through the takeover of existing plants, often overseas, rather than through new investment. Increased profits have been achieved in the short run through the elimination or run down of older plants rather than through modernisation and innovation. The consequent expansion of Vickers' output was thus merely fictitious representing an increase in the share of output controlled by Vickers rather than an absolute increase. This meant that, over the last ten years, trading profits have increased threefold as a percentage of sales and sixfold in absolute terms, while employment has fallen by 10%, a reduction of 6,000 people. If one takes into account the fact that acquisitions during this period have added around 9,000 people to the labour force -- a period in which there has been no nationalisation — the total loss to the labour force is probably around 15,000. This strategy is evidenced in the composition of foreign sales. In the highly competitive advanced industrial markets of West Europe, North America and Australasia, increases in sales have been achieved through the establishment of overseas subsidiaries. Indeed, the *entire* increase in sales of overseas subsidiaries has occurred in these regions. In contrast, exports have been stagnant in real terms. Such increase as there has been has mostly gone to the underdeveloped markets of Asia and South America — areas where tech-

nically backward, cheaper products are more likely to
find a customer.

There may have been gains in employment and output in some areas in Britain; Vickers has undertaken
some new investment in offshore engineering, office
equipment and bottle washing machinery. But its
solution to the declining rate of profit on all but armament work at Elswick has been abandonment rather
than innovation. That this is a long term policy is
evidenced in the run down of designers and the low
apprentice intake. The great weakness at Elswick and
Scotswood was the failure to maintain independent
teams for design, development and testing. In 1970,
only 30 apprentices were accepted at Elswick and some
people say they would be better off apprenticed to
estate agents. For the main asset at Elswick now is
space and land. Hence the growth of warehousing
where there were once productive factories.

The attachment of Vickers to the criterion of short
term profit has to be understood as a consequence
of its growth. Over the years, the management of
Vickers has become hierarchical and traditional. As
one person has put it, there is a kind of notion of the
"divine right to manage, a premium apprenticeship
based on heredity. It leads to terrible inertia". The
heads of the Engineering Group are always Barrow
men. They believe in waiting for orders and not
counting costs. They think they should "make a
crane which lasts for sixty years" which is admirable
no doubt but it does not lead to markets. Even more
important perhaps is the fear of taking risks which
stems from the nature of the hierarchy. The line
management is unwilling to accept new ideas and
tends to oppose new investment for fear of penal-
isation in case of failure. It never puts decisions on
paper and information rarely gets passed up through
the hierarchy. The aim is to preserve things as they

are until retirement. (In fact, the current management of the Engineering Group was responsible for huge fiascos.) The growth of Vickers and the consequent need for increased financial control has led to the replacement of engineers by accountants. They do not understand the production process or may not even be able to tell the difference between a drill and a lathe. They judge a new venture by the number that appears on a calculator and not on a comprehensive view of the long term. It was probably this kind of reason, the unwillingness to anticipate the future, the fear of greater losses, that led to the decision to abandon the tractor scheme. Vickers has been described as a

> ". . . huge animal that has come out of the prehistoric age. It wallows around in the mud and occasionally comes up for sun. It survives because it has got a thick skin"

But the problems are not all of Vickers' making. In many of the commercial fields they entered, they were caught in the fierce competition between established multinational monopolies which militated against the intrusion of newcomers. The market was the market for capital goods and heavily dependent on booms and slumps in investment. To survive a recession in investment like the present one and to build up a new capability in a particular product line in anticipation of the next recovery might well require resources and an ability for risk-taking that would be beyond the capacity of a smaller, more dynamic company.

From the standpoint of the Vickers' shareholders, it was probably true that the decision to pursue rationalisation instead of innovation made sense. But this kind of sense looks altogether different from the standpoint of the people who could have benefited from the products of their skills.

Alternative Products

Out of the stock of Vickers' past experience, it is possible to pick a number of products which may well
have a growing market in the future and which could
be built at Elswick. It is also possible to think of
additional products that are technically feasible and
satisfy some currently unfilled social need. But if such
products are to succeed where earlier products failed,
they would have to entail an entirely new form of
organisation for production. The problem, as we have
seen, is rooted in the basic contradiction of Vickers
as a large corporate organisation. On the one hand,
only an organisation of similar scale can provide
sufficient resources and market protection. On the
other hand, the very size of Vickers and its profit-
seeking nature lead to inertia and timidity. The alternative is a system of national planning in which government support is provided, on a long term basis, for the
build-up of a truly indigenous capability. This would
have to combine design and manufacture with intimate
knowledge of user need. To ensure that the structure
of the state is not patterned by the structure of the
corporation, that real needs are identified and social
priorities shifted accordingly, and that the productive
and creative potential of workers is fully utilised, the
system would have to be based on grass roots participation of workers and consumers. (A proposal for
Workers' Participation at Vickers has already been put
forward by the North East Shop Stewards' Committee
and discussed by the Combine Committee.)[14]

The following list of alternative products is predi-
cated on such structural change. Some of the products
suggested here are theoretically feasible within the
current organisational framework. The money received
by Vickers in compensation for the nationalisation of
aircraft and shipbuilding provides an opportunity to
put the suggestions into practice. Indeed, some of them

have already been put to the management at Scotswood
by members of AUEW Tass. But organisational change
may still be required because of the natural conservat-
ism of Vickers. The management do not encourage
bright ideas — many people have been deterred from
participation in the suggestions scheme because of
the lack of response and the puny remuneration. To ask
Vickers to change, as one person said "is like asking
a brewer to make jam".

The products concentrate on heavy engineering. The
assets at Elswick are large spaces, heavy engineering
skills and a custom-built approach. The fact that there
has never been assembly line production and the plant
is not now geared up for specific production could
prove an advantage in conversion. Where possible the
products have been related to local needs in Newcastle
just as were the original hydraulic cranes built by Armstrong in the mid-nineteenth century.

1. *Manufacturing Machinery*

The main proposal is the design of car presses. Elswick
used to make Clearing Presses until these were transferred to Scotswood. Currently, Scotswood make
Schuler Presses but there are very few orders at the
moment because of the strong European competition.
To stay in the market, Vickers need to have their
own press. The Scotswood draughtsmen have been
thinking about a new economy press. The experience
with Schuler presses has given people ideas about
how the design could be improved and how cheaper
methods could be adopted. They undertook a design
exercise for about 18 months and found that it was
not as easy as they had thought and that there were
reasons for apparent complexities of design. Nevertheless, they concluded that there are real possibilities.
This is probably the most immediately feasible project
and management are considering whether to recruit

seven designers to undertake the project. Another suggestion is the manufacture of plant and machinery needed at Elswick which would be designed around the kind of conditions of work which workers consider to be most appropriate for productive and satisfying labour.

2. *Mining Machinery*

In the medium to long term, there is a huge potential market. The future of British coal mining depends to a large extent on the relative price of coal and oil, but there is a world wide thirst for minerals and with it, a demand for heavy earth moving equipment, such as dragline or bucket wheel excavators, large tracked vehicles somewhat similar to a tank. Management hair goes grey at the mention of heavy earthmoving tractors. But, as we have seen, the problem with the Vickers tractors was not, in the end, a problem of quality. The need for improved health and safety standards in the mines could also provide a challenge to the designers of mining equipment.

3. *Inland Waterways*

There are a number of proposals for making better use of Britain's canal system as an alternative form of transport. This would require a firm Government policy to resuscitate the canal system. This includes:

a. Pumps. As a result of the suggestions made by draughtsmen at Scotswood, the management asked British Waterways if there was any possibility of work for Vickers. The Manchester Shipping Canal wants barges to clean the canal and pump houses. The canal gets silted up and the pumps are used to separate the silt into water and gravel. There is stiff competition from the Dutch who normally do this kind of work.

b. Canal gates, particularly power-driven lock gates which

would speed up transport through the canals.

c. Earth moving equipment for widening the canals.

d. Barges. A specific suggestion is floating containers hitched to a single power unit like a kind of water going cargo train.

4. *Energy Equipment*

a. Fluidized bed boilers. Currently, boilers provide about 20% of energy sources in Britain. There has been very little technical change in boilers and there is considerable potential for energy conservation in their design. Fluidized bed boilers pulverise coal and burn it over limestone like a liquid so that the limestone catches the sulphur. It is possible to improve the pressure control over oxygen and to minimise heat loss by burying the boiler tubes in the bed of limestone. The Americans are very interested because of the high sulphur content in American coal. Over the next ten years, there is widely considered to be a real scope for this kind of boiler.

b. Heat pumps for industrial or office use. Heat pumps function like refrigerators in reverse. They extract heat from the environment and reproduce it in a purer form. The Lucas Aerospace Workers are designing a heat pump to be used in old peoples' homes. But heat pumps on a larger scale for heating office blocks have already been proved to be not only feasible but also economic. The Manweb building in Manchester, the office of Manchester's electricity board already uses a heat pump and the Board is advertising for new designs. Heat pumps are also useful in industry and could be ideal for bottle washing machinery, like that which Vickers manufactures at Crayford and Thetford. The heat pumps would act as kind of heat recyclers extracting heat from used water at the end of the bottle washing process for reuse in the newly sterilised water at the beginning of the process.

5. *Environmental Equipment*

a. Recycling plants. Currently, Vickers make the Logeman domestic refuse recycling plant at Scotswood and the Seerdrum pulverising plant at Southampton. The Logeman equipment bails (squashes) scrap metal and shreds and separates tin from steel. Currently, there are snags in the separating process which Vickers might try to solve. The Seerdrum plant, which used to be made at Elswick, separates metal from domestic refuses and turns the residual into fertilisers. Seerdrum was taken over by Vickers and Vickers could consider a development of the plant. Another suggestion is recycling plants for other materials. An obvious candidate is brass in order to service the non-ferrous metals division. Several people think that the non-ferrous metals division should have gone into plastics. A plastics recycling plant would involve chemical engineering problems which Vickers is not equipped to solve but it might be possible to collaborate with workers in a chemical plant. Vickers could make the heat exchangers and the pressure vessels.

b Tree transplantation equipment. Currently, tree and timber sources are running out. The Dutch Elm disease has made the situation especially serious. It is possible to use an hydraulic cylinder system for the rapid up-rooting and transplantation of trees. The system is very simple and tree transplantation would have to be done on a very large scale to make production worthwhile.

c. Oil spillage pumps. These are pumps which would reclaim spilled oil through a kind of sweep. They would save marine life and stop pollution on the beaches. They are very expensive and difficult to make, however, and would require a heavy social commitment to the environment.

6. *Agricultural Equipment*

The main ideas centre around agricultural systems for the Third World. Vickers has helped India to establish a factory for tanks; this experience might be extended to tractors or other equipment. The very simplicity required might, as one person said, be "right up Vickers' street". A specific suggestion is the design of irrigation systems to replace primitive systems in the Third World. This would involve a combination of pumps and earth moving equipment, such as tractors. The pumps would need to be operated by a local source of power — perhaps people, oxen, or camels. And there would need to be repair shops for local maintenance and future construction. Ideally, a team of workers could spend time in a village making their skills available to the local people to help them build their own systems.

The major impediment here is not so much the social organisation in Britain but the social structure of the villages in which landlords with little interest in improving the land live off interest or rent paid by dependent tenants or smallholders who cannot finance their own investment.

7. *Brewing Equipment*

There is a general feeling that the variety and wholesomeness of beer in the North East could be improved. Currently the pubs are dominated by two large breweries and the beer contains artificial chemicals which are designed to preserve a standard quality in pubs, and to remove the instabilities that result from lack of control over temperaure and humidity. Elswick could build small scale brewery plant which would boost brewery employment and improve the beer. It could also build pumps and vessels, with built-in temperature and humidity control, for the pubs. The main problem is how to wrest control of the pubs from the main breweries. It might be necessary to think about alternative pubs.

8. *The Reconstruction of Britain's Piers*

Britain's piers are falling down. Rebuilding them is essentially a nineteenth century engineering job for which the Elswick plant was built. One could start with the Saltburn pier which gives pleasure to many people in Newcastle.

In addition to the suggestions on this list, there were numerous other ideas. Some, like solar panels, mopeds, pedal cars, windmills, hydrofoils for rapid service along the Tyne, were ruled out because they were suitable for light and medium engineering involving assembly lines or small plants. Others, like hospital equipment or electro-mechanical devices for controlling polluting emissions, required very specialised skills in chemical or electronic engineering. Many of the suggestions made by workers in other plants might also be adopted. These include the proposals for wave and tidal power and offshore engineering made by workers at the Barrow Shipbuilding works[15] or the proposals for fire-fighting equipment or for a hybrid road/rail vehicle made by Lucas Aerospace workers.[16] There are plenty of ideas around. It would be surprising if workers who spend their lives in a factory environment had not thought about different ways in which they might use their skills and talents, about what they could be making and how. Most of the ideas are apparently technically feasible. The problem is political and social. The problem is the organisation of Vickers, the current structure of the world market, and the priorities of the Government. Yet once the possibilities for alternative products are explored and the political context provided, the *mobilisation* of human resources to replace the current *wastage* offers extraordinary opportunities. People who can build a Chieftain tank can and should build a whole range of engineering products that society needs.

REFERENCES

1. National Economic Development Office: *Mechanical Engineering. Summary of findings and recommendations of the industrial review to 1977,* London, April 1974.
2. Based on figures provided by the Stockholm International Peace Research Institute, the value per ton of Main Battle Tanks is as follows: AMX-30: $10,000(?), Chieftain: $6,000, Leopard: $5,000, M-60: $4,000, T-54: $4,000.
3. For a description of the decline of West Newcastle, see Benwell Community Project, *West Newcastle: Its Growth and Decline,* July 1976 and *Social Change in Benwell,* October 1977.
4. Ministry of Defence News Release, Jun 17, 1976.
5. Vickers Annual Report, 1976.
6. Vickers tanks sold to the Soviet Union under the picturesque name "the English Workman" are said to have played a key role in the subsequent evolution of Soviet tanks.
7. M.M. Postan, *British War Production,* HMSO and Longmans Green, London 1952.
8. See Jane's Weapon Systems, 1974-5.
9. J.D. Scott, *Vickers: A History,* Weidenfeld and Nicolson, London, 1962, p.284.
10. Whitesmiths are a Vickers' speciality. They work in cold metal as opposed to blacksmiths who work in hot metal. They were introduced in the 1920s to counter the militancy of the boiler-makers, who do roughly the same job. They belong to a separate union, the National Union of Sheet Metal Workers and Heating and Domestic Engineers.
11. Vickers Annual Report, 1960.
12. J.D. Scott, op.cit., p.145.
13. Clive Trebilock: "'Spin-off' in British Economic History: Armaments and Industry, 1860-1914", *Economic History Review* XXII (1969).
14. "Vickers: A Proposal for Worker Involvement in Management."
15. *Sense About Defence,* The Report of the Labour Party Study Group, Appendix XV, Mary Kaldor and Albert Booth, "Alternative employment for naval shipbuilding workers: A case study of the resources devoted to the production of the ASW Cruiser".
16. See Chapters 8 and 9.

Chapter XI

Conclusion : Corporate Planning, Workers' Control and Employment

Steve Bodington and Ken Coates

The socialist, Labour and Trade Union movements are, up to now, not fully grasping the significance of the corporate plan strategies which have been initiated by the Lucas Aerospace, Vickers and other shop stewards' combine committees (henceforward called SSCCs for short). Such strategies are in fact fundamental to any realistic struggle for full employment. In essence a SSCC corporate plan is a study by employees of the resources, output potential and outlets for products of industrially advanced, high technology firms. The point is to plan for utilisation of resources of which they themselves are a part, to plan *full* employment of these resources but also *socially useful* employment. This is a mode of struggle against redundancies but it is also much more than that; it extends to include, as well as bargaining on wages and conditions of work, demands about the social use of labour; and it also looks from within the teams of workers who constitute productive resources, the human beings that give productive forces life, out towards the social potentials that these resources might be used to realise.

What is so significant about this? How does it differ from workers' participation as advocated by almost any modern management? The best way to see what is different about the SSCC corporate plan strategy is to look at the economic strategy which most of the Labour movement is uncritically accepting (sometimes explicitly, sometimes implicitly) *de facto* by virtue of 'preferring not to get involved in problems of management'. The presently prevailing economic strategy governs policy in nationalised industries (such as coal and steel, for example) every bit as much as in the privately owned firms; its guiding hope is to increase competitive strength to win more markets by raising productivity, thereby improving both the national balance of payments surplus and the enterprise surplus of profits out of which funds can be derived for new investment and for the public purse via taxation. Then, the argument runs, we will be well enough off to spend more on social services and other forms of community expenditure.

No one, if he is honest, argues that this strategy will solve the problem of unemployment in productive industries. Indeed, following the 'Neddy' reviews early in 1978, it was pointed out that the success of their development plans might even lead to falling employment in the sectors examined.[1] Being competitive involves higher productivity which translates itself simply into the fact of fewer men and women producing more products. If markets were gigantically enlarged this could theoretically mean higher employment as well as higher productivity. But for contemporary Britain, faced with German, Japanese and American rivalry, such an outcome even under conditions of world boom — and today we are in a worldwide employment slump — is improbable in the extreme. (If productivity increases 50%, sales must increase 50% merely to maintain existing levels of employment.) We should not fail to note also that the bulk of British large-scale manufacture and export based on advanced technology

is in the hands of multinational companies. In pursuit
of their own global competition with other multinationals it is far from necessary that they will, left
to their own devices, wish to enlarge employment
in Britain even if they do take steps to increase
productivity in British plants. Indeed, a number of
them seem keen to pare down the productive capacity
they own in countries such as Britain for a very
simple reason: if they limit employment and productive capacity in their own plants, they are then likely
to be able to keep this capacity more or less fully
utilised and thereby maintain a higher rate of profit
on their invested capital. When they need to enlarge
output they have a number of alternatives open to
them without tying up funds in additional investment;
for example, they can use sub-contractors or other
capacity available to them which may or may not be
in Britain.

Quite clearly then higher productivity — the 'star
in the East' for the strategy of industrial recovery as
conceived by officialdom at present — is not going
to touch the unemployment problem, and it is entirely
possible that higher productivity and increased output
could go hand in hand with higher unemployment. Job
creation projects? Without the stimulus of new
economic philosophies, engendering new attitudes in
the Labour movement towards the main objectives
of economic struggle, Job Creation Programmes would
resemble battery farms for breeding diminutive
lame ducks, so many are the crippling conditions
imposed upon the use which may be made of their
special funds. And anyhow where are the funds?
Britons are still suffering from overwhelming cuts
in public expenditure despite the fractional reliefs
that have been here and there returned in attempts
to mitigate their ravages.[2] So where, being realistic,
is there the slightest hope of getting back to full

employment? The dream of a boom in markets for
British products, based upon a sudden leap forward
in British productivity, outstripping all our competitors, is a romance for a start. But it is only
a start! Next the surplus profits have somehow
to be snatched from the multinationals and from
the nationalised industries and somehow converted
into job-creating expenditures to mop up nationwide
unemployment. New services and new forms of non-
productive community activities are vaguely referred
to but nothing yet has been worked out economically,
socially or politically to demonstrate how these new
employment creating activities are to be generated.
There is little indeed in existing economic policies,
or in the traditional thinking of economists and
administrators, that points to their feasibility. The
thrust of those economic philosophies prevailing
today cannot lead to full employment: and those
who imagine otherwise are living with the birds
in Aristophanes' happy dominion, Cloud Cuckoo Land.

Though it is not the purpose of this book to deal in
detail with community economics, it must be stressed
that this is an area to which the struggle for full
employment must also address itself very vigorously.
Under no circumstances is large-scale industry going
to generate all the worthwhile forms of activity and
all the need-satisfying output that fully employed
society must require. Democratic and labour organisations at community level need very much to co-
ordinate their forces in order to harness the resources
available to them, and to help communities to define
their own needs as a counterpart to the attempts at
corporate planning in big industry which the shop
stewards' combine committees are initating. Big, technically advanced industry is a key factor in wealth
creation. How it uses capacity not absorbed by the
competitive market will depend in great part on social

needs defined in the community where other forms
of socially useful employment also need to be generated. Full utilisation of the potential of technically
advanced big industry is important in the struggle for
full employment, not merely to conserve jobs, but
also because such resources properly directed are
needed to create foundations for a new kind of social
wealth. But large scale industry cannot provide socially
meaningful activity for all who need and seek it. To
take one example – the most burning problem of our
times, youth unemployment. Without a basic change
of economic strategy, come boom come slump, there
is no prospect of ending mass youth unemployment.
A part of the most vital, energetic, creative age-group
is being rejected by society and turns against it. The
social cost of this is gigantic. (And the cash cost is
not small: on average £5,000 a year for every individual detained in prison and a substantial bill for
relief for unemployed persons.)

How, then, does the strategy of corporate planning
as posed by shop stewards' combine committees differ
from the 'competitive productivity' strategy in which
the corporate planning is done by a multinational
company or a nationalised industry? The essential difference is that the shop stewards combine committee's
corporate planning is about *the matching of resources
to needs,* whereas 'management planning', unless con-
strained by new economic criteria, is about the strength
and market viability of competitive groupings, discip-
lined and tested by the merciless struggle for realisation
of money values.

This is not to say that SSCC corporate planning
is not interested in money values. They play an important part in a number of ways but do not dominate
decision-making. Nor is the economic strategy of planning socially useful production for unused resources
uninterested in competitive market production. The

organisation of production for use, moving into new
territory where economic relations are not primarily
articulated by money and profit criteria, will be a
tough assignment, facing many unexplored problems;
and so where traditional economic mechanisms are
tolerably sustaining economic life, it is an advantage
in the complex struggle for social change to enable
them so to continue. Even an inadequately functioning
apparatus of social production is better than total
disruption of economic reproduction processes, creating
further deserts of unemployment and collapsing social
services. SSCC planning evaluates prospects for 'market-
generated' employment and will even make proposals
for underpinning it.

The alternative strategy of 'socially audited' plans for
socially useful production attacks, first, territory that
has been or threatens to be made waste land by the
failures of production motivated and regulated by
market criteria and by the strategies which multinational
companies have based on such criteria. Let us look (in a
very oversimplified way) at what a SSCC plan is doing.
It asks first how, on the present tack, resources will be
used. There is a work force, say, of 50,000. Expected
orders, sales and investment plans, say, will keep this
labour force employed for six months and thereafter it is
expected to fall to 40,000. Question number one is obvious: for what could the released resources, represented
by the 10,000 people to be made redundant, be used?
But it is also necessary to ask, what is the production
on which those continuing in work are expected to
remain employed? Suppose this includes armaments,
the manufacture of which the political arm of the
Labour movement is insisting be cut: then, if there
is to be consistency between the political and economic
demands of that movement, proposals must also be
made for alternative use of this capacity. So the first
stage of SSCC planning is to examine critically the

present and projected use of resources. The next
stage is to propose 'socially useful products' to the
production of which available unused (or about to be
unused) resources could be put. It is possible, even,
in some cases, probable, that the socially useful alternative products will not be readily marketable through
existing channels. If they could easily be produced and
sold at a profit, it is likely that the existing management would already be doing this. However, this is
no more than probable; for two reasons at least it is
possible that ordinary profit-motivated market production could be successfully undertaken in suggested
new areas: a) because the workers and employees
may commonly have a more intimate understanding
of the potentialities of the teams of people and the
plant in which they work and b) because big-firm
policies — and those of multinationals in particular —
follow political lines designed to defend for themselves
certain product territories in pursuit of which they
come to arrangements (be they tacit or explicit) not
to invade other product territories so long as other
firms do not invade their own.

The corporate plans of the multinational companies
cannot coincide with SSCC corporate plans. The
policies followed by the great economic combines
at present are part of a worldwide strategy in a
tense power struggle to gain positions of competitive
advantage. They also comprise struggles by top
managerial personnel to maintain for themselves their
own positions of power. Tough opposition is therefore
to be expected to alternative plans originated by the
SSCCs — even where the objective may be commercially
profitable. Against such tough opposition an SSCC
whose plans carry clearsighted and committed support
from employees, can also bring to bear strong pressures:
since it is on the skills and efforts of these same employees that the managements and owners are depen-

dent for production of those goods whose sale at
present yields to them their money and their profits.
However the degree of commitment of employees to
an alternative plan must depend upon its realisability.
For its technical feasibility employees are often better
placed to speak than anyone else. The wider problem
is 'commercial' and 'social' realisability. This means,
first of all, considering under what circumstances the
autonomy of management might be overridden. Very
clearly this would be impossible without wide and
convinced support throughout the country and particularly from the trade unions and the labour movement. Widespread recognition of the importance of
SSCC planning to the whole strategy of an economic
policy of full employment is at present lacking; to
succeed the struggle for full employment will need
campaigns in support of SSCC planning similar to
those which backed the Upper Clyde Shipbuilders'
struggle against unemployment during 1971 and 1972.[3]

It also is impossible to override managerial decision-
making if there are no practically accessible outlets for
the alternative products. Once the saleability of products
is assured the struggle for production of socially useful
products becomes realistic. Powerful multinationals
may try to get tough. Then the case for Government
intervention, requisitioning or nationalisation becomes
very strong. Widely presented and explained as an alternative to unemployment, it could then command
popular support. Under such circumstances managements faced with the alternative of retaining a foothold
and income or loss of investments and an economic
base, would often modify their earlier policies. If they
did not then corporate planning for socially useful
production coupled with nationalised ownership of
plant and equipment would have to be carried, very
rapidly, to an advanced form.

A classic example of the impasse in which trade

unions have frequently been confined is that of Imperial
Typewriters at Hull and Leicester.[4] One Friday afternoon
in January 1975, the workers in these plants were laid
off by their employer, the American transnational,
Litton Industries. The Hull workers quickly occupied
their plant, and began to agitate for the formation of
a workers' co-operative. "We stay in 'til Benn says
when!" read their placards, and they received strong
and immediate support from their unions, notably
from the T&GWU Regional Office in Hull, but actively
also from the ASTMS and the AUEW. Delegations were
sent off to visit the previously established worker co-
operatives at Fisher Bendix, Triumph Meriden and
the Scottish Daily News. The Department of Trade and
Industry promised to secure time for a feasibility
study, and prolonged negotiations then began.

Litton Industries seem to have planned, from the
moment of their initial take over, to run the worn-out
machines in Hull, manufacturing aged models (which
could not be adapted to become electrically operated)
for an interim period during which a more urgent
strategem was maturing. This major plot involved using
the short breathing space left for profitable operation
of a typewriter *manufactory* in Britain in order to
secure optimal control, on a permanent basis, of typewriter *distribution.* Suitably modern office machines
could then be imported from the Litton subsidiary
in Germany, and the company would, within its own
base of calculation, have furthered its interests in the
most comprehensive way. Unfortunately these interests
were in no way identical with those of the redundant
workforce, or with those of a client nation State, left,
in the midst of a ramified engineering industry, without
the national capacity to produce even so apparently
simple a product as a typewriter. The social costs of
this lack were evident, and the shop stewards rightly
stressed the adverse effect upon the balance of pay-

ments, as well as the human cost of unemployment, in their appeals for support. Hull dockers immediately blacked imported Adler typewriters, marooning a whole consignment at the port.

Meantime, working in their home garages with amateur do-it-yourself equipment, the unemployed technicians of the Imperial factory set about the task of designing and building an alternative prototype, capable of being made on the antiquated factory equipment during a hoped-for transitional period of modernising investment. This remarkable project needed to be adapted for production as a manual keyboard, and at the same time potentially convertible as an electrically operated model. And while this unique R&D team were working against time, other volunteers were trying to calculate the potential outlets for a British typewriter, first of all in Government and Public Service offices.

Midway in this prodigious effort, the personnel at the Department of Industry were all changed. Tony Benn was relegated to superintend Energy, Eric Heffer had been provoked into resigning during the referendum on the EEC, and Michael Meacher was shifted sideways to another department. Now, after the purge, no-one in the Government wanted to know. The Imperial Typewriters occupation struggled on, but was defeated.

This is a case which typifies a complex of problems faced by numerous others, not only in the difficulties encountered in diversifying a product range, but also in securing outlets to some form of market.

In all such cases, for success to attend the workers' efforts, it is necessary, where a normal commercial outlet does not exist, or where a simple Government guarantee to buy planned output, would not suffice, for new forms of economic calculation to be applied. In such cases the products would, of course,

have to be purchased by public agencies. Because
then money and market criteria would no longer
directly apply, production which such criteria would
not sanction, might still be undertaken, because it met
quite different criteria of employment and social need.
Before considering what these might be, some number
of puzzling questions suggest themselves. For example,
how might 'social usefulness' be determined? What
forms (be they good for individual use, social amenities,
or equipment for use in social services) could 'desirable'
but 'non-marketable' products take? How should
these new types of economic production be financed,
monitored and controlled? Since some of the 'financing' might simply be using public expenditure in new
ways, it is worth noting that at present sums running
into thousands of millions of pounds sterling are
annually paid in support of production which is otherwise entirely guided by money and market criteria of
profitability. What instruments are there currently in
public hands, in the form of direct subsidy payments,
indirect costs arising from unemployment and industrial
decline, orders on public account and so forth? If the
use of resources is to be differently oriented and differently motivated, what new criteria become appropriate, how may they be applied, and by whom?[5]

One begins to see how some of these conundrums
might be tackled when one considers what 'social
usefulness' implies, how it might be interpreted and
meaningfully used as a guide. The Lucas Aerospace
SSCC has long been aware that they as producers
could hardly be in a position to decide what is or is
not 'socially useful'.

Ultimate verdicts about usefulness can be passed
only by users. It is argued in defence of the market
economy that it enables the user to "vote" products
useful or otherwise with the pennies in his or her
purse. This claim, though it has some limited validity,

is far too sweeping. However, that is a debate in which we need not here engage. Our concern is with the areas of economic activity in which market mechanisms fail to function to social satisfaction, and we are trying to devise a structure of economic relationships which will work effectively where the market and money mechanisms and criteria have either failed or could never have been applied. What Lucas SSCC in fact did was to guess at some of the social needs which their resources could meet and which in all probability would win wide social approval and be welcome to the users; at the same time they began exploring the views of people involved in community politics and community work. As the corporate plans of SSCCs are as yet no more than pointers to a direction in which the use of resources might be steered, one can expect at this stage no more than a tentative exploration of means by which 'social usefulness' is to be determined. When forms of production for social use within corporate plans first begin to be realised, the criteria of 'social usefulness' are likely to be pretty rough and ready. With experience these criteria and democratisation of the decision-making process in respect of 'socially useful products' would certainly be greatly improved, but the key point to be remembered is that if these new products (which will use resources that otherwise go to waste) are at all useful, then they represent a considerable net social gain. The community will have products which otherwise would not have come into existence, and there will be useful work to do and incomes to be earned by men and women who would otherwise be rejects from the economic and social community in which they live. There will also be a 'multiplier' effect insofar as new social resources create new employment prospects and new social needs. Nobody 'needed' a kidney machine before there was one. Now there are never enough of them.

Some of the products suggested by the Lucas SSCC seem by simple commonsense to be strong candidates for social usefulness: as again with kidney machines (when kidney failure is a death sentence for many simply for lack of machines), electronic go-carts for spina bifida children, energy saving devices and similar items. One can quite easily imagine a calculus of worthwhileness for energy saving. Measuring energy saved in equivalent of tons of coal or barrels of oil may enable us to see it as replacing these finds which would become available for sale in overseas markets, or for alternative more comprehensive raw material uses. In principle such a calculus is simple; it could without great difficulty determine how much it might be worth paying for the production of energy saving devices. In practice, however, there would be complications of two kinds (i) getting all the data straight and (ii) recognising that the economic measures and principles to be applied in administering such a strategy would be quite different from those currently used in business management and financial control.

From (i) it follows that a very substantial technical and research back-up will be needed; but this is available in educational and research bodies (in particular, universities and polytechnics). Indeed, involvement of these bodies in 'real-life' community problems would be an excellent thing educationally as well as for the community at large.

(ii) Implies a separate and parallel system of accounting and financing. The non-market production would require funds and loans at the production end to pay for resources used (labour, materials etc.) and at the user end to pay for the products. On the other side of the balance the social value of the product would be weighed and savings of other forms of social expenditure would be reckoned — and, it is to be remembered, at present the monetary cost (quite apart from 'social

cost') when the market-mechanism malfunctions, runs
into thousands of millions of pounds annually — as
has already been insisted. The point would be to keep
separate accounts of 'socially useful production' (current expenditure as well as loan capital and advances)
so that the disposition of resources for social, non-
market purposes could be seen separately from trans-
actions in the competitive world-market economy
(in whose money-value terms all public accounting
and private accounting are currently indiscriminately
presented so that social accounting becomes a meaning-
less jumble with consequences that are tending towards
political disaster).

The separate accounting of socially useful production does not present any fundamental difficulty in
principle, although it would be worth giving a great
deal of deep thought and wide discussion to methods
of accounting and to the assessment of social usefulness. The first crude beginning would require ear-
marking 'socially useful' products (as distinct from
ordinary, market products), determining how they
were to be costed and inspected, and fixing the
money payments to producers. Loans and payments
to producers would have to be administered through
banking accounts and following principles that are
distinct from those of the ordinary banking system.
Since money payments would ultimately flow back
into the ordinary monetary system in a number of
ways, strong checks against abuse would be necessary.

It is at this point in this new territory of 'socially
useful production' that people-control (in the community) and worker-control (in production) may be
seen to be fulfilling *an indispensable economic function*. Effective use of productive resources in production and of goods produced in consumption (since
the automatic checks of money-cost, profitability and
purchasing power in the hands of consumers can only,

in this new economic territory, be secondary and
auxiliary instruments) can be ensured primarily by
producers themselves and consumers themselves con-
cretely and knowledgeably watching how resources
are used, and having powers to render such democratic
controls effective. Such supervision would be in fact a
powerful instrument for developing new techniques
of economic control and for shaping new structures of
economic relationships in production and consumption, transforming the separateness of production from
consumption that is accentuated by market and
commodity relationships. But this much fuller involvement of people in economic decision-making would
take a lot of working out and would involve new forms
of knowledge and technical support. For this reason
it is important that facilities for discussion of economic
problems by all workers interested to be involved
should be provided at work, within the working day,
with pay. Alongside such discussion facilities a great
expansion of relevant educational facilities for workers
is also urgently needed. They have a very practical
political purpose here and now. (Analogous facilities
are also needed in respect of people-controlled community economics.)

Such a new type of economic strategy – and only
some such strategy can make our way to full employment – cannot succeed if it is not democratically
based. SSCC corporate plans are *alternatives* to conventional plans based on the worldwide commercial
interests of multinationals or the 'efficiency' aims of
nationalised industries evolved within criteria of international market competition; a corporate plan strategy
succeeds only insofar as it is based on the fullest involvement and convinced support of a majority of employees.
Moreover when such a plan comes to be implemented,
since the crude pressures of money wages and market
profitability no longer provide the essential dynamic, the

monitoring of production by a well-informed industrial democracy, seeking to match performance to the social aims of the corporate plan, will become an essential part of the new structure of economic relationships. The territory of production for social use cannot be entered by autocrats. This is why industrial democracy becomes a key component of the new economic mechanisms which are needed in the development of a new economic strategy. It becomes equally essential to establish community involvement and popular control over the decision as to what is socially most useful. Priorities in the allocation of products need to be determined in the framework of a democratic decision about overall priorities of need.

Whilst we are presently primarily considering the use of industrial resources, it is no less important to recognise that democratic planning and control in industry needs to be complemented by democratic control over the social uses to which products are put. There are also, already present in modern society, large organisational complexes standing close to the consumer. It is clearly relevant to consider whether some parallel forms of democratic corporate planning could not appropriately be developed within them (for example in the National Health Service or perhaps in the Cooperative Movement).

It will not, however, escape students of political manifestos that much of this argument is strongly implied in the Labour Party's 1973 Programme, which sought to make planning agreements between Government, employers and unions compulsory.

"The key to our planning effort is the domination of the economy by a few leading firms. For by concentrating our efforts on to these firms — and especially the 100 or so major firms in manufacturing — we can ensure that our planning is kept both manageable and straightforward. We will harness directly the energies of these giants — leaving the numerous smaller firms to our more general planning policies. Two points of principle, however, we must make clear:

First, that in seeking to operate directly upon the activities of these leading firms, we are interested not so much in the day-to-day or month-to-month *tactics* which they will need to employ – how much they should produce, say, of each particular product – but in their medium and longer term *strategies*. That is, we are concerned to influence and shape their strategic programmes on investment, on location, on training, on import substitution and the like.

Second, that we will not attempt to meet precisely a set of over-detailed economic targets or expect to bring about a miraculous spurt in economic growth. Certainly, we do intend to make a major forecasting effort, and to establish – in consultation with both sides of industry – clear and identifiable targets. But our *prime* aim will be to achieve certain very broad objectives in terms of jobs in certain regions, for example, in investment, or in exports. It is the fulfilment of these objectives, indeed, which is critical to our whole economic strategy."[6]

A far-reaching scheme for monitoring this process was set forth in a seven-point programme.

"To get up-to-date information, on a systematic and continuing basis, from all companies within the system. This information will concern both past performance and *advance* programmes – programmes which can be checked at a later date, against results. And it will cover such areas as investment, prices, product development, marketing, exports and import requirements.

To use this information to help the Labour Government to identify and achieve its planning objectives and to plan for the redistribution of resource which will be needed to meet those objectives.

To get the agreement of the firms within the system – the written Planning Agreement – that they will help the Government to meet certain clearly defined objectives (e.g. a certain number of new jobs in a Development Area) – whilst leaving the *tactics* which will be needed to achieve these objectives to the companies themselves.

To provide for the regular revision of those agreements, in the light of experience and progress.

> To provide a basis for channelling selective Government assistance directly to those firms which agree to help us to meet the nation's planning objectives.

> To provide a systematic basis for making large companies accountable for their behaviour, and for bringing into line those which refuse to co-operate — using, where necessary, both the extensive powers under our proposed Industry Act, the activities of our new and existing public enterprises, and the powers of public purchasing.

> To publish and publicise a detailed annual report to the nation on the record of the companies within the system, and on the progress — or lack of it — towards meeting the nation's economic objectives."[7]

It was insisted that trade unions "must have the right to take part" both in drawing up the plans which were to be presented to the Government, and in the consultations about the final agreements. Later plans were announced to involve the 30 most important companies in such agreements by December 1976, and to comprehend the top 100 by the end of 1978. Twelve items for discussion were listed in the White Paper *The Regeneration of British Industry:*

1. Economic prospects
2. The Company's broad strategy and long term objectives
3. UK sales (sales for each main product line and the Company's market share)
4. Exports
5. Investment
6. Employment and Training
7. Productivity
8. Finance
9. Prices policy
10. Industrial Relations and arrangements for negotiation and consultation.
11. Interests of consumers and community
12. Product and process development.[8]

The last five of these items being more complex than the first seven, it was suggested that they might not be tabled for consideration until 1976.

In fact, nothing at all has happened, because in the cold coup d'etat which Mr Wilson carried through after the EEC referendum, planning agreements were made "voluntary" instead of compulsory. Hence, by February 1978 only one such agreement had been concluded, and that by Chrysler at the moment of their bankruptcy and receipt of Governmental doles. The annual report upon them has had nothing to say, and has therefore not appeared.

Not surprisingly, the workers of Lucas Aerospace have been anxious to activate all these legislative permissions, in order to compel tripartite negotiations on the basis of their Corporate Plan. The following telling exchange took place in the *New Statesman,* after the publication of a sympathetic article praising the original scheme.

"I cannot accept the accusation of Government lethargy over the Lucas Aerospace Shop Stewards' Corporate Plan.

We have made it abundantly clear in innumerable letters to MPs and other interested parties that we very much welcome the idea of workers getting together to put forward positive proposals for the future of their company. In an effort to get the Lucas shop stewards' initiative moving forward, Ministers here and at the Department of Employment have repeatedly met backbench MPs, raised the subject with trade unionists and sought clarification from the company management.

In the end, though, the main reason why so little progress has been made is the failure of the combine itself to use the proper channels that already exist both in their own unions and in the Confederation of Shipbuilding and Engineering Unions for this kind of discussion. If the shop stewards want discussions of the plan with the company's central management, there is only one way that can happen democratically and that is through a properly constituted body involving all the interested unions. That is why, for almost a year now, Ministers have been urging the shop stewards to work through the Confed.

Individual unions and the Confed can only take up the

Corporate Plan if they are asked by the appropriate elected union representatives. So the way ahead is clear.[9]

> – *Les Huckfield, Parliamentary Under*
> *Secretary of State, Department of*
> *Industry"*

"Les Huckfield's letter underlines his Department's mishandling of the Lucas problem, and displays an abysmal knowledge of the workings of the trade union movement. For over a year Mr Huckfield has been informing fellow MPs, including Christopher Price, that meetings were taking place between Lucas management and the workforce to discuss the Lucas Aerospace workers' Corporate Plan for socially useful production. This he continued to do in spite of repeated denials, in writing, by the Combine Shop Stewards Committee that any such meetings were taking place. When, in March last year, 72 elected shop stewards from all 17 sites of Lucas Aerospace converged on the House of Commons, they made it absolutely clear to the MPs and junior ministers that no meetings were taking place. Subsequently, Jeff Rooker and Audrey Wise, with 11 of their fellow MPs, called the Lucas Directors to the House of Commons and they were told bluntly by the company that no discussions were taking place about the 'Corporate Plan', nor were they willing to have any such discussions.

When this message finally got through to Mr Huckfield, he then switched his tack and said that discussions should take place through the Confederation of Shipbuilding and Engineering Unions and the Company. We pursued Mr Huckfield's suggestions with the CSEU, and he has had copies of our letters to that effect. But he knows full well that no meetings have taken place. He is now apparently hiding behind the fact that no structures exist in the trade union movement for meetings with multi-national, multi-site, multi-union companies. It is clear to us that Lucas now interpret the DoI's inactivity as a licence to embark on further sackings. They have reduced the workforce by 1,000 over the last year (in addition to 5,000 since 1970) and are now planning a further 4,000 sackings! We have documentary evidence that we have pursued all the steps proposed by Mr Huckfield and his colleagues, but to no avail. We now want to know what specific steps the DoI intends taking to support us in preventing the sacking of a further 4,000 of some of the most

highly skilled engineers in Britain. Otherwise we shall have
to conclude that the Government is powerless when confronted with a subtly aggressive and intransigent multinational.[10]

> — *Ernie Scarbrow, Secretary*
> *Lucas Aerospace Combine"*

Clearly the Labour Movement will need to resolve
this issue before any advances can be made towards
democratic planning, even at the most rudimentary
level. Yet the existence of the Lucas plan has already
been a powerful influence, in that it has encouraged
other combines with similar problems to take up
similar initiatives; it has indicted the lack of reform-
ing will in the administration, merely in its reproachful
existence; and it has given a sharply practical momentum
to the otherwise abstract argument rehearsed above,
which has evoked a sympathetic response all over the
world, from environmentalists in Australia to aerospace
workers in the USA.

In one sense, the most urgent need of the Lucas
workers is for reinforcements. If 30 companies could
not be induced from the ministerial heights to talk
planning policies, then it has obviously become time
for 30 combine committees to make the running in
the depths of workplaces and the factory shop steward
organisations. A convergence of real pressures from
below might not break through unaided, but would
certainly polarize the argument within the political
movement of Labour, and thus sharpen all our wits
about the alternative possibilities. It is in this spirit
that it seems to us urgent, in spite of official indifference,
to develop the argument further.

'Productive forces' are often thought of as if they
consisted primarily in items of plant and equipment.
This is far from true. The technical potential of a
productive unit (a factory for example, or a department in a large complex) is essentially the well-

established connections between people who have developed experience of working together. For sure, there is a tendency for capitalist production to reduce much of its labour to homogenous routine work so that employees have little consciousness of their place in the complex structure of human skills, knowledge and effort that constitutes a productive unit as an integrated whole. Equally certainly, one aspect of the social usefulness after which the alternative forms of corporate planning are striving is reduction of alienation in work and of the degradation that this means in the quality of working lives. Thus one of the key objectives of SSCC corporate planning is to consider the potential of the workforce as a team and to consider new methods of work organisation. This will not only be an internal matter; it will also involve investment in new forms of equipment. (Miners who advocate workers' control in the mines make a strong point of the need for miners who intimately know pit conditions to advise on design and be involved in the placing of orders for mining machinery. It has to suit specific conditions in a specific pit which they know better than anyone else; also it must improve working conditions, minimise dust and noise, and so forth).[11]

Once the economic strategy of worker initiated corporate planning begins to gain momentum it will compel consideration of a number of fundamental issues about the relationship between advanced science-based technology and democracy. The economic power of the most technically advanced multinationals (and the same goes for nationalised industries) rests more and more on project planning by science-based interdisciplinary teams. The objectives towards which such project teams work are dictated by the power strategies of the industrial complexes and other collossi by whom they are em-

ployed. As such they are commonly quite ruthlessly
single-minded without regard to the possible effects
of their actions socially and politically (ITT in Chile for
example). However the technological significance of the
interdisciplinary team needs to be clearly recognised.
When a team of specialists with strongly rooted connections to research institutions, university departments
and sources of technical, social, political and economic
data, are well funded to work out the feasibility and
means of realising a specified objective, they construct
by the very process of their work a kind of new technology. They write a recipe, as it were, for a vast and
new integrated process that combines existing skills
and generalised human knowledge from a multiplicity
of sciences and so creates an altogether new industrial
and social technique. As combine planning under
workers' control advances and is developed, this technology of interdisciplinary teamwork could very well
be reshaped and redirected to socially more desirable
purposes.

It is not difficult to imagine the kind of objectives
that profit-maximising and power-struggle strategies
might dictate. For example, a project team may be set
the goal of designing a production process whose
labour input would be routine and repetitive requiring
no experience so that plant could be located wherever
labour was raw, cheapest and most controllable. Such
an aim is tantamount to deliberately increasing labour
alienation. Newspaper readers might easily imagine
another type of project involving in its aims the maximisation of political control and domination over some
weak newly independent government, thereby to enlarge the market outlets of a multinational company.
Since the strength of a project team rests upon the
collective knowledge and skills of team members, it is
more than probable that there will be project team
members who have little sympathy with the aims of

the project on which they are working; but they would hardly be in a position to take a critical attitude without outside support. Such support is precisely what at some stage SSCCs might be able to give: on the other hand reciprocal relations between SSCCs and inter-disciplinary teams of scientific workers could be a means to great social improvement in the use of resources. Techniques of interdisciplinary teamwork could strengthen and enlarge the scope of corporate planning; on the other hand the input of experience and judgements from the workforce *as a whole* in a productive unit, would enrich a planning team's ability to assess productive potential which — to repeat — rests more than anything else on the human beings in a productive unit, collectively in their structural interrelationships as well as individually, in their talents and enthusiasms.

To convince oneself of the importance of the inter-disciplinary team as a productive force, one has only to consider the potential — for all its ambivalences — of the American Space Agency (NASA) and the methods of work it has adopted. On a smaller scale consider a project team exploring the possibility of getting gas from the Arctic or oil from beneath the sea. It studies technical problems, equipment needed, human skills required, psychological problems of work under strange conditions, costs of this that and the other, capacity to produce oil rigs, pipes, platforms etc., international law, political reactions and so forth and so on. It comes up with a project for using human science, human knowledge, human skills and effort to create a source of energy in a totally new way.

A movement for social change must have a strategy for controlling and subordinating to its purposes the most advanced technological potentials. Science, if not controlled by democratic forces, will destroy human society; democracy on the other hand should (indeed to be fully democracy, *must*) be able to meet the human needs of all without exploitation; so it requires to meet science as a means of reducing that amount of social effort needed to adapt the environment in which we live to the necessities of our existence.

The strategy of the worker-controlled corporate plan opens a path towards the socially useful employment of science. It offers a means for taking over those economic areas in which the market/money structure fails, whilst leaving existing structures to operate insofar as their functioning continues to be socially tolerable. It is a strategy that realistically faces up to the problems involved in recreating full employment. Alone among the options open to us, it depends upon the encouragement of individual initiative and personal development, at the very instant that it forces people to look their social needs directly in the face, instead of refracting their perceptions through the ill-smelling fog of money-valued market decisions.

We may be forgiven for hoping that more and more people will find such a choice to be an interesting one.

REFERENCES

1.   Indeed, Sir Ronald McIntosh, retiring director-general of NEDC, was reported in *The Guardian* (2 December 1977) as saying "the industrial strategy, even it if is successful, will not lead to any significant increase in employment." A year previously, it had been announced as "a key step" towards developing "a high output, high wage, full employment economy." *Full Employment – Priority,* Spokesman 1978, pp.139-40.
2.   See John Hughes: *The Cuts, Strange Arithmetic,* IWC Pamphlet No.57, 1978.
3.   See *Trade Union Register 3,* Spokesman, 1973, pp.9-46, 253-59.
4.   See *Why Imperial Typewriters Must Not Close,* IWC pamphlet No.46, 1975.
5.   See *Beyond Wage-Slavery,* Spokesman, 1977.
6.   Labour's Programme, 1973.
7.   *Ibid.,* p.18.
8.   HMSO: *The Regeneration of British Industry,* August 1974.

9. *New Statesman,* 3 February, 1978.
10. *New Statesman,* 10 February, 1978.
11. *Bulletin* of the Institute for Workers' Control, December 1975, February 1976, December 1977.